Citizenship in a global age

ISSUES IN SOCIETY

Series Editor: Tim May

Current and forthcoming titles

Zygmunt Bauman: *Work, Consumerism and the New Poor*
David Byrne: *Social Exclusion*
Graham Crow: *Social Solidarities*
Gerard Delanty: *Citizenship in a Global Age*
Steve Fuller: *The Governance of Science*
Les Johnston: *Crime, Justice and Late Modernity*
David Knights and Darren McCabe: *Organizational Change*
Nick Lee: *Childhood and Society*
David Lyon: *Surveillance Society*
Graham Scambler: *Health and Social Change*

Citizenship in a global age

Society, culture, politics

GERARD DELANTY

OPEN UNIVERSITY PRESS
Buckingham • Philadelphia

Open University Press
Celtic Court
22 Ballmoor
Buckingham
MK18 1XW

email: enquiries@openup.co.uk
world wide web: www.openup.co.uk

and
325 Chestnut Street
Philadelphia, PA 19106, USA

First Published 2000
Reprinted 2002

A catalogue record of this book is available from the British Library

ISBN 0 335 20489 9 (pbk)   0 335 20490 2 (hbk)

Library of Congress Cataloging-in-Publication Data
Delanty, Gerard.
    Citizenship in a global age : society, culture, politics / Gerard Delanty.
      p.   cm. — (Issues in society)
    Includes bibliographical references and index.
    ISBN 0–335–20490–2 — ISBN 0–335–20489–9 (pbk.)
    1. World citizenship. 2. Internationalism. I. Title. II. Series.

JZ1320.4.D45   2000
323.6—dc21   00–022511

Typeset by Graphicraft Limited, Hong Kong
Printed in Great Britain by Biddles Limited, Guildford and Kings Lynn

The peoples of the earth have thus entered in varying degrees into a universal community, and it has developed to the point where a violation of rights in one part of the world is felt everywhere. The idea of a cosmopolitan right is therefore not fantastic and overstrained; it is a necessary complement to the unwritten code of political and international right, transforming it into a universal right of humanity. Only under this condition can we flatter ourselves that we are continually advancing towards a perpetual peace.

Immanuel Kant *Perpetual Peace* [1798]

The bourgeoisie has through its exploitation of the world market given a cosmopolitan character to production and consumption in every country.

Karl Marx and Friedrich Engels
The Communist Manifesto [1848]

[A]mong European peoples there is a tendency to form, by spontaneous movement, a European society which has, at present, some idea of itself and the beginning of organization. If the formation of a single human society is forever impossible, a fact which has not been proven, at least the formation of continually larger societies brings us vaguely near the goal.

Emile Durkheim *The Division of
Labour in Society* [1893]

Contents

Series editor's foreword

The social sciences contribute to a greater understanding of the dynamics of social life and to explanations for the workings of societies in general. They are often not given due credit for this role and much writing has been devoted to why this should be the case. At the same time, we are living in an age in which the role of science in society is being re-evaluated. This has led to both a defence of science as the disinterested pursuit of knowledge and an attack on science as nothing more than an institutionalized assertion of faith, with no greater claim to validity than mythology and folklore. These debates tend to generate more heat than light.

In the meantime, the social sciences, in order to remain vibrant and relevant, will reflect the changing nature of these public debates. In so doing, they provide mirrors upon which we can gaze in order to understand not only what we have been and what we are now, but also in order to inform ideas about what we might become. This is not simply about understanding the reasons people give for their actions in terms of the contexts in which they act, as well as analysing the relations of cause and effect in the social, political and economic spheres, but also concerns the hopes, wishes and aspirations that people, in their different cultural ways, hold.

In any society that claims to have democratic aspirations, these hopes and wishes are not for the social scientist to prescribe. For this to happen it would mean that the social sciences were able to predict human behaviour with certainty. One theory and one method, applicable to all times and places, would be required for this purpose. The physical sciences do not live up to such stringent criteria, while the conditions in societies which provided for this outcome, were it even possible, would be intolerable. Why? Because a necessary condition of human freedom is the ability to have acted otherwise and thus to imagine and practise different ways of organizing societies and living together.

It does not follow from the above that social scientists do not have a valued role to play, as is often assumed in ideological attacks upon their place and function within society. After all, in focusing upon what we have been and what we are now, what we might become is inevitably illuminated. Therefore, while it may not be the province of social scientists to predict our futures, they are, given not only their understandings and explanations, but equal positions as citizens, entitled to engage in public debates concerning future prospects.

This new international series was devised with this general ethos in mind. It seeks to offer students of the sciences, at all levels, a forum in which ideas and topics of interest are interrogated in terms of their importance for understanding key social issues. This is achieved through a connection between style, structure and context that aims to be both illuminating and challenging in terms of its evaluation of those issues, as well as representing an original contribution to the subject under discussion.

Given this underlying philosophy, the series will contain books on topics which are driven by substantive interests. This is not simply a reactive endeavour in terms of reflecting dominant social and political preoccupations, it is also proactive in terms of an examination of issues which relate to and inform the dynamics of social life and the structures of society that are often not part of public discourse. Thus, what is distinctive about this series is an interrogation of the assumed characteristics of our current epoch in relation to its consequences for the organization of society and social life, as well as its appropriate mode of study.

Each contribution will contain, for the purposes of general orientation, as opposed to rigid structure, three parts. First, an interrogation of the topic which is conducted in a manner that renders explicit core assumptions surrounding the issues and/or an examination of the consequences of historical trends for contemporary social practices. Second, a section which aims to 'bring alive' ideas and practices by considering the ways in which they directly inform the dynamics of social relations. A third section will then move on to make an original contribution to the topic. This will encompass possible future forms and content, likely directions for the study of the phenomena in question, or an original analysis of the topic itself. Of course, it might be a combination of all three.

In *Citizenship in a Global Age*, Gerard Delanty reflects the ethos of the series by engaging with contemporary issues surrounding capitalism, globalization, identity, belonging and the nation state. In respect of these, we are living through times of rapid change. How these changes are characterized is not just a matter for scientific debate concerning the validity of various claims to reflect reality, for these contain within them, or have implications for, evaluations concerning the possible effects of social, political and economic trajectories. In the process terms abound that often lose their specificity in relating to particular forces of change: globalization being a case in point. Is this an opportunity for the expansion of a sense of association among different peoples, or yet another manifestation of the unbridled forces of capitalism enacted in the name of large corporations whose concerns are with profit to the exclusion of such considerations? These questions have important ramifications for our futures and those of our children.

Gerard Delanty commences his investigation of these concerns with the observation that both capitalism and democracy have become forces that have lost their connection with a sense of unity and the rule of law. To this extent, globalization is based upon a release of political and economic considerations from public culture. This produces a fragmentation that was once checked by democracy, but is now often apparent in resurgences of nationalist sentiments whose claims are thought to legitimate the genocides that have become a tragic and appalling feature of our contemporary era. Such manifestations represent celebrations of identities that are afforded through an exclusion of the 'Other'. Allusions to unities of the 'self' then become problematic in times of a plurality of selves.

A core problematic and central concern of *Citizenship in a Global Age* now becomes whether a sense of citizenship can flourish in such circumstances and act to both resist and temper those contemporary forces that seek to undermine it? It is here that the arguments for what Gerard Delanty calls a civic cosmopolitanism come to the fore in bringing the ideas of community and autonomy together, whilst recognizing that allusions to older notions of citizenship are no longer tenable. For this purpose, it is necessary to consider approaches to citizenship, in terms of their strengths and weaknesses, which is the subject of the first part of the book. A basis is then provided upon which to consider the ideas and implications of cosmopolitan citizenship which, as a recent development, is not restricted by the geographical boundaries associated with the nation state; hence its associations with globalization.

The central issue now becomes the capability of a civic cosmopolitanism, based on communication rather than concentrating exclusively on legal and political governance, to withstand the corrosive effects of current changes, whilst recognizing the contingent and decentred aspects of contemporary identities. Here we turn to human rights, not as a reflection of a universal human nature, but something to be achieved. In addition, drawing upon the argument of Jürgen Habermas, the author notes that this is not about the cultural imposition of western ideas upon societies in general, but the local conditions of their realization. Sensitivity to context then comes in the recognition that there is no universal and autonomous human nature to which we can appeal, but the frailty and incompleteness of the human condition. Difference is now recognized without resort to a universal humanity, but relativism and its accompanying retreat to indifference is checked by human rights becoming something that is to be achieved, not assumed, against such a background.

With this possibility in mind, the author then proceeds to an engagement with globalization, nationalism, the city, migration, multiculturalism and the European Union. Themes may be drawn from this extensive and interesting survey. First, with residence becoming an increasing dimension of citizenship, its links with nationality are no longer so important. That noted, the European Union still operates on the basis of the conferment of citizenship on the basis of birth and so it remains linked to nationality. The ability to confront the forces of globalization is thus limited unless accompanied by a move towards citizenship in terms of residence. In turn, this would require not only a concept of European Union citizenship, but the empowering of subnational forms at the level of the region and local authorities: that is, a principle of subsidiarity as applied to citizenship that takes account of the contemporary forces of fragmentation, without a corresponding capitulation to the irrationality of global economic forces.

A recognition of the need for citizenship to operate at these levels is a response to democracy now operating at different levels, thus leaving allusions to the nation state and birth as guarantees redundant and inapplicable to modern times. Inclusion then also operates at different levels and reflections upon cultural traditions, as well as celebrations of their past, exist alongside each other. A reflexive attitude in a post-national cosmopolitanism thereby acts as a check upon nationalism, as well as requiring public spaces of communication in which pluralism may flourish and communities grow. In being context bound and yet also context transcendent, the problems of liberal allusions to a false universalism and retreats into the particularity of worldviews may be avoided.

Arguments such as those contained in this book are part of the vibrancy and relevance of the sociological imagination. Refusing past categories of thought that have become so much part of our thinking that we rarely reflect upon them, is one task of this series in particular and sociological thought in general. As C. Wright Mills noted in *The Sociological Imagination*, several decades ago, these 'standard categories of thought', if generalized to contemporary situations, 'become unwieldy, irrelevant, not convincing' (1967: x). Once questioned, however, uncertainty is generated and to move on to engagement requires the generation of ideas that are prepared to contribute to new ways of living together. It is for this reason that this book deserves a wide readership among academics, students, politicians and an interested public in general.

Tim May

Reference

Wright Mills, C. (1967) *The Sociological Imagination*. New York: Oxford University Press Inc. USA.

Preface and acknowledgements

The debate on citizenship has been dominated by normative political theory, as in the controversies between liberals and communitarians. The older debate within sociology and social policy over the work of T.H. Marshall also became very much entwined in normative issues concerning the possibility of radical social change. While approaches deriving from radical democracy, including feminism and cultural pluralism, offered different perspectives on what membership of political community entails, the social sciences have been notably silent on citizenship. The interventions of radical democracy brought citizenship, which has traditionally been a pre-political category, closer to democracy but on the whole the debate has been dominated by political philosophy. Though many of the accounts of cosmopolitan citizenship are also highly normative, the contemporary challenge to citizenship from globalization, the subject of this book, offers a way of overcoming this deficit. Changes in the nature of society have forced us to rethink the meaning of citizenship. Citizenship has become a major new area of debate in the social sciences. The growing literature on this topic and journals such as *Citizenship Studies* have highlighted challenges such as technology, ecology, the media, group rights and consumerism for a new kind of citizenship beyond nationality. One of the striking aspects of this new citizenship is the move from a concern with equality to difference. Citizenship today has become a major site of battles over identity and demands for the recognition of group difference.

One of the aims of this book, then, is to bridge the gap between the political theory of citizenship and sociology in an assessment of the prospects of cosmopolitan citizenship in what is now a global age. A second objective is to explain to the student as concisely as possible of what cosmopolitan citizenship consists and how this development can be located in the context of the classical debates on citizenship. There is also a third objective, which it is hoped will be of interest to the theorist of citizenship. This concerns a critical account of the dominant conceptions of cosmopolitanism and the proposal for an alternative concept, which I have termed civic cosmopolitanism.

Briefly stated, my argument is that most conceptions of cosmopolitan citizenship are in fact about the prospects of global civil society and concern the possibility of legal and political forms of governance. In my view a more important question is that of the possibility of a cosmopolitan public sphere as a domain not only of transnational communication and governance, but also of the internal transformation of public spheres at national and subnational levels. Cosmopolitanism is increasingly becoming a significant force in the world in terms of culture, civic ties, law, technological innovations and political mobilization. But cosmopolitanism is not the same as globalization and therefore does not just take place on the transnational level. That is why cosmopolitanism can succeed only if it is connected to civic communities from which it draws the strength to resist globalization.

The book is organized into three parts. Part one deals with the classical models of citizenship. Following a short introduction in which the central ideas of the book are elaborated, Chapter 1 discusses the liberal theory of citizenship and focuses on the debate around Marshall. Chapter 2 presents the communitarian critique of liberalism and Chapter 3 brings theories of radical democracy to bear on citizenship. Part two concerns the implications of globalization for citizenship. Chapter 4 outlines the various cosmopolitan theories of citizenship. Chapter 5 deals with the implications of changed relations between human rights and the rights of citizenship. Chapter 6 focuses on the concept of globalization. Chapter 7 looks at the transformation of the nation state with respect to such issues as nationalism, migration, multiculturalism and the resurgence of the city as a space of citizenship. Chapter 8 brings the focus of post-nationalization to bear on European integration. In Part three a more precise interpretation of the implications of globalization for cosmopolitan citizenship is attempted. Chapter 9 presents a comprehensive theory of the reconfiguration of citizenship in the multi-level polity and, in conclusion, in Chapter 10 the idea of civic cosmopolitanism is outlined.

I would like to thank Tim May, the series editor, for advice on the book. I am also grateful to Justin Vaughan, the publisher, and four anonymous referees for advice and assistance in the preparation of this book which derives from a seminar on citizenship and social theory I gave while I was a Visiting Professor of Sociology at York University, Toronto in 1998.

All the material in this book is previously unpublished but I have drawn from a number of published papers, these being: Beyond the nation state: national identity and citizenship in a multicultural society: a response to Rex, *Sociological Research Online*, 1996, 1(3) <http://www.socresonline.org.uk/socresonline/1/3/1.html>; Models of citizenship: defining European identity and citizenship, *Citizenship Studies*, 1997, 1(3): 285–303; Social exclusion and the new nationalism: European trends and their implications for Ireland, *Innovation:*

The European Journal of Social Sciences, 1997, 10(2): 127–44; Social theory and European integration: is there a European society?, *Sociological Research Online*, 1998, 3(1) <http://www.socresonline.org.uk/socresonline/3/1/1.html>; Self, other and world: discourses of nationalism and cosmopolitanism, *Cultural Values*, 1999, 3(3): 365–75.

Introduction

This is a book about the theory and practice of citizenship in our global age. It is now widely recognized that various processes of globalization have greatly undermined the sovereignty of the nation state. While views differ on the extent to which the nation state may be exhausted, there is much evidence to suggest that our age is one less shaped by the nation state than was the case in the past. We are living in a global age in the sense that citizens are exposed to a far greater range of influences, resources and dangers than was formerly the case. Geography is less constraining for many people who also have more leisure time; the primary function of the state is no longer the permanent preparation for war as was the case up until the middle of the twentieth century; new technologies of communication and production have forced the state to become as much a regulatory agency as a provider; the internationalization of crime has given rise to the need for new kinds of security policy; following decolonization, formerly distinctive national cultures have been transformed by the encounter with other cultures; European cultural identity is no longer specific to Europe, not only having become westernized, but also it is a core component of all cultural identities; and the universal culture of risk and envir-onmental destruction is shaping the political imagination.

Perhaps one of the most far-reaching changes is that in the west and much of the rest of world we are leaving industrial society behind and entering a post-industrial society with what some claim to be a postmodern culture. It is fateful that this transition is being made when much of the rest of the developing world is making the transition to industrial society and that in the former communist world the double transition to modern political culture is taking place, with the contradictory logics of capitalism and democracy unfolding under the aegis of what is widely recognized to be post-communism (Sakwa 1999). These three societal models, post-industrial, the industrial and post-communism, as they emerge from divergent modernities, are now colliding in the global age whose geopolitical configurations will be very different from what has previously prevailed.

In the view of many, this situation has had huge implications for citizenship with globalization opening up the possibility of something like cosmopolitan citizenship, a new practice of citizenship that goes beyond the parameters of the nation state. Cosmopolitan citizens, according to this increasingly influential position, are citizens of the world community, not of any particular state, for cosmopolitan community is replacing national community. This book is written as a critical engagement with this thesis which can be associated with the work of Jürgen Habermas, Richard Falk, Bryan Turner, John Urry, Andrew Linklater, David Held, Saskia Sassen, Anthony Giddens and many other social and political scientists (Linklater 1998; Isin and Wood 1999). My position is one that acknowledges the massive onslaught on the nation state that has come with the globalization of markets, new kinds of war, increased migration, technological changes, changes in communication and cultural production but questions the adequacy of cosmopolitanism, while at the same time acknowledging its necessity. It is capitalism, not citizenship, that is truly cosmopolitan today, a tendency that Marx and Engels noted: 'The bourgeoisie has through its exploitation of the world market given a cosmopolitan character to production and consumption in every country' (Marx and Engels 1967: 83). If democracy has become global, it has done so only by becoming allied with nationalism and populist ideology. The global age has created a highly fragmented world in which the struggle for democracy and the expansion of capitalism is not always contained within the structures of a civil society based on the institution of citizenship. Having been released from the contours of the nation state, capitalism and democracy have lost their moorings in the spirit of civic community that had made modern society possible. In the global age – which is assumed by many to be both postmodern and neo-liberal – there is no 'invisible hand' guiding a common purpose, as Adam Smith believed characterized an earlier capitalism; no 'cunning reason' leading to a rational polity, as Hegel discerned in the post-Enlightenment state; no benign principle of equality compensating for the inequalities that the pursuit of wealth brings in its wake, as T.H. Marshall (1992) said of the institution of social citizenship in the twentieth century. It is a world that is highly disconnected, even fragmented (Delanty 1999a; Touraine 2000).

One major dimension of globalization, according to my analysis, is that capitalism (the economic pursuit of profit) and democracy (the political rule of the majority) have become untamed forces, having lost their connection with the institution of citizenship. Capitalism and democracy, in their pure forms of money and self-determination and unconnected with a principle of unity, are among the most pervasive forces in the world today. The identification of society with economy or with politics, the pursuit of wealth or the means of influence unconstrained by a civic commitment and the rule of law has provided the principal dynamic of globalization: the release of economy and politics from the public culture of citizenship and a conception of space shaped by the civic ties of community. In this view, the global age is a highly fragmented order for what has disintegrated is the stable force of a civic realm and its replacement by disembodied space.

Democracy of course has been the principal challenge to capitalism in the formation of modernity, but democracy in the modern age has mostly been based on citizenship. The danger today is that democracy may become disconnected from citizenship, as well as from the rule of law. Thus, in many parts of the world democracy is providing a legitimation of triumphalist kinds of nationalism, with demands for self-determination being the other face of the determination of the other by the self (de Vries and Weber 1997). Michael Mann (1999) has criticized the view that democracies are essentially pacific and almost never go to war with each other. He has argued that many democracies have conducted genocidal acts and that these genocides have been justified 'in the name of the people':

> By claiming legitimacy in the name of 'the People', genocidal regimes claim kinship to movements which are usually recognized as the bearers of a true modernity, like liberalism or social democracy. Indeed, I argue that modern genocide can be regarded as 'the dark side of democracy'.
>
> (Mann 1999: 19)

Mann goes on to argue that it was class struggle and its institutionalization that have restrained liberal democracies from cleansing atrocities and genocides. I agree with this argument but take the view that class struggle – the struggle for social justice – has led to the institutionalization of an active and deeper kind of citizenship which has become a major dimension of democracy. Though I do not see class struggle as dead, it has taken a new and more more plural form in contemporary societies (Eder 1993). In our late modern societies a new range of issues has arisen, many of which go beyond questions of class, which has become only one site of struggle.

Modernity was a discourse of the emancipation of the self, but the question of the other is being asked only now. The problem with 'self-determination' in postmodern times is that there is no one single self but a plurality of selves. In this move beyond the contours of the modern age we have to ask the question of the responsibility of the self for the other. The rethinking of democracy – which is a discourse of self-determination – that this entails will force us to re-establish a link with citizenship – where self and other find a point of reconciliation. This is the central thesis of several recent works on the reconciliation of the political frameworks of modernity with the cultural aspirations of late modernity. As the Canadian political philosopher, James Tully (1995), argues in his *Strange Multiplicity: Constitutionalism in an Age of Diversity*, the struggle for cultural recognition – aboriginal self-government, ethnic minorities, feminism – presents constitutionalism with its most important challenge since constitutionalism was never designed to deal with cultural diversity. It is the merit of his work and others, such as Jürgen Habermas's (1998a) *The Inclusion of the Other*, William Connolly's (1995) *The Ethos of Pluralization*, Engin Isin and Patricia Wood's (1999) *Citizenship and Identity*, Andrew Linklater's (1998) *The Transformation of Political Community* and the many writings of Alain Touraine and Karl-Otto Apel, that they have sought out within the cosmopolitan heritage a means of reconciling the political achievements of the modern age with the current situation of cultural conflict. I find in these works the basis of a cosmopolitan critique of globalization.

Can cosmopolitanism resist globalization? Can capitalism and democracy be relinked by citizenship? Can a principle of autonomy be recovered from the current reality of fragmentation? These are the basic questions underlying this book which can be read as a critique of the false promises of cosmo-politanism. Allying citizenship with cosmopolitanism, I shall try to explore how something like a post-national citizenship is possible. It seems to me that one of the really major challenges for citizenship is to retain some of the great innovations achieved in the era of the modern nation state while being able to open up new possibilities in line with the current situation and new con-figurations of time and space. The problem can be stated more precisely. Citizenship entails membership of a legally constituted political community, which may be called civil society; it consists of rights, duties, participation and identity. Yet, there is only a very limited civil society beyond the nation state. Civil society emerged along with the rise of the modern state and was the social basis of citizenship. Citizenship was partly a state-led project and partly a project emanating from civil society. It occupied both a political and an economic space in which personal autonomy was guaranteed by the rule of law. These two faces of civil society – the political and the economic – encapsulated the ambivalence of citizenship, which was closely connected with the institutionalizing of democracy and capitalism by law and by public discourse. What prevented this tension within citizenship from collapsing into the ideal either of a totally self-governing society or the legitimation of capitalism – the rule of the self or the rule of self-interest – was the formation of the modern nation state. In short, the modern state provided the institu-tional contexts in which citizenship developed so that modern society was not entirely shaped either by the rule of pure democracy or by an unconstrained capitalism. The problem that conceptions of post-national citizenship, or more broadly, cosmopolitan citizenship, are faced with is that the institutions and social context on which citizenship rests do not exist in any substantive form in the global arena. The essence of this substantive dimension to citizenship is the existence of the public domain as a civic community, for citizens are reducible neither to private, economic beings nor to purely political agents. The basis of citizenship ultimately is a recognition of the autonomy of the *person* – and therefore presupposes the reconciliation of self and other.

To be sure, globalization has eroded much of the authority and resources of the nation state, producing in its wake a whole range of problems which cannot be addressed by the existing structures of civil society: issues relating to international migration, environmental destruction, the control of com-munication, human rights and humanitarian aid, international crime, the increased incidence of civil wars. But on the other hand, citizenship is for the greater part still very much defined by the state which, despite globalization, is the more or less sole upholder of the rights of citizenship. An additonal problem is the absence of a common cultural foundation for cosmopolitan citizenship, for instance, the existence of a common language. Moreover, there is no effective constitutional state in the international arena that can be compared to the nation state, no democracy in the international arena which is still dominated by states, and, to give a final example of the limits of cosmopolitanism, there is no transnational welfare state, for social rights are more or less exclusively arbitrated by the national state.

It would appear, then, that while recognizing the apparent need, even necessity, of cosmopolitan citizenship, we are still confined to the nation state wherein, alone, the potentially destructive forces of capitalism and democracy were tamed. But this would be to draw a too pessimistic conclusion of the prospects of cosmopolitanism. Rejecting a model of cosmopolitanism based on global citizenship, I am advocating a model of civic cosmopolitanism, which I believe is more realistic. What is distinctive about this position is that it seeks to bring the dimension of community and autonomy, the basis of national models of citizenship, closer to the emergent reality of a cosmopolitan citizenship. A central dimension to this conception of citizenship is a sense of citizenship as multi-levelled, cutting across the subnational, the national and the transnational, for citizenship can no longer be located exclusively on any one level. One of the main critical contributions of this book is a defence of the idea of a *cosmopolitan public sphere* while being more critical of the prospect of a *cosmopolitan civil society*, particularly to the extent that the latter is disconnected from the former. The distinction between the concepts of the public sphere and civil society is frequently confused and most of the arguments for cosmopolitanism advocate some notion of a global civil society. But the distinction is an important one and allows us to evade some of the problems of cosmopolitanism as a normative version of globalization. To follow Habermas, the public sphere is prior to civil society for it is the domain of civic communication and cultural contestation; civil society, on the other hand, refers to more specific forms of mobilization and citizenship participation which have some relation to the state (Habermas 1989a, 1996, 1998a). Cosmopolitan public spheres come into existence when transnational, national or local public spheres come into contact with each other and undergo change as a result. This is quite distinct from the question of civil society as a legal and political form of *transnational governance*, for it is a matter of cultural transformation in the values and norms of social and civic relations. A cosmopolitan public sphere gives rise to a limited kind of cosmopolitanism, which I am calling civic cosmopolitanism and which can be contrasted to the broader political and legal conceptions of cosmopolitanism as transnational governance. A cosmopolitan or global civil society, on the other hand, can of course also come about, but this is a different kind of cosmopolitanism and whose possibilities are limited to the tasks of government – the rule of law and public administration – and governance – the political assertion of civil society. The idea of civic cosmopolitanism, in sum, is a qualified kind of cosmopolitanism, one that is cautious about the possibility and desirability of a global civil society. The real power of cosmopolitanism lies in communicative power, that is in the problematizing, the reflexive transformation of cultural models and the raising of 'voice'. Unless global civil society is based on a cosmopolitan politic sphere – which can be on subnational, national and transnational levels – there is the danger that it will become disembodied.

This, then, is a book about the encounter between cosmopolitanism and globalization, the clash between the civic politics of autonomy and the ruthless forces of fragmentation. The understanding of citizenship here is essentially that of a politics of autonomy based on civic community and public discourse. Civic cosmopolitanism is a politics of autonomy that preserves civil society against the new fragmentations, be it those of capitalism or nationalism, the rule of profit or the rule of the self. A politics of autonomy entails the con-nectivness of self and other, as Axel Honneth (1995) has argued. Written in 1999 as the war in Kosovo unfolded, this book is a reminder that not just capitalism, but also nationalism thinly disguised by democracy can be a de-structive force. Destroyed initially by post-communist transition to capitalism, the violent forces of nationalism allied to democracy brought that part of the world further along the path to devastation. So long as capitalism and democracy remain unconnected with the institution of citizenship the chances are very great that the global age will be one that has seen the demise of the social itself. The example of Kosovo was a further reminder, too, that there is no global civil society. A local event suddenly became a global stage – with a potential confrontation with Russia and China on separate occasions – but one where the protagonists were states, regional blocs and military alliances. This three-month long episode presented a disturbing picture of 'cosmo-politanism' – in effect globalization – allied to militarism and an exhausted civil society. One of its most notable characteristics was the division of the European intellectual liberal-left into those who supported the North Atlantic Treaty Organization (NATO)-led campaign and those who resisted in the name of an alternative but non-existent civic order. A concern with civic cosmopolitanism in the sense advocated here of a stronger emphasis on the public sphere as a domain prior to civil society is essential and suggests the need to address communication and the building of civic ties.

PART ONE

Models of citizenship

The liberal theory of citizenship: rights and duties

In the most general sense citizenship is about group membership. More especially we might say it entails membership of a particular kind of group, namely political community. Much of the debate about citizenship concerns the nature of group membership. Of what does it consist? What does it mean to be a member of political community? Does citizenship enhance or limit the possibility of democratic politics?

Citizenship as membership of a political community involves a set of relationships between rights, duties, participation and identity. These may be termed the components of citizenship, the defining tenets of group membership. Citizenship in the classical tradition of modern liberal thought has generally been held to be a particular relationship of rights and duties. In this tradition the emphasis has been on a market-based reduction of citizenship, though in its later, left-wing and more social democratic form the emphasis shifted towards the administrative state. In more recent times, but harkening back to Renaissance and later civic republican ideas of political community, an alternative tradition emphasizes citizenship as participation in the civic community. It is useful to distinguish these two dominant models of citizenship, on the one hand market and state-centred conceptions of citizenship which is a formal and legally coded status and, on the other, citizenship as entailing the more substantive dimension of participation in the civic community (Stewart 1995). In the first case what is usually intended is nationality, while in the second sense what is normally meant is a more active kind of citizenship, not in the sense of the conservative discourse of the 1980s but of participation and democratization (D. King 1987; Clarke 1996; Rimmerman 1997). In this chapter I shall be discussing mainly formal citizenship and in Chapters 2 and 3 some active conceptions of citizenship will be examined. Anticipating the argument that will be developed in these chapters, it may be stated here that the formalistic conception of citizenship is based on a reduction of citizenship to a privatistic and pre-political status.

In a variety of ways the main theoretical traditions in modern social and political thought have reflected these very different dimensions of membership of political community, as formal membership of the state or as an active and essentially public involvement in civil society. Indeed, a good deal of modern political thought is divided between a statist stance and a commitment to civil society. But the distinction is more complicated once we bring in the four components I mentioned above: rights, duties, participation and identity. The liberal tradition, in both its right- and left-wing forms, has principally emphasized citizenship in terms of rights; the conservative tradition has stressed the duties or responsibilities of citizenship; the republican and communitarian traditions have given centrality to participation; while identity has been the core idea in nationalist-inclined conceptions of citizenship, as well as in some communitarian theories. It is even more complicated for (as we shall see) the category of rights can be differentiated into civic, political and social rights and, for instance, identity can refer either to political or to cultural identity. However, on the whole it is possible to discuss the modern theory of citizenship in terms of rights, duties, participation and identity. These components of membership need to be further divided in terms of the formal and substantive dimensions, which roughly correspond to the statist and the civil society traditions in modern social and political thought.

In the first part of this book I critically outline and discuss the classical conceptions of citizenship. In this chapter I look at theories which stress rights and duties and which on the whole reflect the formalist conception of citizenship as a state-centred project; in Chapter 2 I examine communitarian theories that emphasize participation in civil society, and in Chapter 3 the focus shifts to democracy. I shall argue that the two dominant traditions, the liberal and communitarian traditions, have on the whole neglected the link between citizenship and democracy. According to proponents of radical democracy, no theory of a substantive citizenship is complete without a notion of democracy. This, then, presents one of the main debates in the theory of citizenship, the question of the relationship of citizenship to democracy.

In tracing the trajectory of citizenship in terms of a shift from formally held rights and duties to a more substantive concern with participation and identity, a further rupture can be discerned in the discourse on citizenship: the conflict between citizenship as the pursuit of equality and as a recognition of difference. In the classical tradition of modern liberal thought, the subject of this chapter, citizenship was above all based on a principle of equality whereas today one of the most important themes in the debate on citizenship is the recognition of difference, be it group difference or wider issues of cultural difference. This shift brings to the fore a whole series of new conceptions of citizenship which, in highlighting collective rights, make redundant the former separation of the rights of citizenship and human rights. In this book I am arguing that the rupture between equality and difference is one of the greatest challenges to citizenship. Moreover, no discussion of this problem can neglect the question of democracy and in particular the question of global governace, for the extension and transformation of democracy is the dynamic that has led to the increased tension between equality and difference. In undermining nationality as the foundation of citizenship where a measure of equality could be guaranteed, the global age has unleashed new kinds of politics that present both possibilities as well as dangers for citizenship.

Citizenship and the struggle for equality

The concept of citizenship as a legal status based on rights was a Roman development, but with its roots in Greek thought and practice. For the Greeks there was no clear distinction between morality and legality, citizenship and democracy. A citizen was an essentially political being, by which was meant both a moral and a legal entity. Citizenship was an inherited privilege and clearly marked the boundary between non-citizens and citizens, for the polis was based on a restricted principle of equality as well as on a clearly defined territory. Thus from the very beginning the term entails exclusion since not everyone is in possession of it. Exclusion could take either the form of banishment from the geopolitical territory or subordination to non-citizen status, as was the fate of slaves, women and children. The more expansive or inclusionary citizenship becomes the less it has to offer citizens. Consequently it must be restricted. For the Greeks, who valued highly the idea of citizenship, a strong citizenship of exclusion was preferred in order to restrict social resources and political rights to a small number of persons, namely male warriors of known genealogical origin who were also slave owners.

Equality was not central to the Greek conception of citizenship, which was ultimately a privilege. For the Greeks, the citizen achieved equality in the public domain, the world of 'speech' where he was free to engage in political discourse freed from the burden of the household or the world of 'things', the confine of women, children and slaves. No account of citizenship can evade the fact that it was originally constructed in order to exclude and subordinate people. As J.G.A. Pocock (1995) has written, this is the central predicament of the classical ideal of citizenship:

> If one wants to make citizenship available to those to whom it has been denied on the grounds that they are too much involved in the world of things – in material, productive, domestic, or reproductive relationships – one has to choose between emancipating them from these relationships and denying that these relationships are negative components in the definition of citizenship.
>
> (Pocock 1995: 33)

For the Romans citizenship became established as a strictly legal status defining membership of the Roman political community, the *res publica*. This conception of citizenship as a legal category was connected with the rise of the distinction between state and society whereby a legally codified set of relationships defined the rights and duties of the individual. Consequently the individual, in the eyes of the law, was a legal being, a citizen, and no longer entailed a relation to politics as a face to face relationship with other citizens. With this came a firmer recognition of citizenship as a question of formal equality in the public domain. From then onwards the link between citizenship and democracy was broken. Yet it is clear from such works as Cicero's *De Re Publica* (in 52 BCE) that the Roman idea of citizenship sought to preserve a link with the Greek emphasis on participation in public life with its universalistic status as a legal category. This was very much connected with the need for the legal regulation of the possession of property in what was now a much more societally complex society than the Greek polis, where democracy was coeval with citizenship. Thus law and property now become the paramount indicators of citizenship, which can be termed participation in the community of shared common law. By the time of the Renaissance, when there was a revival of interest in the ancient Roman Republic, republican concepts of citizenship offered a new political identity for the Italian city states. The main departure from the ancient ideas was that republican citizenship must reconcile itself with a society organized through a state, the basic model of which was the Roman rather than the Athenian system. This turn to the state also marked another step in the separation of citizenship from democracy, since Renaissance republicanism made no claims to democracy. In this it was very different from American Enlightenment republicanism.

For a long time the word 'citizen' meant simply the inhabitant of a town and as Max Weber (1958) has documented of the medieval period, this was a legal conception of the person and therefore a contrast to the word 'subject' (Nisbet 1974). At this time, it is important to mention, the term citizen did not mean nationality with which it has become coterminus in modern times. It was not a bond between the individual and the state or nation but a specifically urban relationship concerning rights and duties in a town, for as Weber points out in his classic study of the European city, the existence of independent courts and autonomous administration in the medieval cities in effect offered local forms of citizenship which were later taken over by the centralizing nation state in the age of absolutism and mercantilism (Weber 1958). There was, then, historically a very clear relationship between the condition of citizenship and membership of a city.

With the rise of the central bureaucratic state from the sixteenth century also came a discernible social domain, for state formation and the rise of a market society were closely connected and began to extend beyond the confines of the autonomous city. As the moral philosophers of the Scottish Enlightenment recognized, the social domain became a more diffuse web of relations, extending beyond the strictly public domain. This is evident in Ferguson's *Essay on the Origin of Civil Society* in 1767 (see Delanty 1999d). With these developments it thus becomes meaningful to speak of civil society to refer to the public domain between state and society. Civil society refers less to the general economic and social space than to the specifically *public* sphere and is also distinct from the official organs of the state as such (Habermas 1989a).

Equal in the eyes of the law, citizens increasingly came to be ostensibly equal in the public sphere as the domain between the private arena and the political realm of the state. This domain was partly regulated by law but was also open to communicative practices (Strydom 2000). However, in its eighteenth-century form, this public domain was very much based on the prior exist-ence of a private domain composed of unequal relationships in terms of class, race and gender.

This essentially legal conception of citizenship as the public representation of the individual has remained the basis of the entire modern liberal tradition of citizenship; it opened up into two principal paths in the eighteenth century, when civil society became consolidated, these being the tension between citizenship as defined by reference to the political or the economic. What I am claiming is that civil society never fully occupied the intermediate ground of the public domain, for it was always inclined towards either the political or the economic. From the Enlightenment and revolutionary period onwards, the two conceptions of citizenship emerged around the dual face of civil society as the domain of wealth creation and the sphere of political activity. One tradition, which has been closely identified with modern liber-alism, has stressed the idea of citizenship in terms of a market society and is reflected in the pursuit of the rights to possess property and to enter into contracts. This might be called the bourgeois conception of citizenship. Another tradition, associated with modern democracy and republican thought, has stressed citizenship in terms of civic and political rights. In the early the-orists, such as Thomas Hobbes, John Locke, Adam Smith and G.W.F. Hegel, these traditions are not always clearly discernible – as is epitomized in Locke's political theory of the natural rights of 'life, liberty and property' – but by the time of Karl Marx a more pronounced distinction became more visible than in the previous two centuries. Now the citizen suggests a category that was being undermined by its corruption into the 'bourgeois'. Unable to seek the political emancipation promised by their own ideology, the bourgerisic opted for the non-political world of possession. Individualism thus became, in the famous term of C.P. MacPherson (1962), 'possessive individualism'. To recover the civic conception of citizenship was central to the political theory of the early Marx for whom, as in for example his critique of Hegel, it held out the promise of asserting the priority of democracy over capitalism (O'Neill 1996). While this provided the animus for socialism, the tradition of radical democracy from the Levellers through Rousseau to Thomas Paine also looked to democracy and the idea of the *political* citizen rather than the *economic* con-ception of the citizen. However, the specifically *social* conception of citizenship was taken up only by the socialist tradition as a theory of class struggle.

There is no doubt that the dominant tradition in citizenship has been the market-based model, which goes back to the British thinkers Thomas Hobbes, John Locke and Adam Smith. In this tradition, citizenship is related to the emergence of a conception of civil society that is basically pre-political. The civic body of citizens is seen as under threat from government, which constantly becomes a necessary evil, required in order to secure the conditions of market exchange, but undesirable in itself. Liberty as a political condition thus becomes negative liberty, the freedom to be free of unnecessary government (Berlin 1969). Positive freedom, then, is the condition of civil society – the freedom of private individuals to pursue their interests, which have generally been seen to be wealth creation. As Somers (1995) has shown, this understanding of civil society in Anglo-Saxon political thought has had the effect of reducing citizenship to a pre-political status. The citizen is private in that the public face of civil society serves a pre-political purpose. The pre-political foundations of civil society are further anchored in a notion of natural rights.

The rise of sociological thought from the late nineteenth century did much to dispel the myth of a pre-social order of natural rights and the rise of the social democratic inspired social policy shifted the focus of citizenship from the market to the state. The sociology of Emile Durkheim is the best example of this and his work *Professional Ethics and Civic Morals* represents one of the first sociological reflections on citizenship as a form of social integration in modern society (Durkheim 1957). One of Durkheim's abiding questions concerned the nature of what he called civic morals in the context of the social divisions produced by industrialism and the growing differentiation of modern society. For Dukheim the state alone is unable to provide sufficient social integration and consequently social integration must depend on other sources, such as the intermediary bonds of citizenship in associations and civic forms of public service. Durkheim's work on citizenship was incomplete by the time of his early death in 1917 and has been overshadowed by T.H. Marshall's theory of citizenship; a theory that is not too far removed from Durkheim's ideas, but differs in that citizenship is conceived less as a set of civic ties that exist in the intermediary domain between the state and the individual than a bundle of rights that tie the individual through social class to the state.

Marshall's theory of citizenship: from the market to the state

In the most general sense, the modern conception of citizenship has been based on the idea that membership of society must rest on a principle of formal equality. This principle has generally been understood to be defined in terms of a particular understanding of rights. Duties also come into this, but first let us deal with the question of rights. Taking T.H. Marshall's (1992) seminal essay, *Citizenship and Social Class*, originally published in 1950 and based on a lecture the previous year, as a reference point, I shall discuss one of the main debates on citizenship in terms of a relation of formal equality based on rights. What I wish to demonstrate is that Marshall marks a tendency to shift citizenship from its previously too heavy reliance on a market-based model of civil society to a state-based model. This shift from market to state reflects the gradual confluence of liberalism with social democracy. However, it would be a mistake to assume that this facilitates the recovery of the lost public conception of citizenship. It will become evident in the following discussion that Marshall's theory of citizenship retained the basic pre-political notion of civil society that was central to the classical tradition. In fact in his analysis the very idea of civil society disappears and is replaced by social classes.

According to Marshall (1992: 18) in a famous formulation: 'Citizenship is a status bestowed on those who are full members of a community. All who possess the status are equal with respect to the rights and duties with which the status is endowed'. His conception of citizenship was an evolutionary one in that it was, he held in the same passage, a 'developing institution in England since the latter part of the seventeenth century' (Marshall 1992: 18). In this he has been severely criticized since Britain, let alone England, has not been a model of universal applicability and citizenship has not always unfolded according to a single developmental logic (Mann 1987). It should be mentioned, however, that his concern clearly was with Britain, as is perhaps more explicit in his later work, *Social Policy* (Marshall 1965). The developmental path through which citizenship has evolved, he claimed, was the movement from the acquisition of civic rights to political rights to social rights. Each of these sets of rights were achievements, respectively, of the eighteenth century, the nineteenth century and the twentieth century.

Civic rights emerged in the seventeenth century around the struggle for the freedom of the individual with respect to freedom of conscience, freedom of worship, freedom of speech, the right to enter contract and ownership of private property. Lying at the very core of citizenship right from the very beginning was the recognition of the equality of all citizens in the eyes of the law. As a legal status consisting of rights, citizenship could be upheld by recourse to the courts of justice. Rights were thus ultimately secured by justice. This orientation to the civic conception of justice, according to Marshall, means that citizenship is inescapably linked to the pursuit of equality, for in the eyes of the law all citizens are equal.

In the nineteenth century, in Marshall's model, the struggle for political rights was added to the previous emphasis on civil rights. This is more than a question of anchoring rights in justice, but in securing their political enactment in the institution of parliament. This was less based on the creation of new rights than the extension of existing rights to a wider franchise, extending from adult males to full adult franchise. Civil rights had become universal, at least in England according to Marshall, but the struggle for political rights was not won until the first quarter of the twentieth century. Clearly Marshall had only Britain in mind here since in many countries, franchise had yet to be extended to all adults regardless of race. However, his principal aim was to assess the impact of social rights on what he called social class.

Originally confined to local communities but later coming under the sphere of the Poor Law and the early Factory Acts, social rights by the early twentieth century became one of the central dimensions of state provision. But the link has first to be broken from the Poor Law, which was based on the divorce of citizenship from social rights: 'The Poor Law treated the claims of the poor, not as an integral part of the rights of the citizen, but as an alternative to them – as claims which could be met only if the claimants ceased to be citizens in any true sense of the word' (Marshall 1992: 15). The poor had to forfeit any civil rights in order to benefit from the social rights of the Poor Law, which was clearly more an attempt to control the poor than enhance their inclusion in society. It is Marshall's thesis that the foundations for social citizenship were laid in the nineteenth century, especially with public elementary education, but the link between citizenship and social rights did not become apparent until the twentieth century. His argument is that social citizenship, when it eventually came with the modern welfare state, alleviated the social inequalities produced by capitalism. Thus citizenship, in its full and completed form of social citizenship, is a means of minimizing inequality. For Marshall inequality, which derives from the economic order, is inevitable given the reality of capitalism, while citizenship is compensatory and, as the case of civil rights illustrates, can even be complementary to capitalism. As he said, 'these rights did not conflict with the inequalities of capitalist society; they were, on the contrary, necessary to the maintenance of that particular form of inequality' (Marshall 1992: 20). This was so because civil rights were indispensable to a market-driven economy and allowed individuals to become independent economic units. There is, then, some justification in the Marxist critique that civic citizenship was a legitimation of capitalism (Hindess 1998). With the rise of political rights this was less clear cut but formal equality did not translate into actual equality.

Marshall recognized equality in law and in politics could be compatible with real social inequality, or at least have little real impact on it. Social rights in the form of social welfare – whether in housing, health, education, unemployment benefits or pensions – brought to completion the purely formal rights of civic and political citizenship by alleviating the structural inequalities of capitalism. Social rights created 'a universal right to real income which is not proportionate to the market value of the claimant' (Marshall 1992: 28). Social citizenship thus has an equalizing effect, bringing about equality of social opportunity. 'Equalization is not so much between classes as between individuals within a population which is now treated for this purpose as though it were one class. Equality of status is more important than equality of income' (Marshall 1992: 33). What Marshall saw emerging was a growing tension between citizenship and capitalism, a conflict that could be said to be one between the state, as the guarantor of social citizenship, and economy as the producer of inequalities. He saw this antagonism to be a healthy one in that citizenship would act upon capitalism, reducing the inequalities that are inevitably produced by the market. For Marshall this conflict between citizenship and capitalism was one that was leading towards the incorporation of the working class into society, for through the institution of citizenship the state was taking over the role of class conflict by taking conflict out of the social domain. In effect, his vision, partly reality and partly ideology, was one that looked to the state rather than social actors as the arbitrators of social conflict. It is therefore with some justification that he has been seen as a theorist of social integration, from standpoints ranging from functionalism to Marxism (Bendix 1964; Hindess 1987).

Finally I would like to remark on the question of the duties of citizenship. Marshall was primarily writing about the rights of citizenship, but towards the end of his essay he remarked on the corresponding duties that rights entail (Marshall 1992: 41–3, 45–6). This was a largely undeveloped theme in his thought although he clearly had some notion that corresponding to social rights is a public duty. Examples of duties are the obligation to pay taxes and insurance contributions, as well as mandatory schooling and, in times of war, military service. But as pointed out, these duties are compulsory and no wilful action is required. Most duties are vague, such as the duty to work or to promote the welfare of the community. The limits of his conception of duty become apparent in an often quoted sentence: 'A successful appeal to the duties of citizenship can be made in times of emergency, but the Dunkirk spirit cannot be a permanent feature of any civilization' (Marshall 1992: 46). Clearly, he had a wider understanding of citizenship as participation in society but he lacked a conception of social action. His overly formal conception of citizenship led to a view of involvement in the community as purely passive.

The limits of Marshall's theory of citizenship

There are many problems with Marshall's theory of citizenship. There is some uncertainty as to whether he was offering a normative or an empirical outline of citizenship. It was clearly both. It was primarily a description of the development of citizenship in England, though one that had a strong normative edge to it. The normative ideal of citizenship is not unrelated to the actual institution of citizenship, for as he wrote: 'societies in which citizenship is a developing institution create an image of an ideal citizenship against which achievement can be measured and toward which aspiration can be directed' (Marshall 1992: 18). It was his firm conviction that the institution of citizenship contained within it an ideal of imperfect equality, which he saw as more or less realized in the post-war welfare state. That the welfare state has not alleviated inequality to the degree he believed was likely to be the case, is only one of the serious flaws in his theory. I will not rehearse the familiar argument that the welfare state has not merely alleviated inequality but has contributed to it, beyond remarking that social citizenship has in effect bought off dissent and become a form of crisis management (Offe 1984). What is noteworthy is that his theory of social citizenship never progressed into economic or industrial rights. This was not unrelated to Marshall's conviction that the dynamic of inequality and equality was essential to modern society and that, to a degree, socialist measures had been realized by all political parties (Marshall 1992: 47). The conservative slant to his argument has been the subject of many debates on his work (Giddens 1982; Mann 1987; Barbalet 1988; Turner 1990; Hindess 1993). Yet his work has been of enduring significance and in the age of globalization some of the achievements of the European welfare state cannot be lightly dismissed, as Holmwood (2000) argues. Though social class may no longer be the primary source of group ties and solidarity, having been displaced by other bonds, such as race, gender, ethnicity and other forms of collective identity, it is still one of the most important forms of structural inequality in late modern societies (Grusky and Sorensen 1998; Byrne 1999).

My main concern is to assess the limits of Marshall's theory of citizenship from the vantage point of the contemporary situation and of alternative conceptions of citizenship. I do not think that the Marxist emphasis on economic and industrial citizenship presents the principal challenge to citizenship theory today, though a comprehensive theory of citizenship will need to take account of the deepening of social citizenship with respect to economic rights (Roche 1992; Twine 1994). It would indeed appear that the Marshallian notion of social rights has now been taken up by other discourses of citizenship which will be introduced shortly. In other words, the problem with his account of citizenship relates to its presuppositions, many of which have been rendered invalid by more recent discourses and by social change. I shall comment on five central problems with Marshall's theory of citizenship.

First, the challenge of cultural rights. Today there are other kinds of exclusion which cannot be accommodated by a model of social rights. One of the main contending theories of citizenship, to be discussed towards the end of Chapter 3, concerns the contemporary politicization of gender and race-related forms of exclusion. The recognition of these forms of exclusion has committed many to the view that policies of universal equality will not be adequate and that therefore some kind of radical difference is necessary in the recognition of group right (I.M. Young 1990; Isin and Wood 1999). The rise of cultural or collective rights might be heralded as yet a further model of rights (see Chapter 5). As I have already intimated, and which will be explored in more detail later, there is now a tension between equality and the recognition of difference. To this might also be added the growing importance of ecological questions, such as the idea of the rights of animals and of nature.

Second, the challenge of globalization and multiple modernities. Cultural rights, which also relate to issues concerning the media and information, the protection of cultural heritage, linguistic rights and so on, cannot be simply added on to Marshall's developmental model. This is because there is no singly developmental logic by which citizenship unfolds along a historical trajectory (Mann 1987). Thus, as has frequently been pointed out, the world-wide experience has not been that of convergence but of divergence. In the USA there is a notable absence of social rights, while in the former USSR under communist rule there was a strong recognition of citizenship in terms of social rights. In general, totalitarian rule, as the cases of Nazi Germany or Chile under Pinochet attest, is compatible with social rights. Also, as already noted, civic rights were not fully institutionalized in the USA until the late 1960s with the removal of racial discrimination. In many parts of the world today the struggle for cultural rights seems to be given priority over other kinds of rights. In sum, there is no simple trajectory along which a logic of rights unfolds.

Third, the challenge of substantive over formal citizenship. One of the main problems with Marshall's theory is that he ignored the salience of participation as a dimension of citizenship. His account of citizenship entailed a very passive conception of the citizen. As he clearly put it, his concern was with the impact of citizenship on social classes, not of social classes on citizenship. Citizenship may entail a relationship between rights and duties, but his analysis ignored the fact that where citizenship was not simply a 'ruling class strategy', as Mann (1987) termed it, by which a dominant class or the state controlled the masses and maintained the class system, it was also a means of empowerment. Citizenship was not only a ruling class strategy or a strategy of divide and rule (Hindess 1998) but also a product of centuries of popular mobilization leading to the winning of rights (see Chapter 3). The rights of citizenship did not simply come automatically from a benevolent state by some kind of preordained evolutionary path, but arose out of the historical struggles between capital and labour (Therborn 1977). In the context of the theme of this book, the important point here is that the question of rights cannot be posed aside from the question of participation. In other words, citizenship entails an *active* dimension. For Marshall it was purely passive, having little to do with agency and, moreover, was highly privatistic. Social classes were the passive recipients of state-given rights and all that was required of them were minimal duties, most of which were unspecific and largely irrelevant to the institution of citizenship. The point that this leads to is that citizenship as membership of a political community is more than a matter of rights; it also entails an identification and commitment to the community. Thus, the two main components of citizenship that have given expression to an alternative tradition of citizenship – the civic republican and more broadly the communitarian tradition – have focused on identity and participation. Marshall's uncertain words on invoking the spirit of Dunkirk not only are a reminder of his inability to accommodate an active dimension of citizenship, but also epitomizes his tacit equation of citizenship with nationality (Marshall 1992: 46).

Fourth, the decoupling of citizenship and nationality. Marshall recognized that in peacetime the national community is too large and remote to command loyalty (Marshall 1992: 46–7), but he did not question the tie of nation and state; the state as the provider and guarantor of rights and the nation as the focus of identity. Today in the global age this linkage cannot be taken for granted. The state is no longer entirely in command of all the forces that shape it and sovereignty has been eroded both downwards to subnational units, such as cities and regions, and upwards to transnational agencies, such as the European Union. With respect to citizenship, what this means is that the marriage between citizenship and nationality is broken. At least there is no perfect equivalence between nationality, as membership of the political community of the state, and citizenship, as membership of the political community of civil society. This is clearly evident in the case of immigrants who can possess formal citizenship in the sense of nationality and yet be excluded from participation in the society in which they live (Brubaker 1989, 1990,

1992). No theory of citizenship can ignore the growing number of non-citizens, immigrants and dual citizens. Turner (1986a; see also Klausen and Tilly 1997), for instance, has drawn attention to the relationship between citizenship and migration, arguing that in fact it was migration, both within and across states, that led to modern citizenship.

Fifth, the confluence of private and public. Marshall took for granted the strict separation of the private and public realm. The former he equated with the members of social classes and the latter with the sphere of the state. This is an extremely reductionist treatment of these domains and robs them of the political ties that cut across them. As beneficiaries of social rights, citizenship becomes purely privatistic, for civil society is reduced to social classes. But there is more to civil society than the culture of entitlements and the administrative welfare state does not entirely absorb the public sphere, which also contains informal networks of organization and mobilization.

The concept of citizenship in Marshall's theory was essentially the social democratic alternative to liberalism, and could be termed left-wing liberalism. Liberalism rested on a conception of civic and political citizenship, which Marshall held to be too formalistic to be able to offer an adequate balance against the real inequalities in the world produced by the market and which were partly legitimized by civic and political rights. In the classical tradition the other principal tradition, conservatism, offered no real alternative. Where liberalism stressed rights, conservatism stressed duties. Marshall's social democratic vision of citizenship gave expression to what he believed was a fuller kind of citizenship entailing both rights and duties, with social rights offering a substantive embedding of citizenship. We can now see that the social democratic idea has itself become yet another formal kind of citizenship, lacking the substantive dimension it allegedly offered and ultimately accepted the pre-political and privatistic understanding of civil society. Much of the contemporary debate on citizenship concerns this question of the recovery of a substantive dimension to citizenship.

Finally, we can remark on the fate of citizenship with the arrival of neo-liberalism, or 'neo-conservativism' as it is conventionally termed in the USA. It is associated with some major theoretical works (Hayek 1973–9; Nozick 1974; Oakeshott 1975) but had a wider resonance in government policies in the 1980s, such as decentralization, deregulation, privatization and monetarism (King 1987). Neo-liberalism marks the end of the liberal concept of citizenship with the return of citizenship to the market. Ostensibly an attack on the 'big government' of social democracy, neo-liberalism claims to stand for the classical ideal of liberal negative liberty (Berlin 1969). But whereas negative liberty originally referred to a notion of freedom from state-led oppression in the period of early absolutism, the neo-liberal concept of freedom has nothing to do with the liberties of citizenship but of market forces. The negative freedom required for the basic rights of citizenship is quite different from laissez-faire free market principles which were a nineteenth-century development and had little to do with citizenship. Neo-liberalism, while appealing to laissez-faire economic principles, in fact led not to a minimal state but to the strengthening power of the state over society. Classic liberalism spoke in the name of civil society; neo-liberalism – as in the famous statement of Margaret Thatcher, 'there is no such thing as society, only individuals' – denies the social in favour of individual consumers.

The concept of citizenship in neo-liberal discourse replaces the citizen with the consumer. This tendency towards privatism was partly an extension of social citizenship into the world of consumption. The increased consumption of goods has created the need for new kinds of rights which have little to do with inequality. The post-industrial society of today is a society of consumers and therefore quite different from what was still an industrial society when Marshall wrote his essay on citizenship. Citizenship in neo-liberal discourse loses its equalizing function and becomes a highly privatized matter requiring often only regulating bodies to secure its effectiveness.

Summary

In this chapter I have traced the dominant tradition in modern liberal thought concerning citizenship. Particularly in Anglo-Saxon thought this has been predominantly conceived in terms of a model of civil society based on either the market or the state. In the seventeenth and eighteenth centuries, the space of citizenship was the rising order of a market-based society. As Somers (1995) has pointed out, this has had the consequence that citizenship has been pre-judiced by a pre-political and private definition of civil society. In the classical tradition emanating from Hobbes and Locke, the sphere of the state was seen as intruding on the pre-political autonomy of civil society. The state-centred model of Marshall reversed this tendency somewhat by shifting the focus of citizenship from the market to the state. However, what was retained was the essentially pre-political conception of citizenship. As a state-centred project, social citizenship is in effect taken out of civil society and becomes absorbed into mass society. Indeed, the concept of civil society plays no role in Marshall's analysis, where the emphasis instead rests on social class. The result is that social citizenship degenerates into the pre-political privatism of consumer rights.

This situation has led many left-inclined theorists to be dismissive of citizenship. Many of Marshall's critics, such as Giddens (1981, 1982, 1985), Hindess (1998) and Mann (1987), tend to dismiss citizenship as a state-centred strategy of social control. These Marxist-influenced criticisms of citizenship do not see the institution of modern citizenship connected to democracy, preferring to see it in terms of class and state power. Rather than enhance the power of people, citizenship is seen as an elite-led project that serves the structures of capitalist inequality. Fortunately, many critics do not follow this route of analysis and see citizenship as essential to democracy (Held 1989). However, in general, the relationship of citizenship to democracy has not been the subject of debate within the liberal tradition.

In Chapter 3 I shall explore some theories which try to bring citizenship closer to democracy. First, in Chapter 2, we look at the communitarian critique of liberal conceptions of citizenship. The challenge of community and the challege of democracy represent the two main lines of attack on the liberal model of citizenship.

2

Communitarian theories of citizenship: participation and identity

The classical theory of modern citizenship suffered from a failure to grasp the significance of the public sphere as the location of citizenship. In its various forms, citizenship was ultimately reducible to the pre-political private domain. As we have seen, in the classical theory of modern liberalism from Hobbes to Locke to Smith, the market was the model for the shared public culture of civil society. With the emergence of social democracy the market was replaced by the state and, as epitomized in the Marshallian theory of citizenship, civil society eventually becomes subsumed into social classes. In the pre-political privatism of social class, citizenship is reduced to a formalistic relationship to the state as one of rights and duties. It has thus been the fate of citizenship that it has been absorbed into either the realm of the market or the sphere of the state. In this chapter the focus shifts to the communitarian critique of citizenship and the attempt to relocate civil society, not in the market, as liberalism attempts, or in the state, as in social democracy.

If civil society is to be located in neither the market nor the state, what then remains? The broad range of positions that can be termed communitarian would locate civil society in community. Rather than rights and duties, it is participation and identity that is emphasized. As I indicated at the beginning of Chapter 1, there is an alternative conception of civil society to the tendentially privatistic philosophy of modern individualism. This tradition has diverse origins, partly in pre-modern ideas of politics and partly the modern notion of democratic participation. Some would trace it back to Aristotle and the Greek idea of praxis, the fusion of the ethical and the political (Arendt 1958); others to the Renaissance idea of virtue (Pocock 1995); while for many the modern champion is Rousseau and the ideal of a self-governing political community (Cohen and Arato 1992). However, what is common is the appeal to community as the foundation of civil society rather than the individual. This tradition has little faith in the market or the state as the model of society for what has generally been emphasized is the public realm as the domain of community. While community can take many forms – for instance political community, cultural community – what is distinctive about communitarianism is the rejection of individualism and contractualism. It is this move from 'contract to community' (Dallymayr 1978) that marks it off not only from liberalism, but also from social democracy, which as we have seen in rejecting collectivism came to stand for a similar kind of privatism as liberalism. Viewed in the context of Chapter 1, communitarian theories of citizenship can be seen as gradually extending citizenship into the domain of politics, but as I shall demonstrate in Chapter 3, their concept of politics does not extend as far as democracy. Yet, the politicization of citizenship in communitarian discourse is an important part of the contemporary renewal of citizenship.

Much of the debate on communitarianism has been confused by a failure to address the different forms it has taken. In the following discussion, communitarianism will be looked at under three categories: liberal communitarianism, conservative communitarianism and civic republicanism. It is important to appreciate that these are frequently overlapping. Yet, as I shall demonstrate, there are clearly discernible differences in their stances. In this chapter I shall not be looking at the radical democratic theories of civil society, which are the subject of Chapter 3.

Liberal communitarianism

Communitarianism has been closely identified with the critique of liberal political philosophy in the 1980s. Despite the revival of neo-liberalism in those years, the target here is a strictly philosophical version of an older liberalism. Much of the debate has been addressed to John Rawls's *A Theory of Justice*, originally published in 1971. As the title of Rawls's book suggests, his concern was with the foundations of a notion of justice rather than citizenship as such. Though predominantly seen as a liberal, his liberalism is a left liberalism and is not too far removed from Marshall's concern with social justice.

The communitarian thesis in political philosophy has been associated with Michael Sandel, Michael Walzer and Alisdair MacIntyre, to mention the most famous proponents of communitarianism. Walzer's (1983) *Spheres of Justice*, Sandel's (1982) *Liberalism and the Limits of Justice* and MacIntyre's *After Virtue* (1981) were the works that made communitarianism the main challenge to Rawls's revival of classical liberalism and his attempt to wed it to notions of social justice. While communitarianism has now become a diffuse body of thought on the role of community in modern society, the liberal communitarian debate must be discussed separately from other debates on communitarianism since it has been concerned with some very specific philosophical issues. Indeed communitarianism has been a negatively elaborated position, defined by contraposition to liberalism. This has not been true of some of the later works in this tradition, for instance Selznick's (1992) *The Moral Commonwealth*, which does attempt to offer the foundation of a substantive theory of community. The following section of this chapter will discuss some of the later communitarian positions, such as that of Etzioni (1995).

In any discussion of communitarianism one must be mindful that the differences between communitarians are often greater than those between any particular group of communitarians and liberals. This is particularly the case concerning the communitarian critique of liberalism, since what has often been at issue is less substantive differences than differences in meta-theoretical justification and methodology, and it is for this reason that the communitarian position is perhaps best termed liberal communitarianism, since these are no longer exclusive positions (Miller and Walzer 1995; Mulhall and Swift 1996). This term liberal communitarianism pertains to the work of one of the best known communitarian thinkers, Charles Taylor (1990), whose *Sources of the Self* has become a major statement of the mature political philosophy of communitarianism. It might be suggested that while liberalism was modified by social democracy, communitarianism has modified liberalism in yet another direction to produce liberal communitarianism. That this debate on membership of community has occurred largely in North America is not surprising since there the impact of social citizenship has been less pronounced. In the absence of a state historically committed to social rights, the terms of debate on citizenship have tended to be posed as ones of membership of community. Community has appeared to many to hold out the promise of a utopia destroyed by both society and the state. Rather than retrieve the state project, communitarianism seeks to recover a lost dimension of community, the utopia that modernity promised but destroyed. Communitarians can be seen as liberals disenchanted by liberal individualism.

In any case what we shall term liberal communitarian theory has been an important contribution to a notion of citizenship as participation in the community. It has also had an impact on highlighting the problem of identity in citizenship. For communitarians, liberal conceptions of group membership, in particular rights, are too formalistic, neglecting the substantive dimensions of identity and participation, the real ties that bind members of a community together. Rejecting moral individualism for a collectivist conception of citizenship, liberal communitarianism seeks to anchor political community in a prior cultural community and it is in this that identity is to be found, according to a particular tradition in communitarian thinking. The kind of collectivism that is advocated is a moral collectivism and one that is less individualistic than cultural. In this it differs from socialist notions of collectivism since the values that communitarians appeal to are essentially cultural rather than material. What is at issue is a particular conception of the self. For communitarians the self is always culturally specific and it is for this reason that communitarianism can be seen as a defence of cultural particularism against liberalism's moral universalism. Thus we find some of the more recent contributions to the debate focusing on the challenge of multiculturalism. This again reflects the American preoccupation with community and the failure of its project to create a community of community, a nation built of nations. For many communitarians multiculturalism has failed to establish a common political community. However, despite these background issues, the liberal communitarian debate has centred on the question of the self and the limits of individualism.

Communitarians object to the asocial concept of the self in liberalism. The self is not only socially constructed but also embedded in a cultural context. Rawls (1971) never gave consideration to the possibility that different cultural groups might have different ideas of the common good. Communitarians have responded to precisely this weakness in Rawls. Three features of the communitarian theory of citizenship must be highlighted: participation, identity and cultural particularity. Citizenship is about participation in the political community but it is also about identity and, therefore, it is always specific to a particular community. Thus it would appear that the price paid for the introduction of a substantive dimension to citizenship has been the loss of the absolute commitment to universalism that has typified liberalism. Indeed, communitarianism can be seen as an attack on moral universalism, which is seen as an empty formalism and as potentially hegemonic.

The liberal communitarian debate in political philosophy, it must be noted, has been conducted at a very abstract level and mostly has not explicitly addressed concrete issues concerning citizenship. Charles Taylor has offered the most specific analysis in this regard. One of the features of his work is a pronounced tendency to turn away from the emphasis on formal equality which has been central to the dominant tradition in modern thought. According to Taylor, who has become a major theorist of citizenship as the recognition of cultural difference, the essential problem is the integration of self and other (Taylor 1994). For Taylor what is at stake is not just participation but also identity. For him the crucial feature of social life is its dialogical character for the encounter between self and other is embedded in a shared language. In this encounter what is of central importance is a discourse of recognition. With respect to the politics of recognition – that is recognition on the public as opposed to the interpersonal level – this can take the form of an emphasis on equality, for instance the equal dignity of all citizens with respect to their rights and moral worth, or an emphasis on difference, the need of the majority culture to make concessions to particular groups, generally minorities but also, and for communitarians, more importantly, for the state to give official recognition to cultural community, be it that of the majority or minority: 'Where the politics of universal dignity fought for forms of non-discrimination that were quite "blind" to the ways in which citizens differ, the politics of difference often redefines non-discrimination as requiring that we make these distinctions the basis of differential treatment' (Taylor 1994: 39). In order for a cultural community to retain its integrity and flourish there must be some public recognition by the state of cultural community. This is particularly the case with minority cultures to which concessions must be granted by the majority culture. However, as is clear from the case of the French-speaking community in Quebec whose cause is philosophically defended by Taylor, his main concern is with the cultural majority seeking to preserve their identity. For liberals this is a betrayal of the principle of equality, though some liberals believe that liberalism can be reconcilable with multiculturalism in so far as this requires the positive recognition of cultural difference (Kymlicka 1989). As Bauman (1993) has argued in respect of the conflict between liberalism and communitarianism, the liberal idea of 'difference' stands for individual freedom, while the communitarian 'difference' stands for the group's power to limit individual freedom (Bauman 1993). Taylor, however, is cautious about polarizing the principles of liberal equality and communitarian difference. What he stands for is a liberal communitarianism that seeks to modify liberalism by compelling it to accommodate the reality of cultural difference and the need for the preservation of cultural community. Yet the differences are quite strong. Because of the atomism underlying it, liberalism for Taylor has no sense of a common good in the narrow sense of a common way of life. 'Procedural liberalism cannot have a common good in the narrow sense, because society must be neutral on the question of the common good life' (Taylor 1989: 172). Liberalism however does recognize a common good in the broader sense of a rule. But for Taylor there is also a common good in the more specific sense of 'patriotism', an identification with a political community which itself embodies a deeper cultural way of life. It is for this reason that he is strongly supportive of patriotic causes, such as the demands of the French-speaking Quebecois for the official recognition of their language and francophone culture by the state as in the interests of the common good. It would appear that real recognition is recognition of a self-declared majority capable of defining the common good. So long as this culture respects diversity, it has a reasonable claim for official recognition. But this of course fails to take account of a plurality of cultures – which may entail a plurality of conceptions of the common good – and what may be a minority in one context may be a majority in another.

For philosophers such as Taylor and Walzer, the contrast between liberalism and communitarianism is not quite so stark as having to chose between two fundamentally opposed positions. While their preference is clearly for liberal communitarianism – the need for a positive recognition of cultural community – this is anchored in a basic commitment to the liberal principle of equality. Liberal communitarianism is not a postmodernist theory of radical group difference. While liberals get around the problem of protecting minority groups by a commitment to tolerance (Kymlicka 1995), communitarians are on the whole more concerned with protecting the majority culture; this is not an issue for liberals, since this is largely taken for granted, or, as in a recent formulation of Rawls's (1987), it is a matter of looking for an 'overlapping consensus'. It is this concern with reconciling cultural community to citizenship that allows communitarians to claim the liberal mantle. The concept of community in communitarian discourse is the community of the dominant culture which is officially recognized by the state. Since political community, in which citizenship exists, rests on a prior cultural community minorities and incoming groups must adapt to this community in order to participate in its political community. Thus, liberal communitarianism is simply forcing liberalism to make explicit the existence of the cultural community that underlies political community. In his later work, *Political Liberalism* (Rawls 1993) and *The Law of Peoples* (Rawls 1999), he recognized that some of the assumptions of his early position were untenable, in particular the assumption of cultural consensus on a common conception of the good. In an age of cultural diversity rational assent cannot be taken as given. But by this time the communitarian intervention had overtaken Rawls's attempt to revise his theory. It may be observed in this context that the problem of competing definitions of the common good has proven to be just as difficult for communitarianism as it is for Rawls. Both the notion of an overlapping consensus and the communitarian adocation of public recognition of cultural difference leaves the contending groups untouched. Multiculturalism thus becomes the last resort of cultural conflict and incommensurable conceptions of the common good.

In sum, the liberal communitarian debate marks the beginning of the decent from universalism to particularism. While drawing attention to the dimension of participation in community as a central dimension to citizenship, its greatest impact has been in highlighting identity, thus opening up the way to a citizenship of particularism. However, this element of particularism is more of a relativization of the dominant culture than an appeal to cultural relativism as such. It is a communitarianism that has retained some of the basic tenets of liberalism.

Conservative communitarianism

Liberal communitarianism was centrally concerned to modify liberalism by introducing the salience of cultural identity. In more recent times a version of communitarianism has gained widespread influence by a variety of intellectuals and politicians. This can be seen as the continuation of liberal communitarianism but the debate has been less philosophical and more bound up with substantive sociological issues of citizenship. Not too surprisingly this has led to a largely uncritical appraisal of national identity, though one that is not populist in the sense of authoritarianism. Indeed, there has been a growing interest in rethinking populism from within left-wing political theory (Taguieff 1995; Canovan 1999). As David Miller has argued, the promise of community is that it allows people to regard themselves as active subjects shaping the world according to their will: 'The collective identities that people currently possess are predominantly national identities. Here, if anywhere, it seems, the promise of overall community must be redeemed' (Miller 1992: 86). This position might be called 'nations without nationalism'; it goes beyond liberal communitarian political philosophy in addressing key social issues and can take a socialist direction as in the work of Miller (1995) and O'Neill (1994) or a conservative and populist direction.

A conservative populist kind of communitarianism was central to the political rhetoric of the British Labour Party in its election campaign in 1997 when the terms 'nation' and 'society' became interchangeable. The appeal to trust and solidarity as British civic values allowed the Labour Party to take over the Conservative Party's previous monopoly of the discourse of the nation. Thus what had been a nationalist populist rhetoric – focused on traditional nationalism: the Second World War, heritage, the cultural mystique of Englishness – now became a communitarian discourse. The nation had become disengaged from patriotic nationalism and could be deployed for the purpose of social reconstruction. The Conservative Party had spearheaded the neo-liberal attack on social citizenship with its market-led policies of decentralization and privatization. In Britain in the 1980s, when neo-liberalism had replaced the citizen with the consumer, the nation was identified with nationalist rhetoric, which was fuelled by the Falklands War. By the late 1990s, the idea of society was eventually able to re-emerge around the idea of the nation disconnected from the state. This was not just a British development, for the appeal to community as a belief in the social bond and in civic values has been central to the revival of social democracy in many countries in the latter part of the 1990s. It might be suggested, then, that while liberalism communitarianism in the 1980s had been a response to left-wing liberalism, such as that of Rawls, conservative communitarianism was a reaction to the rise of neo-liberalism (which liberal communitarianism largely ignored). In fact the liberalism espoused by Rawls was essentially social democracy. Though his work has had little real political impact, in contrast to its importance in political philosophy, it has mostly been read as a work in left-wing liberalism on social justice. In this he is a contrast to Robert Nozick (1974) who in *Anarchy, State, and Utopia* presented a more right-wing libertarian theory.

The particular kind of popular communitarianism that arose in the 1990s was very close to civic republicanism, which I discuss below. But it differs from it in many respects. Conservative communitarianism must be distinguished from civic republicanism. Communitarian values are more organic than the publicly constituted ones in civic republicanism, where the emphasis is more on voluntary organizations, associations, occupational groups and corporations. The communitarian stance, at least in its more conservative form, tends to stress family, religion, tradition, nation and what in general might be called a culture of consensus. It is for this reason that I have termed it conservative in that it does not have a self-critical moment built into it. It is a variant of old conservativism in its appeal to the ideal of the nation, though this is now linked with civil society. However, that it might become allied with radical conservativism is not to be excluded (Dahl 1999). The appeal to the organic notion of the nation, even when it is not explicitly nationalist, can easily become a form of organized populism.

An influential version of popular conservative communitarianism is to be found in the writings of Amitai Etzioni (1995). His advocacy of community was an American reaction to the dominance of rational choice and neo-liberalism in the 1980s. His call for a recovery of community was designed to create a sense of responsibility, identity and participation in order to make citizenship meaningful to a society that had become highly depoliticized. Community for Etzioni is a moral voice; it is not just a question of entitlements. Though his appeal to community has a radical dimension to it, it lacked a political voice, for according to this vision politics has become exhausted of meaning. It is noteworthy that his formulation of citizenship has very little to say about the role of the state, and democracy hardly figures in it. Also, there is little discussion on social citizenship, which in general has been absent from American debates on citizenship (Fraser and Gordon 1994). John O'Neill argues that 'it is evident that communitarian action without state involvement merely represents another version of voluntarism' (O'Neill 1994: 13). Etzioni's concerns lie with issues relating to schooling, family, policing. Another version of this kind of communitarianism, but with a more radical edge to it, is to be found in the writings of the American cultural critic, Christopher Lasch, who, in his final work, saw the decline of democratic values of citizenship as a consequence of the betrayal of democracy not by the masses but by the elites who have isolated themselves from community (Lasch 1995). Consequently, his call is for a return to the virtues of community, religion and family. Whether conservative or critical, this all reflects the communitarian concern with the micro level of society in contrast to the macro focus of liberalism.

Communitarians such as Etzioni do not see community as incompatible with modernity as Tönnies (1957) did in *Community and Society*. The idea of community in his work is not entirely based on homogeneous traditional communities with a clear geographical location.

> America does not need a simple return to gemeinschaft, to the traditional community. Modern economic prerequisites preclude such a shift, but even if it were possible, such backpedaling would be undesirable because traditional communities have been too constraining and authoritarian. Such traditional communities were usually homogeneous.
>
> (Etzioni 1995: 122)

His version of community is intended to be compatible with diversity and social differentiation. Yet, the communitarian position suffers from a total neglect of democracy, being almost entirely a theory of citizenship as a self-empowering force. Though it has in many respects reconciled itself with cultural diversity, in its concern with voluntarism, it absolves the state from responsibility for society. It is in this stance that it displays a certain conservatism.

In sum, what distinguishes conservative communitarianism is its substantive consensus on identity and its stress on participation as civic responsibility and social reconstruction. In its more populist forms, identity is largely allied with a notion of the nation and participation is seen as access to social goods. In general it is expressed in strong moral terms and can be contrasted with civic republican ideas of citizenship.

Civic republicanism

This is arguably the oldest communitarian tradition and is often associated with participatory democratic theory and what later was to become the theory of civil society (Cohen and Arato 1992). The emphasis is on civic bonds rather than on the market or state as in liberal thinking or on moral communities as in mainstream communitarianism. In this tradition, participation occupies the position given to identity in liberal communitarianism but it takes a more pronounced political form than in the idea of moral responsibility found in other streams of communitarian thinking discussed above. We also find in it a certain resistance to populism. While there are many who would say that populism is the genuine American political tradition, others see the spirit of political community to lie in the republican ideal of civil society. Participation in public life is the essence of the civic bond in the famous theories of Jean-Jacques Rousseau in *The Social Contract* in 1743, Hannah Arendt (1958) and the more recent work of Skinner (1978), Benjamin Barber (1984) and Pocock (1995). This version of communitarianism can be seen as a radical form of liberal individualism, differing from its classical liberal presuppositions in two respects. First, individualism reaches its highest expression in commit-ment to public life, as opposed to the liberal emphasis on the private pursuit of interest or personal autonomy. Rather than self-interest what is at stake is public interest. Second, civic republicanism is an explicitly political conception of citizenship which loses any connection with privatism. While liberalism was based on negative freedom, the civic republican ideal of politics is one of positive freedom, the ideal of a self-governing political community. This is the true meaning of republicanism, as intended by the radical stream within the Enlightenment, though it was only in the United States that it became a real force, as de Tocqueville recognized. In the radical variant, represented by Rousseau, this entailed a confrontation with liberal democracy, or constitu-tional democracy, in that the ideal of a self-governing political community was incompatible with representative government. It may be noted that historically liberal democracy had been tied to constitutional monarchy. But for theorists such as Hannah Arendt (1958), civic republicanism was perfectly compatible with representative government. The challenge rather lay in bring-ing politics out of the state and into the public domain. This was the repub-lican challenge. One of the legacies of this tradition has been an ambivalent relationship with democracy. Classical republicanism like liberalism preceded the democratic revolution and to varying degrees accommodated democracy. But the original impetus of republicanism is a radical doctrine of citizenship as participation in the public domain of civil society. As is evidenced in the writings of Arendt, republicanism exhibits a deep distrust of the modern idea of democracy which is associated with the intrusion of the social question into what is allegedly a purely political domain (see Delanty 2000c: Chapter 3).

The essence of the republican conception of citizenship was the consent of the governed. It owed its early origins to the Italian city states from the eleventh century where a self-governing concept of citizenship emerged in what was still a pre-democratic society (B.J. Smith 1985; Skinner 1992; Springborg 1992). This instrumentalist approach to republicanism was epitomized in the work of Machiavelli for whom citizenship was a means to pursue self-interest. Rejecting democracy, monarchy and aristocracy, he advocated republican mixed government. This rested not on consent as such but on 'virtue', to which consent was subordinated and by which was meant commitment to the common good of the civic polity. With Machiavelli republicanism was clearly linked to strong government and in effect it severed any connection between citizenship and democracy, which were united in ancient republicanism. Citizenship was declared central to politics, the other side of which was statecraft.

While the question of the consent of the governed figured in British liberal theory, it received its republican formulations in the writings of Rousseau and Kant. The British theorists, Hobbes and Locke, had hugely compromised the principle of consent, which in the mature theory of Locke became tied to the sovereignty of parliament. Consent for Hobbes was merely consent to create an all powerful ruler. The social contract as conceived by Rousseau was republican in a way that would have been inconceivable for either Hobbes or Locke. For Hobbes, once the contract to set up a state was made and power handed over to a supreme sovereign – the Leviathan, in effect, the royalist state – it could not be revoked. Locke, as is well known, reversed this caveat of irrevocability in Hobbes and stipulated that the social contract between civil society and the state could be reversed if the sovereign broke the commitment. But this qualification was a legitimation of the 1688 settlement to depose James II; it had little to do with the self-government of civil society and was in effect a Whig ideology. While the English Whig tradition saw sovereignty in terms of a particular relationship between monarchy and parliament, the continental and later the American political tradition saw sovereignty as less parliamentary than popular. It was thus in the idea of popular sovereignty and not in the English notion of parliamentary sovereignty that republican citizenship made its entry. Consent is crucial to it, but without participation it becomes indistinguishable from liberalism, or representative government. But it is important to note that the doctrine of popular sovereignty took a variety of forms, of which the republican tradition was particularly influential. The Enlightenment notion of popular sovereignty allowed the republican tradition to leave behind the patrician heritage of the republican and humanist ethos of the Renaissance and to reinvent itself around a wider notion of popular citizenship.

In the *Social Contract* the citizen is an autonomous individual who is both governed and governs. Rousseau is perhaps the greatest theorist of the view that it is in the public domain of political community that the full expression of individualism is to be found. The Renaissance ideal of virtue, the pursuit of the good life, is to be found neither in the private world nor in the state. Rousseau's republic was the republic of civil society, the city not the state. 'Houses make a town, but citizens make a city,' he stated in the *Social Contract* (Rousseau 1968: 61). The attraction of civil society was its classical association with the Greek polis. But in the age of the Enlightenment when republicanism emerged, the ideal of civil society was faced with a dual challenge from the nascent state on the one side and, on the other, the expansion of a privatized domain of social relations, in family and in the market society. This is what

Rousseau despaired of and possibly explained his famous turn from society to nature.

Kant, Rousseau's great republican successor, took up the cause of republican citizenship in a new key, not from the perspective of Geneva but from Prussia. For Kant civil society is indeed crucial, but for him the republic extends beyond civil society to embrace the state, which, though a reformed monarchy, was answerable to civil society. Kant stands between republicanism and liberalism in that for him civil society must live with the despotic state, for the republic is also a state and therefore extends beyond civil society. He was no champion of democracy and regarded popular sovereignty merely as a matter of institutionalizing civil society as a legally constituted public domain. As we shall see in Chapter 3, civil society also extends into international society, according to Kant. Kant's other problem, and which compounded his entire work, was that the world of morality was derived not from civil society or any conception of the social bond, but from the inner world of the individual. Civil society thus had no moral or political autonomy: morality was the province of a pre-social and pre-political private domain of individualism and politics belonged as much to the state as to civil society. With Hegel, who had succeeded in overcoming the reduction of morality to individualism, there was the recognition of yet another fragmentation of civil society: the rise of the market society and the subsequent transformation of civil society into capitalist social relations. Hegel was the first modern thinker to appreciate that the modern project of autonomy might be undermined by the forces of fragmentation, the other side of the dialectic of modernity (Habermas 1987b; Honneth 1995; O'Neill 1996).

The revival of civic republicanism in the second half of the twentieth century may also be called neo-republicanism. It is a recovery of the Renaissance and Enlightenment ideal of citizenship in much the same way as those ages sought to recover the classical ideal of citizenship. Commitment and participation in public life are its defining features. Few will hold to the absolute integrity of civil society; as we have seen even in Rousseau and Kant, there was the recognition that civil society must live in a world shared with the state and the private world, though Kant was more concerned with reconciling civil society to the state. The challenge for civic republicanism is to preserve as much of the autonomy of the political field as possible, to prevent politics from become privatistic or statist.

Republicanism, while having roots deep in European political history, is a pre-eminently American idea of politics. One of its most distinctive features was noted by de Tocqueville (1969) in his account of his visit to the USA in the 1830s, *Democracy in America*: it was a society without an oppressive state. In Europe the restored state was still autocratic and quasi-absolutist but in America the state was decentralized and associations seemed to play a greater role. This of course was connected with the absence of a feudal state and the fact that the USA was a society of immigrants and did not have a hereditary ruling class. Communitarian republicanism was a feature of what was a civically organized agricultural society, a contrast to the tradition of the city in Europe. While the state as a domain distinct from civil society did eventually triumph in the USA in the latter half of the nineteenth century, the American political tradition was founded on the idea of political community rather than the ideology of a centralized state, as was the case with the French model of the Jacobin Republic.

Civic republicanism strongly emphasizes the associational character of citizenship. Citizenship is about participation, not merely rights and duties. As a private person one has rights and duties but only in public action is citizenship a meaningful category. This was the central idea of Arendt (1958) and has also been echoed in the work of such critics as Pocock (1975), Skinner (1978) and Oldfield (1990). It has received a more pronounced form in Benjamin Barber's (1984) vision of 'strong democracy'. He argues for a new participatory democracy in order to rescue western society from the depolitization into which it has been brought by 'thin democracy'. Democracy must be taken out of the hands of elites and given back to citizens, he argues. This version of communitarian democracy is not to be confused with a unitary vision of democracy where conflict is resolved through community consensus.

> The future of democracy lies with strong democracy – with the revitalization of a form of community that is not collectivist, a form of public reasoning that is not conformist, and a set of civic institutions that is compatible with modern society . . . The crucial terms in this strong formulation of democracy are activity, process, self-legislation, creation, and transformation. Where weak democracy eliminates conflict (the anarchist disposition), represses it (the realist disposition), or tolerates it (the minimalist disposition), strong democracy transforms conflict. It turns dissensus into an occasion for mutualism and private interest into an epistemological tool for public thinking.
>
> (Barber 1984: 150–1)

But not all civic republican positions are as politically radical as Barber. Much of civic republican discourse operates on the pre-political level, valuing associational participation for its non-political benefits. In one of the best known formulations of this 'neo-Tocquevillean' position, Robert Putnam (1993) relates civic engagement with what he calls 'social capital'. The value of civil society is not its ability to overcome conflicts but to promote values of trust, commitment and solidarity, values that allow democracy to flourish. In this version of republicanism, social responsibility primarily falls firmly on the shoulders of civil society rather than on the state, which can function only if civil society already speaks with one voice. In his study of modern Italy he thus found that what matters is not institutions but cultural traditions, in particular those that reinforce civil society (Putnam 1993). It is civil society that makes for a better state and public institutions, not the reverse, he argues. Democracy is a social condition and can flourish without a state, according to de Tocqueville (1969) in his classic work *Democracy in America*. Putnam takes up this Tocquevillean romanticism of American democracy but advances it one step further: a strong civil society will lead to a stronger state in which democracy will flourish. However, Putnam, like de Tocqueville, does not consider the conflicts within civil society and the resolution of such conflicts in translating the demands of social capital into government policy (Whittington 1998; Cohen 1999).

Civic republicanism, then, is a communitarianism of participation, with identity playing relatively little role. Rather than identity or loyalty to an abstract ideal it is more a question of commitment to achieving a common goal. Thus the position of liberal communitarians, such as Taylor, that political community must rest on a prior cultural community which must have official recognition by the state, plays little role in civic republicanism.

Summary

In this chapter I have discussed the three main communitarian critiques of a rights-based conception of citizenship, liberal, conservative and civic communitarianism. All of these share a concern with politicizing citizenship and giving to it a substantive dimension which is missing from the state-centred tradition associated with liberalism and social democracy. Taking community as the defining feature of civil society, these approaches in their different ways give to citizenship a public voice based on identity and participation. It was argued that liberal communitarian stressed the salience of identity while conservative communitarians emphasized participation. The third group, civic republicanism, also made participation central to their discourses but rather than conceive of it in terms of a model of consensus or nationhood, as in conservative communitarianism, the emphasis tends to be on a more radical kind of public commitment.

It was noted that communitarian theories of citizenship share with liberal theories the restriction of citizenship from democracy. In Chapter 3 we look at theories of radical democratic citizenship which address the meso level, where communitarianism looks to the micro (voluntarism) and liberalism the macro (society-state relations). One of the weaknesses of communitiarian-ism is not only that it fails to address the relationship between democracy and citizenship but also that it ignores social struggles in the private domain. Feminist theories of citizenship attempt to remedy this by relinking identity and participation in a way that cuts across the private and public domains.

3

The radical theories of politics: citizenship and democracy

The concept of citizenship in modern social and political thought has been heavily criticized. Marxist-inspired and other left-inclined critics have been dismissive of citizenship, which they see as an institution dominated by either the market or the state. From a different tradition, as we have seen, communitarians opposed the liberal model with an active conception of citizenship as participation in civil society. But this does not appear to have solved the problem of citizenship as far as the proponents of radical democracy are concerned. The project of radical democracy can be seen as an attempt to deepen citizenship in a more political manner than is possible within the communitarian tradition. The various stances on radical democracy, which will be discussed in this chapter, can be seen as advocations of democratic citizenship.

However, radical democracy does not offer a theory of citizenship as such; it is primarily a theory of democracy, a distinction which, as Danilo Zolo has pointed out, is frequently confused (Zolo 1993: 258–9). Its importance with respect to citizenship is that it has been crucial in taking the debate on citizenship out of both communitarian and liberal discourses. In both left- and right-wing liberalism, citizenship was reducible to rights, be it those of the market or of the social welfare, and in communitarian-influenced theories citizenship becomes a substitute for democracy. In radical democracy, on the other hand, citizenship is repoliticized by democracy, allowing us to speak of democratic citizenship. First, I deal with direct democracy as it emerged around the new social movements, second, with discursive democracy in the work of Jürgen Habermas and finally, with feminist citizenship.

Direct democracy and new social movements

In Chapter 2 we saw how the communitarian tradition as represented in the civic republicanism of Barber (1984) comes close to radical democracy. What is specific to civic republicanism in contrast to radical democracy is its concern with mobilizing public commitment rather than bringing about more far-reaching structural change. Its basis lies in the associational ties within the micro domains of society rather than in the 'meso' realm of social movements which are mobilizing society against the state. In the 1970s and 1980s with the revival of civil society around the emergence of new social movements – ranging from what have been called 'post-materialist' movements such as feminism, the peace movement, the environment movement and in central and eastern Europe anti-totalitarian movements, such as Solidarity – it is possible to speak of yet another kind of citizenship, democratic citizenship (Eder 1993; Abramson and Inglehart 1995). These developments, which can be seen as calls for a radical democracy of participatory citizenship, go far beyond civic republicanism in that their aim is the overall transformation of the relationship between state and society (Keane 1984, 1988a, 1998b; Laclau and Mouffe 1985). Civic republicanism is closer to liberalism in that it basically accepts the status quo, seeking merely a more active kind of citizenship within it. Radical democracy as it emerged in the late 1970s and early 1980s in the context of debates around the new social movements and, in a somewhat different context, the democratic opposition against totalitarianism in central and eastern Europe, put citizenship as participation on a new agenda. This cannot be called neo-republican for that was essentially a Tocquevillean political philosophy rooted in a pre-modern, Aristotelian understanding of the political and social world as largely undifferentiated. Community could therefore be, if not an organic underlying totality, at least a means of citizen involvement. In communitarian and civic republican theories, democracy is reducible to citizenship participation, losing any connection with the state. In many civic republican theories, for instance Arendt (1958), democracy is dismissed as statism in favour of a more participatory understanding of citizenship. This is where republicanism differs most strongly from radical democracy, which elevates citizenship to the project of democratic transformation. In radical democracy the aim is to bring about social change by means of transforming politics.

Radical democracy is based on a strong notion of participatory democracy, generally called grassroots democracy or direct democracy. This model is stronger than the predominantly American idea of civic republicanism since it is not anchored in notions of individual duty and virtue but of social movements. Rather than preserve the separation of state and society by confining citizenship to membership of the latter, it seeks to abolish the distinction by radically empowering citizenship as democratic participation. The ecological movement captures the essence of direct democracy as self-government. In its early phase this was a movement concerned with environmental issues but it went on to become a movement that had broader implications for society. In this wider sense, as an ecological movement as opposed to a narrower environmental movement, it brought into question some of the fundamental assumptions about modern society. In the present context of importance was its radicalization of democracy and the need for a citizenship of participation. As the many writings of Manuel Castells demonstrate, radical participatory democracy was both the theory and practice of urban social movements. The city, not the state, became the site of radical grassroots politics in the advanced post-industrial world, as well as in the developing world (Castells 1983; Lowe 1986; Fisher and Kling 1993).

New social movements are defined in opposition to the old social movements, which were based on class and were a product of industrial society and its male workforce. In the present context what is striking is that the new social movements made democracy central to their political project and it is in this that their impact on citizenship is particularly evident. Democracy was not an object of the old socialist-inspired movement and much of its ideology lent itself to the legitimation of anti-democratic regimes. The older movements were based on a stricter separation of leadership and members, and they were closely related to political parties of the left. Social justice, not the democratization of society and the transformation of social relations, was its primary objective. The rise of the new social movements from the late 1960s broke from the older movements in that they sought to bring politics out of the state and into society (Eder 1993). In this their most distinctive feature was their extra-parliamentary nature and their ability to mobilize large segments of the population. The new social movements also brought into question the assumption of the older politics that nature was a resource to be plundered by society (Goldblatt 1996). As a result, social justice could no longer be pursued without consideration of environmental sustainability.

Particularly in their formative phase from the late 1960s to the early 1980s the new social movements appealed to a radicalized popular sovereignty. They were based on mass mobilization and were generally very strongly anti-statist, seeking to recover the political from the domain of the state. They were oppositional movements which pitted society against the state (Tarrow 1994). As specifically *social* movements they gave expression to the political component within the social and it is this that led to the recovery of the idea of civil society. In central and eastern Europe the idea of civil society was an important part of the democratic struggle against totalitarianism, as represented by Solidarity and the radical civil society politics of people such as Adam Michnik in Poland and Václav Haval in the Czech Republic. There, more than in the west, the state represented oppression, and democratic politics consequently was associated with something more specifically social. The idea of civil society perfectly served this task (Konrad 1984; Vajda 1988).

This period, the late 1970s to late 1980s, generally saw a recovery of the idea of civil society (Keane 1988b; Cohen and Arato 1992) which seemed to express the democratic potential of the social and thus give expression to a new kind of politics beyond the state. One important dimension to this which has been the subject of considerable discussion is the question of collective identity (Melucci 1989, 1996a). The politics of radical democracy was based on the formation of collective identity around a common goal. In this it was able to bring a more meaningful dimension to citizenship as not only participation in the civic polity but also the self-creation of society, as Touraine (1977) termed it in one of the major theoretical works on the new politics.

Heller and Feher (1988) see citizenship as crucial to democracy. As in the republican tradition they see citizenship as being based on an ethics of civic virtues. For them the 'civic virtues' of citizenship are radical tolerance, civic courage, solidarity, justice and the intellectual virtues of readiness to rational communication and prudence. Other approaches to radical democracy, such as feminism, which will be discussed separately below, have opened up the private sphere to political transformation. In this the most decisive break with the older social movements is apparent, for the older labour-based social movements did not extend the political into the private sphere of family and presupposed relatively fixed identities and gender roles.

It is of course questionable whether we can actually use the term citizenship to describe the turn to radical democracy, since most of these developments refer to collective action whereas citizenship is based on the individual. This is where the confluence of citizenship and democracy becomes blurred. The liberal and republican traditions (as we have seen) kept citizenship and democracy apart from each other. The latter's politicization of citizenship did not extend into democratization as social transformation. Radical democracy was important in invigorating citizenship and supplementing the civic republican tradition. In its most influential forms it was European, in contrast to the American-influenced communitarian tradition and the British tradition of liberalism. While there are undoubtedly grounds for the claim that citizenship and democracy are two quite different discourses, some are of the view that 'the new sociology of citizenship could be said to have much in common with the sociology of citizenship movements' (Roche 1995: 188).

After fundamentally reshaping the face of western politics during the 1960s, 1970s and 1980s the radical participatory paradigm did not endure and went into decline in the 1990s. In the age of post-communist transition in central and eastern Europe and European integration in western Europe, a new political context arose which was not amenable to participatory politics. Many of these movements, such as the environmental movement, reached the stage of institutionalization and, to an extent, many of their initial objectives were realized (Eder 1996). More importantly, no coalition of interests emerged between the disparate social movements. The promise of such a coalition emerging around the earlier peace movement disappeared with the end of the cold war. In central and eastern Europe post-communist transition to a market society and democracy led to the collapse of civil society into either the free market or nationalism. This is not a pessimistic picture of the fate of the new social movements but a recognition of their powerful impact and their changing nature. A social movement cannot remain 'new' for over three decades. At the end of the 1990s these movements still remained strong but operated in a different context than was previously the case.

Discursive democracy

One of the successors to radical participatory democracy is the notion of discursive democracy. This is still a relatively novel idea and one that is largely associated with the work of Habermas, though it has a broader reception (Dryzek 1990; Fiskin 1991; Alejandro 1993; Rehg 1994; Bohman 1996; Bohman and Rehg 1997). As formulated by Habermas, discursive democracy puts the weight of democracy on its ability to generate communication. It locates democracy both in the state and in society. While direct democracy confined democracy to society and stressed public participation, discursive democracy is primarily concerned with the deliberative process within public communication. It can be seen as a deepening of direct democracy in the direction of institutionalization. While some might see discursive democracy as a weakening of direct democracy, Habermas, as one of its leading proponents, would see it as the contemporary form of radical democracy.

The turn to discursive democracy marks a break from the famous thesis of his earlier work, *The Theory of Communicative Action*, published in 1981, that the carriers of radical democracy are the new social movements (Habermas 1984, 1987a). He concluded that classic work on modern social theory with an interpretation of the new social movements, portraying them as defending the 'life-world' from colonization by the 'system', that is the forces of the state, bureaucracy, law and economy. The new social movements were thus seen as preserving democracy from the state. This led to a notion of democracy as embedded in the social and cultural structures of an embattled life-world and as a result radical democratic politics had to be oppositional, pitting society against the state. It is evident in that work that Habermas did not see the potential for democratic renewal linked to citizenship, which he saw as an expression of the monetarization of services and the consumerist redefinition of the private and public spheres. In the new politics 'the relation of clients to public service agencies is to be opened up and reorganized in a participatory mode, along the lines of self-help organization' and, he argues, 'certain forms of protest negate the definitions of the role of the citizen and the routines for pursuing purposive-rational action' (Habermas 1987a: 395).

Habermas has now restated his position, which no longer sees law as an instrument of colonization but as essential to radical politics (Habermas 1996). This turn to discursive democracy and the cautious embracing of the state domain is epitomized in the changing role of the Green Movement in Germany. No longer an extra-parliamentary voice of opposition, it has now become centrally involved in the parliamentary sphere while at the same time having a strong presence in civil society. The kind of radical democracy that it has fostered is less direct democracy than a 'mediated' democracy which emerges in the opening of communicative spaces around the master theme of ecology.

Discursive democracy differs from communitarian and liberal conceptions in that it does not accept the pre-existing nature of consensus which underlies both of these models. For communitarians consensus is largely located in the worldview of a particular community while for liberals it is more a decision at the hands of elites. The former holds to an ethical-political view of democracy while the latter reduces democracy to the legitimation of an economically determined society. In the liberal model, citizenship is divorced from democracy; in the communitarian model they are collapsed into each other.

Liberals see democracy in terms of representation with citizenship as a depoliticized condition. Communitarianism assumes a pre-existing cultural consensus underlying political community. Rejecting an approach that reduces democracy to either the priority of community or the state, Habermas argues for a mediation of both. Discursive democracy is rooted in argumentative communication and its style is deliberative rather than consensual. His position is closer to the republican version of communitarianism in that he accepts the role of participatory citizenship but differs from it in that the demands of a complex society cannot ignore the need to locate decision-making powers in the state. 'Given the challenges that confront us today', he argues, 'the communicative account of republicanism is more appropriate than either an ethnonational or even a communitarian conception of the nation, the rule of law, and democracy' (Habermas 1998a: 139–40). However, in general, he speaks of republicanism and communitarianism in the same breath, presumably because while the former has a more differentiated view of political community, it shares with the former the assumption of a common cultural community lying in the background. For Habermas, the problem with 'self-determination' is that there is no one single self but a plurality of selves. Discursive democracy, in contrast, extends the deliberative process into what other theories would see as depoliticized zones challenging the philosophy of the subject and liberal privatism at same stroke. 'Discourse theory invests the democratic process with normative connotations stronger than those found in the liberal model but weaker than those found in the republican model' (Habermas 1996: 298). In order to mediate these two positions, Habermas looks to the discursive moment within civil society. Civil society cuts across the informal public sphere and the domain of the state. The importance of it lies in its discursive nature. The public sphere is based on a communicative network of public spheres. 'Like the liberal model, discourse theory respects the boundaries between "state" and "society", but it distinguishes civil society, as the social basis of autonomous public spheres, from both the economic system and public administration' (Habermas 1996: 299). For Habermas, a discursive democracy is a democracy that is based on informed public debate and is responsive to the demands of an active citizenry. The actual capacity of the public sphere to solve problems is limited. However, 'this capacity must be utilized to oversee the further treatment of problems that takes place inside the political system' (Habermas 1996: 359). It is a network for communicating information and articulating problems; it does not deal with solutions: 'the communicative structures of the public sphere relieve the public of the burden of decision making, the postponed decisions are reserved for the institutionalized political system' (Habermas 1996: 362). An important distinction is thus to be made between the public sphere as a domain of communication and the partly institutional political culture of civil society. A discursive democracy is located not only in civil society but also in the public sphere.

One of the implications of this for sovereignty is that discursive democracy dissolves national sovereignty. It does not do this in the name of popular sovereignty since 'the people' is not an alternative for the state. Habermas's discursive democracy corresponds to the image of a decentred and self-critical society: 'Once one gives up the philosophy of the subject, one needs neither to concentrate sovereignty concretely in the people nor to banish it in anonymous constitutional structures and powers' (Habermas 1996: 301). Thus, the 'self' of the self-organizing legal community disappears in the subjectless forms of communication that comprise civil society. In this intersubjective understanding of the self the very idea of the public is also recast as a medium of open-ended communication. Though Habermas does not put it so explicitly, it may be suggested that the public has become divorced from any particular social actor as it has from a unified concept of the self. Since politics belongs partly to the domain of the state, the ideal of a pure political society of self-organizing publics is a romantization of politics. With the increase in competing interest groups, civil society must become discursive rather than self-organizing and compatible with the reality of societal complexity. 'Democratically constituted opinion- and will-formation depends on the supply of informal public opinions that, ideally, develop in structures of an unsubverted political public sphere' (Habermas 1996: 308). Without a constitutional state, discursive democracy would be ineffective since, and this is the point of Habermas's (1996) major work, *Between Facts and Norms*, it requires recourse to law in order to institutionalize the results of democratically generated discourse:

> Only after the public 'struggle for recognition' can the contested interest positions be taken up by the responsible political authorities, put on the responsible political authorities, put on the parliamentary agenda, discussed, and, if need be, worked into legislative proposals and binding decisions.
>
> (Habermas 1996: 314)

Aside from the reality of a high degree of societal complexity, there is also the challenge of cultural pluralism. Given this situation of multiple subjectivities, the assumption of a background consensus cannot be taken for granted. The solution is not to separate politics from citizenship, as liberal theory would have it, but to make citizenship the basis of politics.

Discursive democracy entails a transformative impulse. Rejecting the reduction of democracy to strategies of compromise or to concrete forms of life, it seeks to render positions reflective. This is what Habermas calls the 'public use of reason'. To adopt the public perspective is to accept a third-person perspective, that is neither the perspective of the opponent nor one's own vantage point. The public perspective is the genuinely intersubjective perspective, reducible to neither self nor other. Thus, while Rawls sees the challenge to be in the search for a 'reasonable' overlapping consensus, the public perspective is one that forces the reflexive scrutiny of both positions (Rawls 1993). In other words, a reasonable consensus is one that is held to be true by the corresponding parties, but a reflexive position looks for the critical appropriation of both positions (Habermas 1998a: 87). Habermas finds this public perspective in certain kinds of communication in modern societies and it is empirically related to particular kinds of social movements and intellectual critique. He sees modernity as the progressive expansion in the discursive capacity of society to solve its problems by communication rather than violence. Moreover, complex societies cannot be integrated by resource to substantive values but by abstract norms. Moral conduct toward strangers calls for a generalized disposition for justice which cannot be anchored in culturally particular values. To that extent the constitution is of central import-ance in institutionalizing justice. He describes the process of constitution-making as an ongoing process. The constitutional state does not represent a finished condition but a dynamic and revisable means of extending rights and securing justice. A constitution can be defined as 'the establishment of a fallible learning process through which a society gradually overcomes its ability to engage in normative reflection on itself' (Habermas 1996: 444).

Habermas has been criticized by feminist theorists for not giving suf-ficient consideration of the pre-discursive space, seeing social actors as relat-ively autonomous agents operating in the public sphere (Fraser 1989). This view neglects the deeper forms of power operative in the construction of identity. In the next section I examine the contribution of feminist theories of citizenship.

Feminist citizenship: the politics of cultural pluralism

Civic republicanism did not question the public–private dichotomy that is typical of liberalism. Though this distinction is preserved, its distinctive feature (as we have seen above) was its contribution to the politicization of the public realm. No attempt is made, however, to politicize the private sphere, which lies outside the shared political culture of the public domain. It is precisely this that is the objective of feminist theories of citizenship (Voet 1998). For civic republicans there is only one public. Feminist approaches to citizenship challenge this assumption, arguing that civic republican theories of citizen-ship from the point of view of women and disadvantaged groups have not made a major advance over liberal theories. The problem is that while civic republicanism argues for an intensely political conception of the public domain, it ignores the private realm. Feminist approaches demand the politicization of the private as well as a pluralist view of the public domain. Moreover, for feminists the civic republican virtues are male orientated and have little to say on issues of personal identity and autonomy. Rousseau, for instance, excluded women from citizenship since he held that they were too prone to emotions.

Feminist theories of citizenship thus take a different point of departure from conventional liberal and communitarian approaches. Feminists object as much to the universality of liberal conceptions of equality as they do to the communitarian appeal to a unitary ideal of community. Neither rights nor participation offer adequate models when issues of patriarchy are concerned

(Walby 1990; Kingdom 1991). As we have seen above, liberal communitarians seek to accommodate cultural differences from the vantage point of the dominant group. Communitarianism in general does not begin from the standpoint of multiculturalism but from a dominant group, usually a national group, which must accommodate cultural diversity. For feminists, in contrast, group difference is a starting point and thus there can be no unitary community but a plurality of cultural forms. Perhaps the central problem is that liberal and communitarian, as well as civic republican, theories of citizenship assume that citizenship is simply the expression of already autonomous citizens and is constructed on the ideal of a homogeneous society. Feminist theories of citizenship build upon notions of radical democratic citizenship in that they reject the Aristotelian assumptions of much of communitarian discourse, in particular the assumption of an underlying cultural community which is relatively homogeneous and the idea of a common conception of the good that is typical of liberal ideas.

For some theorists, such as Iris Marion Young (1989, 1990), the homogenous ideal of universality must be rejected for a more differentiated notion of rights. The liberal ideal, which is also reflected in civic republican ideas, privileges a dominant group whose values become falsely universalized and are but a disguised strategy to exclude marginal groups as well as women. She argues:

> The attempt to realize an ideal of universal citizenship that finds the public embodying generality as opposed to particularity, commonness versus difference, will tend to exclude or to put at a disadvantage some groups, even when they have formally equal citizenship status.
>
> (Young 1989: 256–7)

Her position is one that defends the necessity for group rights in order for them to maintain their autonomy against dominant groups. Equality is now firmly challenged by difference, for what is frequently sought is not equality but the right to remain different. So, against Benjamin Barber, she opposed the creation of a unified public realm in which citizens leave behind their private identities since this merely suppresses group differences and excludes them from the public. She argues:

> Instead of a universal citizenship we need a group differentiated citizenship and a heterogeneous public. In a heterogeneous public, differences are publicly recognized and acknowledged as irreducible, by which I mean that persons from one perspective or history can never completely understand and adopt the point of view of those with other group-based perspectives and histories.
>
> (Young 1989: 258)

Does this mean the end of universalism and the arrival of radical relativism? Young does not believe so – arguing that there can be communication across different positions – but this is clearly the direction of many positions on multiculturalism: the irreconcilability of cultural groups. Postmodernism has also contributed to this positive view of group differences. But for those whose concerns are with citizenship, which by definition entails some commitment to a shared community, this presents major problems (Gutmann 1993). Even Young's moderate position, which defends positive discrimination for disadvantaged people, has not won widespread acceptance. Many feminist and theorists of multiculturalism fear that this position leads to cultural essentialism. The reality is that while many groups are disadvantaged they are not clearly definable and to convert them into legal categories runs the risk of fixing their identities into reified and given constructs (Mouffe 1992; Phillips 1993). This is clearly a dilemma for feminists and those concerned with disadvantaged groups because many of these problems can be relativized depending on whether what it is at issue is an aim – that is, an end – or a strategy, that is a means to achieve a desirable end.

As a solution to this dilemma concerning the nature of rights, many theorists argue for what Ruth Lister (1998) has aptly called a 'differentiated universalism' (see also Lister 1995, 1997). She argues that if a politics based on group identity is to avoid the problems of retreating into cultural essentialism, it has to be based on a broader commitment to integrate marginalized groups into society. Some of the key features of this approach lie in linking a politics of solidarity with a politics of difference. As Lister argues: 'The commitment to difference requires a non-essentialist conceptualization of the political subject as made up of manifold, fluid, identities that mirror the multiple differentiation of groups' (Lister 1998: 77). The dimension of solidarity is also crucial since this is also a question about building support links between different groups for the realization of their different objectives (Yeatman 1993). Solidarity and difference in turn need to be complemented by a third dimension, a commitment to dialogue.

Feminist theorists inspired by Habermas have brought issues of group participation to bear on communication. Rejecting Habermas's earlier separation of communication as presuppositionless discourse from the social and cultural context of the life-world, authors such Benhabib (1992, 1996) and Fraser (1989, 1992; Frazer and Lacey 1993) argue for the necessity of a communicative articulation of problems. For these theorists the aim is less to arrive at consensus than to articulate problems and promote as many voices as possible. While Habermas's early work relegated all issues of identity to the pre-political private realm, his later work indicates an increased recognition of the need to promote as many voices as possible (Habermas 1996). However, what is still absent in the view of many feminists is an enabling perspective on dialogue, an emphasis more on the process of communication that an outcome. Too much of the mainstream debate on citizenship has been premised on the assumption that citizens are fully formed individuals able to express their interests in the public domain. But the problem as highlighted by feminists is that many groups in society do not have access to the avenues of communication necessary for them to participate in society. Thus equality of opportunity is itself an interest as opposed to being a means to achieve an interest.

It might be suggested that it is in this area that the most progress can be made for a citizenship of participation. Citizenship is not then a question of rights but of a politics of participation that aims to build bridges across the otherwise separated private and public worlds. Lister (1998) concludes as follows: 'At the theoretical level, the challenge is to pursue a pluralist, feminist conception of citizenship without slipping back into a false universalism within the gender categories and to maintain a genuinely differentiated analysis that moves beyond mere tokenism' (Lister 1998: 85).

One area of citizenship in which feminist theories have introduced new perspectives is identity. In communitarian theories identity was taken for granted as something fixed and belonging either to the private domain or reducible to a public notion of the common good. Feminists and cultural pluralists, such as Parekh (1994, 1995, 1997), see identity as contested and therefore always open to definition. Democratic participation and identity are connected in that radical politics is also an identity politics, a politics of enhancing a society's capacity for communication and dialogue.

In sum, feminists and other cultural pluralists have demonstrated that radical politics is not just a question of participation but a critical awareness about some of the assumptions about power and identity that were taken for granted in the communitarian and liberal theories.

Summary

Radical democratic citizenship takes many forms but underlying these is the recognition that citizenship must be located neither in the state nor in a depoliticized civil society but in collective action. I have tried to show that conceptions of collective action have changed from the purely adversarial mode to the discursive, from action to communication. But the politization of citizenship extends into the domain of the self, which in communitarian discourses remains hidden from the political. Only in the politics of the new social movements have these become an issue for citizenship. As feminist theorists have argued, the citizen is not an already autonomous being. Autonomy is a project; not a given condition as it is for liberals and communitarians. For the proponents of radical democracy the solution to individualism is not community but greater and more intensive democracy in all areas of society, from the self to the state domain.

The various positions on radical democratic citizenship point to a threefold model of citizenship entailing the politics of voice, difference and justice. Citizenship is as much about the articulation of problems as it is about their resolution. This recognition of voice is a position shared by many feminists and is also evident in the later work of Habermas. The second follows from this recognition of communication: the universalistic assumptions of liberalism must be relativized to take account of difference. This is less a retreat into relativism than a qualified particularism, a differentiated universalism. Unlike postmodern celebrations of particularism, differentiated universalism does not abandon the normative and critical edge of universalistic morality. Finally, citizenship entails a commitment to justice, not as a formalistic equality of opportunity but as a substantive goal. This model of justice works only if it is strong on local levels and is organized in a participatory mode and can empower those groups most affected by the exercise of power. Clearly, one of the implications of radical democracy is a shift from a model of consensus to one of dissensus. The more groups that are involved in decision making and the more heterogeneous citizenship becomes, the more dissent will creep into civil society. It can no longer be taken for granted that citizenship can appeal to an underlying consensus such as a common conception of the good, as in liberalism, or community, as in communitarian theories.

The debate on citizenship and radical democracy will continue, having already reshaped the older terms of debate between liberals and communitarians. My concern in this book is to address an even more recent debate. This relates to the idea of cosmopolitan citizenship, the possibility of citizenship beyond the state. In Part two of this book I discuss the cosmopolitan challenge to citizenship and in Part three I assess its possibilities and limits. Some of the basic ideas of this are already suggested by radical democracy, namely the view that citizenship is more than a state-led project, but is an expression of networks of communication that extend beyond the boundaries of the nation state linking into different nodal points in heterogeneous civil societies and social movements. However, as will be seen in Chapter 4, the cosmopolitan thesis concerning citizenship has not always been related to the concern of radical democracy. In fact, the contrary has frequently been the case; cosmopolitanism has often been more closely linked to liberal ideas of the international order.

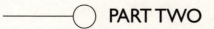 PART TWO

The cosmopolitan challenge

4

Cosmopolitan citizenship:
beyond the nation state

The discussion in Part one has established that the debate on citizenship has been dominated by two quite opposed positions – positions which have been challenged by radical democracy and feminist theory. One the one side are those who see citizenship as a formally held legal status based on rights and duties and, on the other side, are those who see it as a question of participation in, and identity with, the political community. In both cases the nation state is the territorial reference point. While the former group, predominantly liberal, has explicitly tied citizenship to the state, the latter group, largely communitarian, has tied citizenship to the nation. Both liberal and social democratic as well as communitarian conceptions of citizenship have on the whole accepted the nation state as the basis of citizenship, differing only in their emphasis on either the nation or the state. In these positions citizenship and nationality are closely connected, citizenship being the internal or domestic face of nationality. Within a particular state a person is a citizen while outside the borders of the state the individual is a national. To be sure this is a much closer tie in the first group, where citizenship is defined by the state. For communitarians the state is relatively unimportant, and much of communitarianism is a retreat from the state. However, in mainstream communitarian discourse citizenship is confined to relatively narrow limits and instead of the state the nation appears more prominently. The third theoretical strand, radical democracy, brought citizenship closer to democracy and resolved many of the problems with the extremes of universalistism and particularism, rights and participation. In this position we can recognize the basic terms of our concern in this chapter and the debate that concerns the remainder of this book: cosmopolitan citizenship. Radical democracy rejects the definition of citizenship as the property of either the state or the nation and as such it offers a post-national conception of citizenship. However, the concerns of radical democracy have mostly been subnational, or 'meso', rather than cosmopolitan.

Towards cosmopolitan citizenship

Much discussed in recent times is the idea of cosmopolitan citizenship. Cosmopolitan citizenship goes beyond the borders of the nation state, respecting neither state nor nation. Alongside this development is an undermining of citizenship from within the nation state in the form of new kinds of regionally based nationalism and demands for local autonomy. Interest in cosmopolitan citizenship has grown considerably in the 1990s, a development not unconnected with globalization in a wide variety of areas. The older debates on citizenship are poorly equipped to deal with the implications of cosmopolitanism, confined as they are to geographically delimited polities. In this chapter I shall clarify the still confused terms of cosmopolitan citizenship so that in later chapters an assessment can be made of its limits and possibilities. I shall argue against some versions of what can be called global civil society, while defending the possibility of a cosmopolitan citizenship that does not dispense with the nation state.

In speaking of cosmopolitan citizenship we are faced with the problem that, despite the growing interest in it, there is very little of a comprehensive nature written on the subject. In a book published in 1995 Anthony Smith defended the nation state against 'cosmopolitan culture' (Smith 1995). Despite devoting an entire chapter to the cosmopolitan thesis, only one text was cited – a book published five years earlier by the historian Eric Hobsbawm (1990) in which he wrote of the demise of nationalism. Yet Smith felt the need to defend nationalism, though the only critique he identified was one which the author later corrected in light of the rise of nationalism in the early 1990s (Hobsbawm 1991, 1992). In this chapter I shall try not to commit the mistake of attacking a 'straw man' or assuming the existence of an unstated position in support of my argument for a limited cosmopolitanism.

In order to approach what in fact is a very diffuse literature, I take four broad headings under which we can discuss cosmopolitan citizenship: internationalism, globalization, transnationalism and post-nationalism. The first relates to the international politics of states and is manifest in federalist theory, having its origin in Kant and Enlightenment universalism. This is a predominantly legal cosmopolitanism and relates to government as the rule of law. The second concerns the emergence of a global civil society around non-state actors and is mostly an overly political cosmopolitanism. In contrast to the legal conception of cosmopolitan *government*, this is a question of *governance*, that is the political assertion of civil society. This stance is represented in postmodern conceptions of glocality, cultural citizenship as well as in the work of cosmopolitan theorists such as Beck, Castells, Held, Falk, Turner, Urry and proponents of ecological citizenship in the context of the risk society. The third refers to the transnational movement of peoples and is reflected in post-colonial theory. This is characteristically a cultural cosmopolitanism and is also exhibited in the globalized culture of taste. The fourth relates to the reflexive transformation of national sovereignty to the subnational and the supranational, with major theoretical examples being found in the work of Habermas. This approach, I shall argue in Chapter 10, offers the foundation of a civic cosmopolitanism, albeit it is one far removed from Habermas's particular rendering of post-nationalism. My concern in this chapter is less a normative critique of these positions than an interpretative exposition.

These four categories thus correspond to the various conceptions of cosmopolitanism – legal, political, cultural, civic – though most cosmopolitian arguments concerning citizenship cut across them and cannot be limited to any of them. Held and Falk, for instance, belong as much to the first category as to the second. Nevertheless it is possible to discern the various strands that authors have taken. I also believe that, despite these different conceptions, we can point to an emerging cosmopolitan thesis concerning citizenship beyond the state. The key aspect of this, I shall argue, is that citizenship and nationality have today become separated and that the state is no longer the exclusive reference point of sovereignty. This is the negative definition of cosmopolitanism. Cosmopolitan citizenship in the positive sense refers to new possibilities for participation and rights both within and beyond the state. In yet more concrete terms, for cosmopolitan citizenship the fundamental criterion is no longer birth, as is the case with most kinds of national citizenship, but residence. In the cosmopolitan theory of Habermas this crystallizes in an emphasis on citizenship as the 'inclusion of others', in particular immigrants (Habermas 1998a). Cosmopolitanism could thus be seen in the emergence of post-national forms of inclusion and in what might be called the enhanced interconnectivity of cultures.

Internationalism and legal cosmopolitanism

An identification with cosmopolitan community has always been a central feature of western thought ever since the Greeks made a cosmic myth of their civilization. The identification of the early church with the universal community of humanity continued the Roman aspiration for world empire. The medieval universities were also highly cosmopolitan, both in their composition, with scholars coming from all parts of Europe, and in the universality of knowledge upon which they were allegedly based. The use of Latin served for centuries as a common tongue, allowing culturally quite diverse people to communicate and participate in a shared culture. In many ways – in language, religion and the culture of knowledge – the medieval age was cosmopolitan in a way that has been lost today. The cosmopolitanism of the medievals was not unconnected with the fact that their culture was an elite culture with the mass of peoples living sedentary lives untouched by the cosmopolitanism of their rulers. Today that high culture has been replaced by a popular global culture of deverbalized and post-literate communication, largely sport, music and Internet consumerism shared by elites and middle classes alike. But until the beginning of the twentieth century there was considerable movement and identity among elites. To be cosmopolitan was a function of class, allowing the upper classes to distinguish themselves from those below them. Cosmopolitanism was also tied to a notion of western civilization. A cosmopolitan was therefore somebody who was highly mobile, moving largely within elite circles and participating in the consumption of high culture.

A picture of the cosmopolitan emerged as somebody who could renounce the need to identify with any particular community. The cosmopolitan had no ties and therefore no allegiances or loyalties. As in Goldsmith's *A Citizen of the World* (published in 1762), one identified with the world not with a nation. In 1796 Edmund Burke wrote: 'No European can be an exile in any part of Europe'. Voltaire said: 'Today there are no longer Frenchmen, Germans, Spaniards, even Englishmen: whatever people say, there are only Europeans – All have the same tastes, the same feelings, the same customs, because none has experienced any particular national formation'. Rousseau, too, wrote of a coming age when 'there is no longer a France, a Germany, a Spain, not even England, there are only Europeans. All have the same tastes, the same passions, the same way of life' (quoted in Delanty 1995a: 71). This was clearly at a time when the modern nation state had not yet become the primary reference point for identities and elites could still find in a higher order a focus for identity. It was, of course, also at a time when the vision of a single world was a relatively small one, largely confined to that part of Europe where the Enlightenment had left its mark. The American Enlightenment, in contrast, did not embrace the comopolitan ethos that prevailed in Europe and from which the Americans had rebelled. This association of cosmopolitanism with the spirit of Europe has been an enduring tradition (Delanty 1995b). In American literature from Henry James to Hemingway, the cosmopolitan American discovered their identity in a Europe which has lost its identity. If the cosmopolitan was somebody who was capable of renouncing identity, he or she was also somebody who found a new identity, which might quite well be on a voyage of personal recovery, as in James or even the Lost Generation's discovery of Europe. Cosmopolitanism and individualism were thus closely connected. Cosmopolitans went with the assertion of individualism, if not its discovery. From its origins, then, the cosmopolitan spirit was the expression of a globally orientated liberalism, having relatively little to do with republican and communitarian orientated philosophies which tended to stress particularism rather than universalism.

It was not until Immanuel Kant that cosmopolitanism became linked with citizenship. Kant opened the first great modern debate on cosmopolitan citizenship around a notion of an international order based upon civil society. Until now the idea of cosmopolitanism was very much tied to the cultural pursuits of individuals but beyond these postures of class it had little political significance. There were of course some earlier schemes of cosmopolitanism, as in the designs of the seventeenth century Quaker, William Penn, and others, but many of these were in fact connected with struggles between Christendom and the Ottomans and had relatively little to say on citizenship. In these grand designs, peace within Christendom was the other side of war with the infidel

(Delanty 1995a). Kant partly recovered an older idea of cosmopolitanism which was rooted in a fundamentally moral idea of citizenship. First used by the Greek Cynics, the term 'citizen of the world' meant an affiliation with a rational humanity, though the term was more central to later Stoic and Roman thought and meant the community into which one is born and the community of humanity (Nussbaum 1997). This was the sense in which Kant used the term but adapted it to the situation of his time and the need for an international political ethic. Kant himself was no cosmopolitan in the sense of a traveller, being content to remain his whole life in his native city of Königsberg in East Prussia (now Kaliningrad in Russia). His was a cosmopolitanism of spirit and intellect – it had no relation to place. Whereas much of elite cosmopolitanism was counter-revolutionary, looking to the classical civilization rather than modernity, Kant was animated by the French Revolution, which he saw as truly cosmopolitan.

We can say the first modern debate on cosmopolitanism emerged from the late eighteenth century with the growing recognition of the need for a post-Hobbesian order. In Hobbesian political theory the state is created by civil society in order to guarantee the survival of civil society which is always in danger of regressing into the violence of its original condition, the state of nature. To this end, political violence is the function of the all powerful Leviathan. Kant extended Hobbes's theory in two directions leading to two new conceptions of the social contract. First, he radicalized the Lockean theory of the consent of the governed into a theory of civil society whereby the state must anchor itself in public approval. In this he did not go as far as Rousseau in demanding a participatory democracy, for he was content with a degree of despotism so long as it was 'enlightened', that is based on public will. Second, he rejected the Hobbesian view of the international order as an arena of violence. For Hobbes, the state which is internally peaceful is prone to violence in the international sphere, for there is no powerful prince capable of making the states accept his will. A republican state based on civil society can be a warfaring state: 'Although it is largely concealed by governmental constraints in law governed civil society, the depravity of human nature is displayed without disguise in the unrestricted relations which obtain between the various nations' (Kant 1970: 103).

In such works as 'Idea for a Universal History with a Cosmopolitan Purpose' in 1784 and his later and major work, 'Toward Perpetual Peace' in 1795, Kant explored the idea of an international civil society (in Kant 1970). In both of these texts, Kant was advancing the central theme of his entire philosophical work, namely the rule of the principle of reason. For Kant it followed from this principle the need to restrain the exercise of power to law. His ultimate concern was to explore the possibility of having laws in history, but such laws differ from those in nature in that they are the creations of human will and thus require the social contract to bring them about. In his time, Kant appeared to believe that the first social contract had been made – a national or republican one – and the time had come for a second one, a cosmopolitan social contract between free republican states.

The Kantian notion of cosmopolitanism was essentially one of internationalism. In the recent debates this point has not always been stated as clearly as it should be, for Kant's primary concern was with laying the foundations of a theory of international law, not with democratic governance. His ideas were addressed to states, not to citizens as such, and reflected a legal conception of cosmopolitianism. Kant condemned the practice of treaty-making as morally illegitimate since its normative basis was nothing less than the balance of powers rather than a commitment to peace, and as such it only contained violence rather than eliminating it. Kant appears to waver between a cosmopolitan order based on a sovereign, republican authority which recognizes citizens as citizens of the world and one based on a federal order in which there would be within its constituent states strong civil societies within republican states. The first is clearly his preferred option but he seems to recognize that political cosmopolitanism is unrealistic. In his essay, 'Idea for a Universal History with a Cosmopolitan Purpose', there is the suggestion of history leading towards a universal order of humanity based upon a republican constitution but in some later pieces such as 'Perpetual Peace', the question of the political act of creating a cosmopolitan legal framework rather than a republican political order is more central. The problem is in transferring the republican constitution onto the international order. Kant began to see that it is clear that 'the positive idea of a world republic cannot be created' (Kant 1970: 105). Recognizing the limitations of this, he argues for a system of international law, which he calls cosmopolitan law. Though this is a relationship between states, it does have clear implications for citizenship beyond the state. His 'third definitive article of a perpetual peace' refers to the 'conditions of universal hospitality', as he termed it. 'In this context, hospitality means the right of the stranger not to be treated with hostility when he arrives on someone else's territory' (Kant 1970: 105). Kant makes it clear that the stranger cannot claim 'the right of a guest' but only a 'right of resort'. In describing the violence that exists in many parts of the world, as a result of slavery, colonization and the greed of the 'commercial states', Kant sees the possibility of a cosmopolitan constitution emerging simply out of its necessity and, as he argues in the First Supplement, is guaranteed by the providence of nature. However, what is interesting is that Kant appears to recognize that 'continents distant from each other can enter into peaceful mutual relations which may eventually be regulated by public laws, thus bringing the human race nearer and nearer to a cosmopolitan constitution' (Kant 1970: 106). What is compelling about this is the need to overcome what is, in effect, the global state of nature into which nations are thrown as a result of their egoistic inclinations:

the peoples of the earth have thus entered in varying degrees into a universal community, and it has developed to the point where a violation of rights in one part of the world is felt everywhere. The idea of a cosmopolitan right is therefore not fantastic and overstrained; it is a necessary complement to the unwritten code of political and international right,

transforming it into a universal right of humanity. Only under this condition can we flatter ourselves that we are continually advancing towards
a perpetual peace.

(Kant 1970: 107–8)

Kant's theory of cosmopolitanism was the beginning of important debates
on internationalism. However, since Kant the moral dimension receded and
so too did the focus on citizenship. Much of the subsequent debate related
to international society and various kinds of internationalism. Examples of
these could be found in communism, pan-nationalism and federalism. Since
the foundation of the First International, communism was clearly a political
movement which had a global identity as a universal movement based on the
utopia of the 'withering away of the state'. Until the First World War, when
national divisions became apparent, communism had stood for the making
of international society. To an extent some kinds of cosmopolitanism embodied the spirit of nationalism, for instance Mazzini's Young Europe and
some forms of pan-nationalism. Meinecke, in a classic work *Cosmopolitanism
and the National State*, argued that nationalism and cosmopolitan originally
were closely related (Meinecke 1970; see also Lyons 1963; Schlereth 1977).
But the Enlightenment's principle of self-determination was destined to
become the universalism of the particular, as enunciated by V.I. Lenin and
the US president, Woodrow Wilson, who shaped the Versailles order. The
idea of the nation shifted from an association with civil society to the state
and the doctrine was born that every nation must become a state. In the
period immediately after the First World War new federalist ideas emerged
to reconstruct a European civilization destroyed by nationalism. Examples of
these were visions of a European federal state, for instance the pan-European
movement founded by Counenhover-Kalergi in the 1920s (Pegg 1983; Delanty
1995a). But with some exceptions these ideals did not endure or become influential and after the Second World War in Europe the nation state was firmly
established as the basis of an international system. The idea of 'international
society' remained a vague notion of an international normative system to
which states were committed but nevertheless a part of an order dominated
by states (Lyons 1963; Meyer 1987; Luard 1990; Mayall 1990; Watson 1992).

   Within the relatively new science of international relations, two views
emerged, realism and functionalism, on the question of whether the international order was based on autonomous states, realism, or on a functional
system of interacting states. An early example of the growing influence of
the latter is Ernst Haas's (1964) *Beyond the Nation-State*, which was one of the
first books in international relations to look at 'the whole' as constituting a
reality in itself. Hedley Bull (1977) in a famous book, *The Anarchical Society*,
wrote of the rise of an international society, as opposed to an international
system, in terms of a common framework of norms, both moral and legal.
Bull appeared to be arguing for a post-national order in which the state as
a sovereign entity would disappear in a 'new medievalism'. Indeed, he was
the first to use the term 'new medievalism' to describe the anarchy of the

international society in which sovereignty is shared on many levels of over-lapping authority, regional, national and supranational. Bull's (1977) account was very unclear on the nature of the anarchy, however, since it could mean either the anarchy of the international system of states or the anarchy of inter-national society (Hoffman 1995: 181–3). Bull heavily criticized the view that the increasing integration of world society might lead to a world civil society simply because of the presence of the superpowers. His position on the whole tended towards a cautious reading of Kant's cosmopolitanism, a stance that can be contrasted to the stronger thesis of cosmopolitans such as David Held and Richard Falk, to be discussed in the next section.

The general picture that emerges from the discourse of internationalism is that cosmopolitan citizenship has been subordinated to a state-centred world. Despite Kant's work, the question of citizenship beyond the state has not been a central issue in what is still a very Hobbesian view of the international order.

Globalization and political cosmopolitanism: the idea of global civil society

In Chapter 6 I deal in detail with globalization. In this chapter my concern is with the exposition of the normative theory of cosmopolitanism that has partly arisen out of globalization theory but has also had an earlier history. Since the late 1980s the theme of globalization has placed the question of cosmopolitan citizenship on the agenda once again. In these debates there is a stronger focus on the cultural and social nature of cosmopolitan citizenship. Theorists such as Anthony Giddens, who previously saw the international system in terms of statist agendas, have begun to take cosmopolitanism seri-ously, which for Giddens is central to the politics of the 'third way'. 'Global-ization, it should be stressed, is not the same as internationalization. It is not just about closer ties between nations, but concerns processes, such as the emergence of global civil society, that cut across the borders of nations' (Giddens 1998: 137). Initially, in the 1980s, there was considerable interest in new links between local and regional movements and global processes. Nation states were suddenly seen in decline as a result of globalization and subnational forms of politics could find new opportunities in the international context, which is no longer seen as dominated by states. With sovereignty eroded upwards as well as downwards, a whole variety of social actors ranging from the new social movements to regional authorities could bypass the nation state. Thus it was believed that social movements could realize their interests beyond the state more effectively than through it. Melucci (1996a) wrote of the new social movements entering the planetary world:

> the world of which we speak today is a global world of planetary scale, and this is made possible only by information, or the cultural processes with we represent our world to ourselves. The consequences of this change are enormous . . . The planet no longer designates just physical

location; it is also a unified social space which is culturally and symbolically perceived.

(Melucci 1996a: 7–8)

'Glocality' became one of the themes in the new literature on globalization which became associated with transnational social movement activity. This was a very different conception of cosmopolitanism from the Kantian one in that it was more concerned with local and regional attachments than with world governance based on international law. Kant's theory was too much part of a philosophy of history which saw human history as the unfolding of providence and leading along one path to a cosmopolitan order. In essence, Kant's term for globalization was providence, whereas today globalization sits somewhat uncomfortably with cosmopolitanism, having no 'necessary' guarantee by the fundamentally moral nature of humanity, as Kant believed. Globalization theory, in contrast, sees multiple paths of development and cosmopolitanism can also reinforce particularism. In short, globalization contains complex logics of universalism and particularism, and therefore no single conception of the good is possible as it was once conceivable for Aristotle and Kant.

The rise of globalization theory was accompanied by a turn to postmodernism. The key aspect of this was an interest in identity and cultural production as multiple and cross-cutting with respect to space. National identities are no longer the exclusive collective identities of people in an age of cultural pluralism and the anarchy of multiple identity projects. Identities are overlapping, negotiable and contested. The postmodern literature argued that collective identities are irreducible to the fixed identities of class and nation. As argued by Jameson (1991), from a different perspective, late capitalism as a post-industrial society has become based on the extension of capitalism into the cultural domain in what is now a production of cultural objects for a global market (see also Jameson 1998). According to Bryan Turner (1993a):

> it is possible to combine the claims to citizenship status with a postmodernist critique, if postmodernism can be regarded as a form of pluralism. That is, we must avoid the equation of citizenship with sameness. In citizenship, it may be possible to reconcile the claims for pluralism, the need for solidarity and the contingent vagaries of historical change. If citizenship can develop in a context with difference, differentiation and pluralism are tolerated, then citizenship need not assume a repressive character as a political instrument of the state.

(Turner 1993a: 15)

The case for global citizenship can thus be made on the receding significance of nationality and the growing reality of cultural pluralism. The absence of legal institutions for many theorists is not an obstacle, for it simply shifts the focus from law to politics (Rosenau 1990; Lipschutz 1992; McGrew and Lewis 1992).

The view that nationality is no longer the primary reference point for identification has become more and more commonplace. It is a question not only of identity but also of rights. With the new processes of globalization rapidly unfolding there are also new kinds of demands for rights. Steenbergen (1994) writes of ecological citizenship becoming an additional citizenship to civic, political and social citizenship (see also Irwin 1995; Isin and Wood 1999). This is related to wider issues of responsibility for nature and for unborn generations. In *The Risk Society*, Beck (1992) has written on the implications of risk for citizenship. The politics of the risk society are global, he argues, since the problems of ecological sustainability are not specific to any one country. Karl-Otto Apel has written extensively of the need for a global ethic of responsibility, and, in essays going back to the 1970s, he was one of the first to highlight the question of a global political ethics (Apel 1978, 1992, 1996, 2000). The problematic of what he calls 'co-responsibility' has become a central issue in new debates on science and technology. The question of responsibility for nature is not an individualistic position or one that can be entrusted to national elites but is a genuinely global challenge.

The concern with the internationalization of problems has opened a wide-ranging debate on cosmopolitanism with respect to both democracy and citizenship (Jones 1999; Rengger 1999). There is an expanding literature on transnational social movement organizations or international non-govermental organizations (INGOs) as constituting a global civil society based on what Boli and Thomas (1997, 1999) call 'world-cultural principles' (see also Boulding 1990; Walker 1994; Lipschutz 1995; Wapner 1996; J. Smith *et al.* 1997a, 1997b; Goldman 1998; Kriesi *et al.* 1998; J. Smith 1998; Dryzek 1999). 'When we speak of culture as global, we mean definitions, principles, and purposes are cognitively constructed in similar ways throughout the world'; INGOs, Boli and Thomas go on to argue, are becoming increasingly important in 'enacting, codifying, modifying, and propagating world-cultural structures' (Boli and Thomas 1997: 173). For Boli and Thomas INGOs are the primary organizational field in which global civil society operates. There is no doubt that networks of non-state actors are becoming more and more important and to that extent we can speak of global civil society as a domain of radical governance. It may be suggested, then, that to the extent that we can speak of a global civil society, this is largely manifest in *governance* as opposed to *government*, a distinction which John Dryzek (1999) clarifies. In international relations literature, governance is a term used by those who favour spontaneous cooperation in decentralized systems – for example 'governance without government' (Rosenau and Czempiel 1992; Kooiman 1993) – while government is used by those who propose world federalism or a global super-state (Dryzek 1999: 33). The idea of governance suggests a 'stateless society'; it reflects an opposition to government, and is very evident in international social movement literature (O. Young 1994).

Richard Falk (1994: 131; see also Falk 1987, 1995b) believes that globalization is leading to more economic, cultural and social integration and that consequently this will enhance the chances of 'global citizenship'. His view is that global citizenship will come about as a result of the compelling force of its moral necessity. However, as he recognizes, the reality is that the idea of world citizenship is more likely to go with the homogenized elite culture of international business. This is the problem with many notions of global citizenship:

> Its guiding image is that the world is becoming unified around a common business elite, an elite that shares interests and experiences, comes to have more in common with each other than it does with the more rooted, ethnically distinct members of its own particular civil society: the result seems to be a denationalized global elite that at the same time lacks any global civic sense of responsibility.
>
> (Falk 1994: 134–5)

Elsewhere Falk has argued for a global citizenship based more firmly on civil society than states. Only a 'globalization from below' can mobilize transnational democratic forces and challenge the current 'globalization from above', he argues (Falk 1995a: 171). In yet another contribution, the idea of a global constitution is emerging around states, international governmental institutions and non-governmental organizations (Falk 1993). His position is a strong argument for world government based on a legal order, a cosmopolitian constitutionalism. With respect to global civil society there is much unclarity on whether what is being argued for is global constitutionalism or global democracy, with the former position being suggested by Falk and the latter by Held.

This post-statist position has also been stated by David Held in several books (for example, Held 1995, 1996). He argues that states are being challenged by many non-state actors and processes not under the control of the state. In this situation the only option for democracy is the creation of a global civil society based on a network of democratic bodies. In global civil society people would enjoy multiple citizenships:

> They would be citizens of their immediate political communities, and of the wider regional and global networks which impacted upon their lives. This cosmopolitan polity would be one that in form and substance reflected and embraced the diverse forms of power and authority that operate within and across borders and which, if unchecked, threaten a highly fragmented, neo-medieval order.
>
> (Held 1995: 233)

This is a Kantian position to the extent that it is based on the claim that democracy must first be international if it is to be successful. However, his position is post-statist for he is aware that states will not simply 'wither away', but that they will cease to entirely define the field of citizenship.

A major impetus to the debate on global civil society was the coming of the Internet and the idea of the information society. In these debates the question is less concerned with issues relating to global governance than with a citizenship of participation. Castells (1996, 1997, 1998) has written extensively on the information age, which he sees as a network society. The network society is not a nationally based society for it does not have a centre but nodes and is based on the flow of information in electronic forms. If it is a society it is a virtual society and is open to more interactive forms of relationship than was the case with mass society and earlier in bourgeois society. With more and more areas of society dependent on information, access to information is becoming increasingly a foundation of citizenship. But the kind of citizenship that the virtual society fosters is the ultimate global one that has no foundation in the nation state; it can also be seen as driven by the new political economy capitalism which has penetrated into the cultural domain of communication (Garnham 1990). Yet, it does offer states the possibility of creating 'electronic democracy' which may be important in improving public services (Buchstein and Dean 1997; Bellamy and Taylor 1998).

Arising out of the theory of the public sphere initiated by Habermas (1989a; see also Calhoun 1993; Robbins 1993), a number of authors have addressed the question of a global public sphere (Walzer 1995; Bohman 1997; Köhler 1998). Bohman's theory is an alternative to the legal and political versions. Following Habermas, he stressed the salience of communication rather than governance, rejecting the idea of an 'international civil society' for a 'cosmopolitan public sphere'. He argued: 'An emerging cosmopolitan public sphere renews and expands democracy in two ways: via the pluralist public spheres in each state, and through the informal network of communication among the organizations and associations that constitute an international civil society' (Bohman 1997: 191; see also Bohman 1998; Dryzek 1999). In other words, before a mature civil society emerges there must first be a functional public sphere. This is a point that is insufficiently addressed in the debates on cosmopolitanism. Bohman also distinguishes between global and cosmopolitan public spheres. Cosmopolitanism must entail a process of interaction on the local level, whereas globalization can simply be a transnational process from 'above'. He makes the important point that the term 'cosmopolitan public sphere' is really justified only when there is a genuine interaction between two local public spheres: 'Contrary to a global aggregate audience, a cosmopolitan public sphere is created when two or more limited public spheres begin to overlap and intersect' (Bohman 1998: 213). Dryzek (1999) has also extended Habermas's theory of the public sphere to the transnational domain with the argument that the real significance of non-states actors in the international arena is their capacity to change the terms of discourse.

The discourse of globalization has opened up a variety of positions on the possibility of a global civil society based on democratic governance. This can be seen as a real space that has appeared as a result of trends in social, political and economic change. In contrast to the Kantian tradition of internationalism, there is a pronounced anti-statist stance in these debates on political cosmopolitanism. However, interpretations differ as to whether this is to be seen as enhancing the possibility of cosmopolitan citizenship around a global constitution (legal cosmopolitanism) or as global democracy (political cosmopolitanism). It may be concluded that globalization contains possibilities for cosmopolitanism but this is in no way guaranteed. In Chapter 10 I shall argue that we need to distinguish more sharply between globalization and cosmopolitanism, for in much of the literature discussed here there is a pronounced tendency to reduce cosmopolitanism to some kind of trans-national civil society that is produced by globalization. As a result, civil society is reduced to a quasi-corporatist model of large-scale social movements and state actors operating on the trasnational level. I shall return to the public sphere debate in Chapter 10 to explore the feasibility of a more communicative kind of cosmopolitanism.

Transnational communities

Global civil society as discussed in the previous section related to the possibility of post-national governance. I shall now discuss an additional conception of cosmoplitian citizenship which is less directly related to governance, whether legal or political. Coming largely from post-colonial theory, but by no means exclusively, a view is emerging which locates cosmopolitanism in deterritorialized transnational communities and the 'creolization' of culture. Cosmopolitan citizens are those who are highly mobile, such as immigrants, diasporas, refugees and displaced persons. An older view of cosmopolitanism was that it referred to those, largely of the elite, who had no attachments and for whom migration was freely chosen and temporary. But today the cosmopolitan is not the émigré intellectual or the free-floating expatriate, but one of the millions of uprooted people who have had to leave their homeland not out of choice but out of economic or political necessity (Garcia Canelini 1995; Appadurai 1996; Wilson and Dissanayake 1996; Oommen 1997; Cheah and Robbins 1998; Jameson and Miyoshi 1998; Joseph 1999). This means a potential reversal in the relation of cosmopolitanism to nationalism, since the cosmopolitanism of transnational communities often reinforces nationalism. In any case it is a question of attachment not of disattachment. As David Hollinger (1995) argues in *Postethnic America*:

> As 'citizens of the world', many of the great cosmopolitans of history have been proudly rootless. But postethnicity is the critical renewal of cosmopolitanism in the context of today's greater sensitivity to roots. 'Rooted cosmopolitanism' is indeed a label adopted by several theorists of diversity whom I take to be moving in the direction call postethnic.
> (Hollinger 1995: 5)

This view of cosmopolitanism stresses mobility as its key feature. National forms of citizenship rested on the assumption of limited mobility, from country to the town. But today in the global era mobility is more far-reaching. This does not necessarily mean that cosmopolitanism is something good, for the dislocations that it produces can be damaging. The fact is simply that cosmopolitanism has become a real force in the world by virtue of the growing impact of transnational communities whose members can be called cosmopolitan citizens. Thus, rather than look for signs of a global civil society as evidence of a cosmopolitan citizenship, we can find this in the existence of transnational communities. The implication of this view is that ethnicity is not a contrast to the universality of cosmopolitanism but is itself a form of cosmopolitanism. Accordingly, the focus shifts from abstract universalism to the universalism of the particular. Post-colonial theorists argue for a view of transnational communities as having multiple loyalties, often stemming across generations. Their identities are likely to be more negotiable than those of the majority culture and they are more likely to be multilinguistic. To illustrate this situation, Appiah (1998: 91) quotes Gertrude Stein: 'America is my country and Paris is my hometown'. This can also be seen as cultural 'hybridization' or what has also been called the 'creolization' of global culture (Bhabha 1990; Featherstone 1990; Friedman 1990, 1995; Nederveen Pieterse 1995). By this is meant the process by which the global flow of culture is adapted by its recipients in different ways: 'on one end an assimilationist hybridity that leans over towards the centre, adopts the canon and mimics hegemony, and, at the other end, a destabilizing hybridity that blurs the canon, reverses the current, subverts the centre' (Nederveen Pieterse 1995: 56–7). This notion which is becoming increasingly influential is not without problems, for if everything is a hybrid nothing can be authentic and this is precisely what is being claimed by most identity politics (see Friedman 1994).

According to Hannerz (1990) cosmopolitans are not just tourists but those who engage with the other: 'The perspective of the cosmopolitan must entail relationships to a plurality of cultures understood as distinct entities' (Hannerz 1990: 239). In other words, cultural identities have built into them the possibility of change. This flexibility also pertains to citizenship. In the context of Chinese transnationals, Ong (1998) uses the term 'flexible citizenship to refer especially to the strategies and effects of mobile managers, technocrats, and professionals who seek to both circumvent and benefit from different nation-state regimes by selecting different sites for investment, work, and family relocation' (Ong 1998: 136). However for Hannerz, transnational communities are mostly occupational groups and are not genuinely cosmopolitan; in this they are unlike the expatriate who mostly chooses to go abroad (Hannerz 1990: 243).

The discourse of transnationalism brings cosmopolitanism closer to cultural pluralism and communitarianism, and thus away from some of the liberalist assumptions of Kantian cosmopolitanism concerning its legal and political structures. The concern here is less with issues of world governance than the identities of deterritorialized communities. In this case cosmopolitan citizenship is related to residence rather than birth. It also brings the important issue of culture to bear on citizenship for some of the traditional assumptions of the older theories of citizenship, for instance the separation of public and private, can no longer be taken for granted.

Post-nationalism

In the literature on cosmopolitanism there is also to be found a discourse of what might be broadly called post-nationalism. This is a decidedly ambiguous term since it can mean any form of citizenship that is not exclusively defined by the nation state. In the sense used here it is taken to refer to a reflexive transformation of existing national conceptions of group membership. It is primarily built on the recognition of shared sovereignty, whereby subnational and supranational forms of governance have made significant inroads into national sovereignty. Thus a post-national form of citizenship is one that is based primarily on residence (Delanty 1995a). Citizenship as nationality is based on birth, with some exceptions. European citizenship, as codified by the Maastricht Treaty, could be cited as an example of post-national citizenship (see Chapter 7). A useful distinction has been drawn by Thomas Pogge (1992) between legal and moral cosmopolitanism, with the former referring to the global ideal of a world order and the latter meaning an essentially moral relationship between human beings (Pogge 1992: 49). It is in this latter sense that I am using post-nationalism in the present discussion.

One of the major theorists of post-national citizenship is Jürgen Habermas. As argued in Chapter 3, his theory of citizenship is part of a wider theory of democracy which is elaborated in the form of a critique of the two dominant models (also discussed in earlier chapters), the liberal and communitarian conceptions of citizenship. The idea of discursive democracy which he advocates can be seen as the normative basis of cosmopolitan citizenship. His version of cosmopolitanism is largely elaborated from the perspective of the constitutional state but also has implications for the formation of a global civil society. However, what matters for Habermas is the double existence of a constitutional order and a discursively constituted civil society rooted in public spheres.

What is unique about Habermas's work is that it combines a commitment to cosmopolitanism and to the constitutional state. In the present context the important point is that the crucial feature of the state is not that it is a welfare state, a national state, or even a parliamentary based state but that it is a constitutional state. Its constitutionality is the guarantee of its cosmopolitanism. It is post-national in the sense that it does not attempt to anchor itself in formal institutions or in territory or in cultural heritage, or more generally in shared conceptions of cultural community. The essence of post-national identity for Habermas is an identification with the normative principles of the constitution, a 'constitutional patriotism' (Habermas 1998a). This is a minimal identity in that it is a kind of common denominator commonality but it is also what might be called an enactive identity. Originally put forward in the context of the possibility of German national identity discredited by fascism and the Holocaust, Habermas (1989b) argued that a German national identity could be possible only as an identity with the principles of the constitution. This position can be generalized to all post-national societies. With respect to European integration, for instance, he argues: 'the initial impetus to integration in the direction of a postnational society provided by the substrate of a European-wide political public sphere embedded in a shared political culture' (Habermas 1998a: 153). But this shared culture is founded on a *civil* society as opposed to a *national* society composed of interest groups, non-governmental organizations, and citizen initiatives and movements.

Habermas's post-nationalism is less concerned with global civil society than with locating the structures of cosmopolitanism within the confines of the constitutional state. The problems of the global age – ecological disaster, the growing disparity between the northern and southern hemispheres, human rights, international crime – can be solved only by linking the rule of law to democratic politics within the structures of a constitution. But the constitutional state must become a post-national state in that the extension of democracy is not confined to the nation state. He speaks of the emergence of a global public sphere, but in the context of the progressive institutionalization of international law which is leading to the dissolution of national sovereignty. He has argued that Kant's idea of a cosmopolitan order must be reformulated if it is still to be relevant (Habermas 1998a: Chapter 7). One of the main changes is that today international law can become cosmopolitan law since national sovereignty is not as exclusive as it was for Kant. For instance, the United Nations does not leave human rights solely up to the nation states to deal with but has its own mechanisms. Habermas's cosmopolitanism is a qualified one. It is addressed to the growing salience of human rights and the emergence of binding international law which has had implications for national sovereignty. Its impact is as much within the nation state as beyond.

In an essay published in 1990, 'Citizenship and national identity' (Habermas 1996: Appendix 11), Habermas argued against the communitarian thesis claiming that nationality and citizenship are losing their connection. Citizenship is not rooted in a particular form of life that can be identified with a cultural community. With the French Revolution, nationality meant a nation of citizens. In this republican understanding, citizenship was still tied to civil society rather than to a community of descent. But the position he wants to defend is one based on the centrality of communication linked to law, which allows for a more abstract conception of citizenship than in communitarian theories. 'Only a democratic citizenship that does not close itself off in a particularistic fashion can pave the way for a world citizenship, which is already taking shape today in worldwide political communications' (Habermas 1996: 514).

In sum, Habermas looks to the emergence of a 'cosmopolitan matrix of communication' as evidence of a world public sphere. I have tried to demonstrate that what is specific to his position is that he recognizes both the impact of this trend towards post-nationalism on the global level and on the national level, which is no longer homogeneous. His writings intimate a view of cosmopolitanism emerging from within the constitutional state rather than from uncontrolled processes of globalization. The unexplored consequences of this position is that cosmopolitanism can challenge globalization. In my view, there is a basis here for a new conception of cosmopolitanism, which could be called civic as opposed to a legal or political conception of global civil society. But the distinctive feature of this is the public sphere, rather than civil society, as a foundation of cosmopolitanism. This conception of cosmo-politanism stresses to a far greater extent communication rather than legal and political governance. It is the communicative links between these dimensions that Habermas has emphasized.

Summary

In this chapter I looked at the emerging cosmopolitan thesis of citizenship beyond the state. While the various positions I have looked at emphasize different dimensions of cosmopolitanism, there is widespread agreement that citizenship and nationality have today become separated and that the state is no longer the exclusive repository of sovereignty. Views differ on the extent to which global civil society challenges the nation state, with Habermas offering the strongest defence of the continued importance of the constitutional state. However, the constitutional state is no longer exclusively a national state, having been transformed by transnational communities and the growing significance of international law. Perhaps the central question concerns the extent to which citizenship is determined by forces beyond the control of states? It might be concluded that for cosmopolitan citizenship the fundamental criterion of citizenship is no longer birth, as is the case with most kinds of national citizenship, but residence and the cultivation of a critical discourse of identity as multilayered. Developments in this direction will be discussed in Chapter 5, which deals with the undermining of national models of citizenship by new conceptions of human rights.

5

Human rights and citizenship: the emergence of the embodied self

Modernity was born of the recognition that the individual is the measure of all things. This discourse of the individual in modern social and political thought was part of a more general turn to subjectivity in western culture since the Renaissance. In many spheres of life the modern world-picture privileged subjectivity over the rule of external forces, such as God, nature and the divine right of kings. In the Renaissance and Reformation subjectivity emerged as a powerful force capable of challenging the established authorities. The criterion of legitimacy in knowledge, politics, morality and aesthetics ceased to be an external law whose authority derived from the immutable laws of the cosmos. In place of such cosmic laws the idea of human positive law emerged as the source of legitimacy. Natural law became internalized as the inner law of human subjectivity in ethics, aesthetics and inner-worldy asceticism. With the recognition that legitimacy derives from law, the status of the individual changed. Since the Enlightenment the individual has occupied two legally definable positions: as a citizen and as a human being.

These two conceptions of the individual – the individual and the human being – have given rise to two corresponding conceptions of rights: the rights of citizenship and human rights. In the last two hundred years or so since the first declarations of human rights, the two discourses have diverged considerably. There has been a very clear separation of human rights and the rights of citizenship which parallels the separation of national and international law. In this chapter I shall outline how this occurred and how contemporary developments suggest a gradual blurring, or a de-differentiation, of citizenship and human rights which now presents a major challenge to citizenship as membership of a nation state. Human rights are among the best examples we have of a normative global culture (Ruggie 1983; Menand 1993). Once relegated to the status of a pre-political privatism, human rights are now overriding the rights of citizenship and reshaping democratic politics.

The argument advanced here is that with the gradual dissolution of modernity we are witnessing new conceptions of the relationship between citizenship and human rights. This development can be related to the postmodern critique of the self and the emergence of what might be called the embodied self: in place of the Janus-faced individual as a citizen and as a human being we have a new emphasis on personhood whereby the self is contextualized, contingent and decentred (Delanty 2000c). Human rights have become more contextualized and in the resulting loss of their abstractness they can be realized in practice more easily. But this also leads to the decentring of human rights, for the self is not a product of an essence but a constructivist project. The most far-reaching consequence of this is the emergence of legal pluralism and the interpenetration of national and international law. Along with this development is a new conflict between the abstract principle of equality, which was the basis of the older conceptions of citizenship and human rights, and the nascent principle of difference and collective rights. The reconciliation of the right to equality and the right to difference is one of the central challenges facing multicultural societies, and is particularly pertinent to the possibility of cosmopolitan citizenship.

Human rights, modernity and equality

Modernity was the age of rights. With the growing differentiation of social structures, rights served a means of social integration. Under the conditions of modernity – the separation and internal differentiation of the sphere of the state, economy and socio-cultural institutions – social integration cannot be achieved by recourse to traditional forms of authority or by sustained force. More abstract solutions had to be found. The solution modernity found to the problem of social integration was legitimation through the institution of formal law and democratic government. Rights are legal codifications of political and ethical claims; they are formal, procedural rules of justice. Their abstract and depersonalized nature allows modern society a certain degree of integration. It follows from this that rights institutionalize a principle of formal equality, for all individuals are equal in the eyes of the law. The codification of rights and the pursuit of equality are closely connected features of the self-understanding of modernity. The social struggles of the modern age can be seen as the progressive extension of the principle of equality to all social groups.

Human rights are based on an ethical and legal concept of the individual; citizenship rights are based on a political and legal understanding of the individual. They share a legal conception of the individual but differ with respect to their universality. Human rights are basic ethical rights that all individuals enjoy by virtue of their common humanity, whereas citizenship rights are specific to a particular political community. Basic rights are ones that are valid by virtue of ethical arguments and therefore possess a universality that is not characteristic of all kinds of rights. Once certain basic rights were established, more general rights of citizenship could be granted. In the liberal and republican traditions, the citizen as a member of civil society was the source of political sovereignty. Though this emphasis on citizenship was stronger in the republican tradition, the idea remained fundamental to all of modern political thought that the citizen is an individual with a legal status who consequentially possesses rights within the polity. In the early theories, the rights of citizenship and human rights were not quite as separate as they were to become. In some of the early declarations, such as the American Declaration of Independence (1776) and the US Bill of Rights (1791) and in France the Declaration of the Rights of Man and the Citizen (1789) there was no clear demarcation of citizenship rights and human rights, between the rights of 'man' and the rights of the 'citizen'. In the US Declaration of Independence, Thomas Jefferson asserted the inalienability of the basic rights of 'life, liberty and the pursuit of happiness' to which a government must be committed. The US Declaration was also a protest against 'arbitrary government' in the name of popular sovereignty, the 'consent of the governed'. Unlike the idea of citizenship rights and human rights in Europe, in the USA they were part of a project to found a state in a revolt against a colonial power.

With the rise of the nation state the earlier assertion of human rights was overshadowed by the idea of citizenship: both went in their separate directions, one in national law and one in international law. It is true that national constitutions continued to derive their legitimacy from the doctrine of human rights, as is illustrated in the fact that in France the Declaration of 1789 was a preface to the Constitution of 1791 and most national constitutions declared their commitment to basic human rights. However, the understanding of human rights in national legal systems was independent of international law, which was largely minimal as far as human rights was concerned. Indeed in Britain the term civil liberties was more commonly used than the term human rights. Human rights had a largely ethical status, for their legal standing was dependent on their status as citizenship rights. Indeed, the primary function of international law was treaty-making, and it dealt with the relations between states rather than the relationship between states and citizens. The separation of the rights of citizenship and human rights reflected the divorce between politics and ethics, which, since Kant and Hegel, epitomized the vicissitudes of modernity. More fundamentally, the separation of the rights of citizenship from the rights of the human being, along with the polarization of politics and ethics, expressed an even deeper conflict in the self-understanding of modernity: the dualism of universality and particularism.

According to Marx, writing in 1843, in his critique of rights in 'On the Jewish Question', the differentiation of the rights of man from the rights of the citizen was a false distinction and one that served only to legitimize property rights. The rights of man, for instance the right to religion as a matter of one's free choice, is a natural right in the same way as the right to property and as a result do not go beyond 'egoistic man'. Marx thus condemns the bourgeois institution of citizenship as formulated in the 1793 Declaration on the grounds that it was serving to legitimize a pre-social conception of man:

citizenship, the political community, is degraded by the political eman-
cipators to a mere means for the preservation of these so called rights of
man, that the citizen is declared to be the servant of egoistic man, the
sphere in which man behaves as a communal being is degraded below
the sphere in which man behaves as a partial being, finally that it is not
man as a citizen but man as a bourgeois who is the real and true man.

(Marx 1977: 54)

The rights of man thus were destined to become a private emancipation –
religion as a matter of private conscience – and citizenship a matter of political emancipation. Neither secular nor political emancipation amounts to real
social emancipation for Marx. When Marx declared that 'man is no abstract
being squatting outside the world. Man is the world of man, the state, and
society', he was in effect seeking to abolish the distinction between the rights
of man and the rights of the citizen (Marx 1977: 63).

For some two centuries this contradiction within modernity between the
universal and the particular remained unresolved. The modern idea of sovereignty, for instance, rested on an ambivalent relationship to individualism
and nationalism. Some of the early declarations, such as the Declaration of
1789, appealed both to the individual and to the self-determination of civil
society as a nation. Article One states: 'Men are born and remain free and
equal in rights; social distinctions may be based only upon general usefulness',
and Article Two: 'The aim of every political association is the preservation of
the natural and inalienable rights of man; these rights are liberty, property,
security, and resistance to oppression'. However, the third article asserted
the priority of the nation: 'The source of all sovereignty resides in the nation;
no group, no individual may exercise authority not emanating expressly
therefrom'. By the nation was meant civil society, which was supposed to be
compatible with individualism. It was not until the fully fledged doctrine of
national self-determination emerged by the middle of the nineteenth century
that this ambivalence became more contradictory.

Human rights expressed the universalistic assumptions of a normative order
based on the autonomy of the human being, an autonomy which is prior to
all social and political structures. This doctrine was expressed most forcibly
in the moral and political writings of Locke and became central to modern
liberal legal and political philosophy. Its central ideas were embodied in the
constitutions of western democracies and in the universal charters of human
rights whose declarations were supported by most governments, examples
being the United Nations Declaration of Human Rights (1948) and the
European Convention for the Protection of Human Rights (1950).

The rights of citizenship differ from human rights. They are particularistic
and have been very much shaped by the principle of nationality. The rights of
citizenship are not based on an ethical concept of the individual as such, but
on a political understanding of the citizen as a member of civil society, the
political community of a national state. It has been a fact of history that the
nation state has been, on the whole, a territorially specific and sovereign entity.

Citizenship refers to the internal relationship between individuals and the state; its external face is nationality, which defines the rights of citizenship with respect to other states.

Throughout the modern age, by which I mean the era of the nation state, human rights were at the discretion of the nation state to enforce. The international order was largely based on states and international law was not as extensive as it is today. States were also relatively autonomous of each other and much of international law was a matter of the expediency of national security. Between the Congress of Vienna and the First World War, the international order was based on the balance of power, which had little room for ideas of human rights. Democratization had virtually no impact on human rights, the major exception being the anti-slavery movement. This movement can be seen as an early example within the framework of modernity of an international normative culture based on human rights. Aside from this example, it was not until after the Second World War, in the wake of totalitarianism and fascism, that human rights became a serious issue for international law and this period saw the declaration of several charters of human rights, of which the United Nations Declaration of Human Rights of 1948 is the most significant. The legal institutionalization of trials for crimes against humanity in this period was also important for the development of international law. Previously only states were responsible for war crimes, as was the case at the end of the First World War, but from the 1940s onwards the idea of individual responsibility became widely accepted. In 1951 genocide became formally outlawed in the United Nations Convention on the Prevention and Punishment of the Crime of Genocide.

At about this time the older term 'rights of man' began to be replaced by the term 'human rights'. In this period the actual understanding of what constitutes human rights changed considerably. Originally human rights referred to such basic rights as the right to life, the right to personal liberty with respect to conscience, speech, association, and the right to be free from arbitrary violence, such as torture and unwarranted arrest. These rights have often been justified in terms of natural law and divine providence, as self-evident rights of all human beings. These rights became associated with the more specific rights of citizenship relating to civic and political rights. As in the Marshallian theory of citizenship, social justice has also entered the discourses of human rights. Since the 1960s it has been widely recognized that human rights also relate to social, economic and cultural goods, as is represented by the International Covenant on Economic, Social and Cultural Rights (1966) and later in regional declarations such as the African Charter on Human and Peoples' Rights (1986). In these declarations development becomes recognized as a human right, a concept that becomes widened to what is often called solidarity rights. These rights could be called positive rights to distinguish them from the negative rights of the basic liberties in the older conceptions of human rights. The older rights were won against the state, whereas these new kinds of rights are to be won against economic forces. Following Sousa Santos (1999: 215) we can speak of three generations of human rights: 'while the first generation of human rights was designed as a struggle of civil society against the state, considered to be the sole violator of human rights, the second and third generations of human rights resort to the state as the guarantor of human rights'.

With this transformation of human rights the older doctrine of natural law was finally abandoned: natural rights no longer derive from a pre-social nature but from society itself. In other words, human rights have become contextualized. This was a gradual process and one that was considerably hastened by decolonization in the period following the Second World War. The right to work, the right to leisure, the right to education, the right to a share in public goods, such as health welfare and social security, and the right to cultural goods inevitably became bound up with questions about their realizability. Human rights now had to be guaranteed, not merely stated. From the 1960s the right to national self-determination became increasingly recognized as a human right, and not just a question of political expediency as was previously the case. This was expressed in the Helsinki Agreement (1975) and in the United Nations Declaration on the Right to Development (1986). In later declarations, for instance, the Vienna Declaration, which was adopted by the World Conference on Human Rights in 1993, the rights of the child were asserted. In the Beijing Declaration (1995) the rights of women were reaffirmed on the occasion of the fiftieth anniversary of the United Nations. Thus, within the discourse of human rights there has been an internal logic of development leading to an extension of its domain of applicability well beyond the relatively narrow sphere of human rights in the older declarations. Moreover, there is no longer one global order of human rights, but four international regimes, the European, the Inter-American, the African and the Asian (Sousa Santos 1999: 219). The discourse of human rights can be said to constitute a global normative culture of some significance, which states and their national legislative codes began increasingly to respect. This transformation of human rights towards a concern with substantive issues and a considerable expansion in the volume of international law was to have major consequences for citizenship more generally. But to address such issues we need to go beyond the immanent analysis of human rights and look at wider societal and cultural transformation.

Human rights and the postmodern critique of the self

The transformation of human rights has followed the trajectory of modernity. This has been the story of the gradual dissolution of the concept of the abstract individual with which the dominant tradition in modern social and political thought has been burdened. The early feminist declarations of human rights, such as Olympe de Gouge's 'The Declaration of the Rights of Women' (1790) and Mary Wollstonecraft's 'The Rights of Women' (1792), were marginalized by a gender-neutral notion of universal humanity which disguised what in fact was allegedly a masculine bias. Originally a set of pre-social rights founded in an abstract notion of human nature, human rights today have become highly contextualized around gender, race and geographical criteria. With this has come a relativization of the doctrine of universality that originally accompanied the early declarations. The result has been a blurring of the boundary between human rights and the rights of citizenship. I have already suggested that what is replacing the idea of the abstract model of the human being in the discourse of human rights is a notion of the person as a contextualized self. This idea of the embodied self can be related to the transformation of citizenship from a model of individualism to a communitarian-centred one. This can be related to three developments. First, the general postmodern critique of the politics and culture of modernity; second, the post-colonial critique of human rights and western moral universalism that has led to notions of collective rights; third, legal pluralism resulting from the incorporation of international law into national law and the growing importance of multi-levelled polities such as the European Union. I shall discuss these in turn.

The postmodern critique denies the existence of an underlying human essence, a universal humanity. Some extreme versions of postmodernity, such as those associated with the post-structuralist approach, would deny the very idea of humanity itself and declared the death of the citizen. Post-structuralist thought conceived of itself as an attack on the unity of the self, declaring a 'post-humanism' and sought to rewrite history without a subject. Though this movement never addressed the political question of human rights, its rejection of the entire culture of modernity and its political struggles as empty categories was silent on matters relating to suffering, exploitation and emancipation. Yet it had a great impact on how we think of the self (Delanty 2000c). Philip Wexler (1990) writes that 'citizenship is an ideology, a term left over from the past; even its prerequisites no longer exist. Contemporary society killed the Enlightenment's modern individual, first by commodification, then by communication' (Wexler 1990: 165). Postmodernists argue that the terms individual and society, the basis of citizenship, have been dissipated by new cultural forces. Citizenship has declined because the social has been sublimated by culture. The individual subject in the discourses of modernity has been decentred and fragmented. Autonomy can no longer be taken for granted in what is for postmodernists an endlessly fragmenting world.

In the present context what is particularly important is that the development of citizenship, and rights more generally, can no longer be linked to the evolution of society in the way Marshall believed simply because of the collapse of modernity itself into a variety of different projects. This rejection of what Lyotard (1984) has called 'metanarratives' is of course not just a postmodernist theme. Although it is particularly pronounced in postmodernist writing, it is expressed by a whole range of authors from Habermas to Touraine to Wallerstein. In this view, history is not simply the progressive unfolding of human rights in the formation of an international normative culture. While human rights have won considerable assent, they do not reflect a common understanding of their application and even of their content. The postmodern critique has shattered the illusion of progress and the illusion of an underlying self. Instead we have a multiple selves, a plurality of identity projects and multidirectional historical trajectories.

We do not need to enter into a detailed discussion of the postmodern critique of the self here (see Rose 1989; Benhabib 1992; Delanty 2000c). It will suffice to remark that we can no longer take for granted the idea of an underlying universal human nature. Human rights do not refer to something that is self-evident or guaranteed by nature. Moreover, we must also reject the idea of abstract individualism, or methodological individualism. The self is context bound and therefore particular with respect to time and place. This immediately raises the question of the limits of relativism. The term can be used to refer to the impossibility, or at least extreme difficulty, of achieving a universally valid justification for ethical, cognitive and a esthetic claims. It can also refer to the context-bound nature of all ideas. In general, the term has been used in both senses, for if ideas are context bound they cannot be universally valid. But the two uses are distinct and the second use does not commit one to extreme relativism with respect to the possibility of universality. That ideas are context bound does not imply determinism. Habermas, for instance, has defended the possibility of a limited universality based on a communicatively achieved consensus on truth and justice. Popper has defended a limited universality based on the principle of falsification. Rorty (1993, 1998) has offered a pragmatic kind of universality, namely one based on what works best. There is, then, much to choose from without having to go to the extremes of postmodern relativism and modernist universalism. There is a certain consensus on what might be called a differentiated universalism, or an interactive universalism, in recent theory and it is on the basis of this that it is still possible to speak of rights (Benhabib 1992, 1996).

How then are we to understand human rights in the postmodern age? In my view there is much empirical and theoretical evidence to suggest that the present situation is one of a blurring of human rights and the rights of citizenship (Soysal 1994). It is no longer possible to separate these into two separate domains. Several developments point to growing de-differentiation of many parts of society that were previously separated. Postmodern theories of culture point out that economic production and cultural production are interpenetrated (Jameson 1991; Lash and Urry 1994). National and global cultures have become interpenetrated as a result of developments in information technology, Americanization and popular culture, multiculturalism and migration. Other examples of de-differentiation are the interpenetration of private and public, scientific knowledge and lay knowledge, nature and society. Within law we have the growing importance of legal pluralism, for instance in cross-border legal relations (Gessner and Schade 1990). It is inevitable that in this world of interpenetration and de-differentiation discourses of human rights will cross over into other rights rendering diffuse their domains of applicability.

The postmodern critique of rights has been paralleled by the post-colonial critique of human rights (the term post-colonial being used here in the broad sense of a rejection of western Eurocentrism). They both share an appreciation of the relativity of cultural values, though views differ on how far values are to be relativized. Decolonization and the emergence of the non-western world from imperialism have led to the rejection of the European Enlightenment and its universalistic ethos. The post-colonial critique can be divided into four broad stances. First, the extreme position of those who reject human rights as an expression of Eurocentricism and embrace, to varying degrees, cultural relativism. Second, those who seek a common anthropological human rights discourse in all cultures. Third, those who look for a discourse of human rights less in traditional culture than in a transcultural modernity based on a differentiated universalism. Fourth, those who preserve what I have been calling a differentiated universalism in the form of a defence of collective rights.

For the first group many human rights are simply an expression of western civilization and are not universal. Universalism and westernization amount to the same thing if universal morality is reduced to cultural imperialism, which is the extreme position, or, in the more moderate stance, to the culture of the west. In the latter case human rights may not necessarily be imperialistic but culturally specific to the west. Thus it is often held that the doctrine of human rights has no historical basis in many non-western cultures, such as Islamic, African, Chinese and Japanese cultures. However, there are many who would see human rights discourse as a subtle means of legitimizing western influence when questions of national security are at stake. Human rights were once seen as natural; today the tendency is to see them as cultural, and as a result there is a loss in their universal legitimacy. However, this does not need to imply cultural relativism.

A second position would prefer to defend the possibility of human rights as a genuinely transcultural phenomenon, common to all cultures, whether those of the west or of the non-western world (Renteln 1990). In this way the possibility of a non-ethnocentric concept of human rights can be retained. Thus some would argue that a commitment to human rights can be found in Islam and ancient China but the actual forms that human rights take differ very much from culture to culture. Rather than rejecting human rights as western, they are relative to every culture and thus what must be emphasized is the plurality of their forms. The problem with this approach is that many of these allegedly human rights are not in fact what we commonly understand by the term. Donnelly (1989) argues that these are values about the dignity of the person and not in fact rights as such. There is some truth to this, for there has not been a direct relationship in the reception of human rights in non-western countries and some older cultural traditions. Vincent (1986) is also critical of this attempt to find human rights discourse in pre-modern tradition:

> The difficulty with this procedure is that while it might reduce the ethnocentricism of declarations about them, it abandons in the process any notion of universal rights. Drawing up a long list to satisfy everybody merely adds variety together. It does nothing to resolve the differences

between one item or group of items on the list and another, and would invite particular societies to consult only their section of the document.
(Vincent 1986)

Moreover, there is the danger that this approach will essentialize human rights as culturally specific to each culture and the problem of their universality remains unresolved.

A third position, which is best associated with Habermas (1998a, 1998b) and has also been stated by Sousa Santos (1995: 337–42), concedes much of the relativistic critique, admitting that the doctrine of human rights arose in the context of the European Enlightenment and the political struggles within the west in the nineteenth and twentieth centuries. It would concede, too, that human rights have been used by western powers to impose western, and largely American, foreign policy on much of the world. Yet it would be a mistake to assume that human rights are foreign to the non-western world. While being more institutionalized in western culture, human rights can be seen to be universal in the sense of discourses that are interpreted differently by the different historical cultures. This thesis concedes a lot to the extreme post-colonial critique and the more moderate version that sees human rights as common but relative to different cultures, for there is not always a universal consensus on what constitutes specific human rights and how they ought to be implemented. However, what is truly universal is the commitment to human rights as a project to be achieved, rather than in the assumption of the second position discussed above that human rights are embedded in traditional culture. This is not an essentialistic stance, that is the view that rights derive from an underlying cultural essence that is specific to a particular society, since what is being argued is that human rights are legal norms in the first instance, not purely moral, and they enable a society to distance itself from its taken for granted cultural values. Even in the west, as I have argued above, human rights have been understood very differently in the past than they are today, when they were not seen as applicable to women, children and non western peoples. They have only very slowly been extended to the marginalized and socially excluded. It is not surprising, then, that their adoption in the non-western world would not be straightforward. Human rights allow societies to distance themselves from their own particularity and engage in cross-cultural dialogue. This way of looking at human rights makes them compatible with postmodernism rather than a hegemonic model of western modernity: human rights are not pre-given natural rights but rather constructions.

The question is less one of whether human rights are specific to the culture of the west, than of the tension between their universalistic nature and the local conditions of their realization, as Habermas (1998b: 161) has argued. In any case, aside from some polemical positions which in fact have mostly come from western critics themselves, the reality is that human rights have been widely accepted by virtually every country, and their adoption by the UN and other transnational agencies has been crucial for emancipation from dependency. Few would deny the beneficial effects of such UN agencies as the World

Health Organization, the United Nations High Commissioner for Refugees and the United Nations Children's Fund (UNICEF). The questions that have persisted instead are how are we to understand human rights and how can human rights be realized, rather than whether they ought be pursued? In other words, a contextualization of human rights is possible without relativism. We can avoid the extremes of relativism and universalism if we see culture less as integrated and cohesive totality than as differentiated, with overlapping layers of values and as contested in many spheres (Connolly 1995).

The fourth group sees the problems of ethnocentrism and traditionalism as related and postulates, like the third group, that the ethnocentricism of human rights can be overcome by finding post-traditionalist solutions. However, what is distinctive about this group is that, rather than looking for an essentially cultural foundation in pre-modern culture, many human rights theorists and activists argue for a notion of collective rights. There is little consensus on the legitimacy of collective rights, which have recently become the focus of a great deal of debate in areas as wide as philosophy, international relations and anthropology (Vincent 1986, 1992; Donnelly 1989; Renteln 1990; Kukathas 1992; Freeman 1995; Shapiro and Kymlicka 1997; Wilson 1997). Only by embracing the idea of collective rights can the western bias be overcome, it is held. A frequent argument is that individual rights are of little value in cases of rights for self-determination, the rights for the protection of cultural heritage such as language, and rights for economic and social development. The defence of collective rights has itself received some of its strongest support from the west itself. Affirmative action policies have been, to varying degrees, practised in different contexts in the western world, largely in North America. Though not without controversy, these policies have had major implications for citizenship as an enabling practice aimed at creating structures for the participation of the socially disadvantaged. Within the framework of human rights they have been seen as particularly relevant to the claims of indigenous peoples concerning rights to territory. As Sousa Santos (1995) argues, they represent the most far-reaching challenge to the modern equation among nation, state and law, not least because they have been the victims of multiple forms of discrimination. Moreover, the indigenous peoples' rights are different from the rights of immigrant ethnic minorities since the latter do not include claims to land but to the preservation of cultural identity (Sousa Santos 1995: 318–19). The idea of collective rights has further implications for the older ideal of formal equality, since what is implied by the notion of collective rights is a commitment to difference.

The challenge of collective rights has direct implications for one of the most important transformations of human rights and international law: legal pluralism and the transnationalization of law. According to Sousa Santos, the transnationalization of national legal regulation occurs whenever it can be determined that the changes in the state law of a given country have been influenced by formal or informal pressures by other states, international agencies or other transnational actors (Sousa Santos 1995: 274). In his view, there is considerable evidence that national law is no longer entirely sovereign as a result of the impact on it of international law. Previously international law operated outside national law, whereas today it has led to changes within national law. This is particularly apparent in the European Union where EU law has resulted in tremendous transformation of national law, and in the international context it can also be seen in terms of the impact of human rights on national law. The international human rights regime is comprised of more than states and transnational agencies such as the UN. Important, too, are INGOs, which have been crucial in the process of standard setting and monitoring of human rights as well as their implementation (Smith *et al*. 1997b; Beetham 1998: 61–4).

What this amounts to is legal pluralism, the coincidence of more than one legal system with overlapping legal layers of authority. The case of the collective rights of indigenous peoples, who demand the recognition of customary law, is also an apt illustration of legal plurality. The older framework of human rights simply entailed declarations of human rights; today human rights have to be more than just stated, they also have to be guaranteed by national law. This has been the principal change in the relationship of national and international law which has undermined the very idea of sovereignty being located on one level of governance.

Yasemin Soysal (1994), in one of the most far-reaching studies on the confluence of human rights and citizenship, has argued we have now effectively reached the end of citizenship. She has shown how transnational communities can make huge demands on national governments as a result of the incorporation of international laws concerning human rights into national laws. Such groups can also appeal directly to the EU, thus undermining national law (see Chapters 6 and 8; Preuss 1998). It is not only as a result of human rights, but also because of the impact of the post-war internationalization of labour markets, decolonization and the emergence of multi-levelled polities. However, the growing global discourse on human rights, whether individual or collective, has led to an ever greater intensification of legal pluralism and the emergence of deterritorialized rights. Soysal argues that citizenship is no longer based solely on nationality but on human rights, which having become considerably contextualized, are coming increasingly to play an even more important role. Universal personhood is now coming to replace nationhood as much as it is making the idea of the abstract human being redundant. The idea of personhood as the basis of both citizenship and human rights is also increasingly becoming a theme in recent literature, see Melucci (1996b) and Turner (1986b).

According to Bryan Turner (1993b: 185), human rights can be justified by a view of the essential frailty of the human person and precarious nature of social institutions. Human rights relate to the problem of suffering, misery and frailty. In his view

the universality of the concept of rights can be defended through a sociology of the body. If it is possible to identify such a foundation, then this sociology of the body could function discursively as a substitute for the ancient notion of natural law.

(Turner 1993b: 180)

In place of the idea of a common humanity, the body draws attention to social constructiveness and the uncertainty of the postmodern situation which does not have the certainty of natural law to which it can appeal. What is a universal feature of the human condition is not the autonomous or fully formed person but human frailty and the corresponding values of sympathy and concern. This notion of personhood as one of weakness and incompleteness offers the basis of a postmodern philosophical anthropology of human rights. Barrington Moore (1972) has provided a foundation for a universalistic notion of personhood with the argument that while conceptions of happiness may differ, there is widespread agreement on what constitutes misery.

Summary

I hope to have demonstrated in this chapter that there are good grounds for believing that human rights constitute a discourse capable of challenging national sovereignty. It is now possible for human rights regimes to intervene in the affairs of other states, as the much publicized case of the Pinochet trial in 1998 and 1999 illustrates, or the prosecution of Serbian war criminals in the aftermath of the genocide in Bosnia. The idea of the rights of children also has major implications for undermining the distinction between the rights of citizens and human rights. The discourse of human rights is no longer confined to international law but has entered national legal systems as a result of legal pluralism, in the sense of overlapping and interpenetrating systems of law, a development that is more pronounced in the countries of the European Union. I have argued for a notion of personhood as contextualized and decentred in place of the older polarity of an abstract human nature, on the one hand, and, on the other, the territorially bounded citizen. The present situation points to a differentiated universalism: the end of the grand narrative of universal humanity. Equality must now be accommodated by the recognition of difference. But rather than retreat into the extremes of moral neutrality or cultural relativism, a limited universalism remains as a project of cultural transformation. In sum, human rights are not the product of the natural certainties of a pre-social human essence, but constitute a constructivist project; they have to be achieved rather than being discovered. As such, they require social consensus on what constitutes them. It is not surprising, then, that we find growing discussion on what constitutes a human right and what constitutes a crime against humanity since neither of these can easily be defined in absolutely definitive terms.

6

Globalization and the deterritorialization of space: between order and chaos

The debate on citizenship has been very much dominated by political philosophy and, though citizenship has become a topic of pressing concern in sociology in recent years, sociology has not, on the whole, made a major contribution to it. Many sociological accounts of citizenship have tended to suffer from the same normative stance that is prevalent in political philosophy. In this chapter I shall try to bring some sociological perspectives to bear on the challenge of cosmopolitanism. In Chapter 4 I introduced the idea of cosmopolitan citizenship as a challenge to the three dominant normative models discussed in Part one. To an extent, Chapter 5 attempted to bridge a normative with a sociological analysis with an account of human rights as an expression of a global transformation in world cultural principles. The third generation of human rights, that is those concerned with social and cultural issues, I argued, constitute one of the most important empirical expressions of cosmopolitan citizenship. I shall now move yet further beyond the normative statement of cosmopolitanism to examine the nature of globalization with a view to assessing its implications for cosmopolitanism. The analysis of the implications of globalization will largely be done in Chapter 10. Here my concern is to understand the nature and dynamics of globalization, which is widely believed to create the conditions for cosmopolitan citizenship and a democracy beyond the nation state. As I have previously indicated, there are good grounds to be sceptical that globalization provides the conditions for cosmopolitanism. At least, the connection cannot be taken for granted. A examination of globalization is therefore a necessary step in the direction of a theory of cosmopolitanism.

The first section discusses in general terms the globalization and attempts to offer a definition, the second critically discusses the main sociological analyses of globalization, and the third deals with two of the main dynamics of globalization: capitalism and democracy.

What is globalization?

Globalization has become one of the central themes in social science in the 1990s (Sklair 1991; Axford 1995; Waters 1995; Smelser 1997; Jameson 1998; Held *et al*. 1999). One of its first uses was in an article in the *American Journal of Sociology* in 1966 (W.E. Moore 1966). Its widespread use today is clearly connected to the series of major social transformations of the 1990s, the fall of communism and the end of the cold war, the decline of the left, the unification of Germany, the end of apartheid, the international military operations that followed in the wake of Iraq's invasion of Kuwait, the war in Bosnia and Kosovo, the expansion of the World Wide Web, the enhanced momentum of European integration and the growing concern about global warming and worldwide ecological crisis. The approach of the millennium added to this a sense of an epoch ending. All these transformations have had a huge impact on the cultural perception of the world as uncertain, paradoxical and directionless. The world suddenly appeared more connected than it ever had been and, at the same, all the more fragile – for the new modes of integration do not make for certainty or stability. The nation state once defined the outer limits of the larger community; these limits have now lost their ability to provide certain markers of belonging. As a result globalization is as much about the search for community as it is about the transnationalization of the world market. The everyday consciousness is more exposed to events far beyond the parameters of the nation state. Space matters less, accordingly, as time is shortened. These changes in our perception of time and space have transformed the cultural models by which we interpret the world.

There is certainly a case for thinking that globalization might be best understood as something cognitive, as opposed to an account of real changes going on in the world. Many times in history there have been explosions in world consciousness, the Greek cosmopolis, the Chinese world kingdom, the Christian ecumene, the late medieval 'great chain of being'. The present global consciousness can be compared to the cosmic mind of the Renaissance, which was both an 'age of discovery' and also created the 'New Learning' of modern science. But the contemporary situation is different, for the early moderns were conscious of the insurmountable obstacles of time and space, which perhaps explains the Renaissance's fascination with utopia as both a real and imaginary place. The world today is perceived as global in a more real sense, as an interconnected web of relations with nationally mediated forms of perception less important than they were previously. That would appear to be one of the main ideas underlying Roland Robertson's (1992) writings on globalization. For him, the important feature of globalization is the consciousness of the world being a global place. 'Globalization refers both to the compression of the world and to the intensification of the consequences of the world as a whole', he argues (Robertson 1992: 8). Friedman (1994), too, emphasizes the question of meaning as the central characteristic of globalization. But the question of globalization as a real force in the world still remains despite the growing power of the discourse of globality. How are we to define globalization? Globalization is best defined, I would suggest, in negative terms, as the diminishing importance of geographical constraints. It is, as Waters (1995) puts it in a definition that is difficult to improve: 'A social process in which the constraints of geography on social and cultural arrangements recede and in which people become increasingly aware that they are receding' (Waters 1995: 3). Globalization, then, is primarily about the transformation of space. In this it is clearly connected with modernity, which was primarily a discourse of time. In modernity people saw in historical time visions of emancipation, which explains why all modern utopias were located in a particular time consciousness. Today, it would appear that the focus has shifted from time to space, from utopia to 'heteropologies', as Foucault (1986) believed was the case (see also Soja 1996). The global transformation of space is radically different from the modern project, which sought to delimit space: it concerns the deterritorialization of space. This view of global society is not too far removed from Luhmann's (1975, 1990) theory of 'world society' (see also Beyer 1994: 33–41). For Luhmann, world society is based on communication and comes into existence with the transition from a society based on integration to one based on functional differentiation. Luhmann associates this shift with modernity but sees it as intensified in communication systems.

We might, then, ask the question what is different about globalization, for one can see it, at least superficially, as another word for such processes as modernization, westernization and internationalization, to take the main contenders. There is no doubt that the term has been too vaguely used and yet, it does appear to express something that the other terms do not quite capture. Modernization as a process of structural development through functional differentiation fails to capture the essence of globalization which cannot be defined by reference to the myth of progress, rationalization, secularism and individualism. Above all, modernization was a process that was spearheaded by the nation state, which globalization has greatly undermined. Modernization entailed a process of convergence, or what Parsons called adaptation; first within the nation state where there would be a gradual convergence of economic, political, social and cultural structures. The entire edifice of Parsonian functionalism was devoted to explaining how this comes about and how the convergence of societal structures is part of the wider evolution of modernity and its 'societal community'. But the global age has witnessed as much divergence as convergence, as is evidenced by the plurality of societal frameworks. Some theorists, such as Robertson (1992), see globalization as being more fundamental than modernization and having a much earlier origin. If globalization is nothing more than the weakening of the constraints of geography, then it certainly can be brought back to the early formation of civilizations and world religions. Randall Collins (1997) thus projects globalization back to early civilizations in his monumental global theory of intellectual change. In this context mention can also be made of debates on 'global history' or 'world history' (Mazlish and Buultjens 1993).

Globalization, too, is more than westernization. To be sure, in many of its forms it can be said to be merely the latest version of Americanization, but that is inadequate since globalization also entails the worldwide displacement and diffusion of all culture, not just American culture. It is less a process emanating from one origin than a multidirectional web. Certain developments in postmodernism capture this sense of globalization as a directionless and decentred processes. For instance, the postmodernist emphasis on de-differentiation, Derrida's (1977, 1978) notion of decentring, the diffusness of the 'rhizome', to use a term of Deleuze and Guattari (1983), or the end of the grand narratives, as described by Lyotard (1984). Globalization cannot be explained as a system of hegemony as such. That is why the Marxist analyses of the world system, such as those of Wallerstein (1974, 1979), do not fully explain globalization. These analyses concern the dynamics of dependency and the advance of capitalism from the centre to peripheries rather than the dynamics of global convergences and divergences in cultural, economic and political forms of interaction. In other words, the myth of hegemony cannot be attributed to globalization, which, as a theoretical term, is not merely the extension of one national or geopolitical sphere of influence. Above all, globalization suggests the absence of agency, which was central to modern-ization and westernization. To reiterate, globalization is merely a process of deterritorialization, the vanishing of space. With the reduction in the signific-ance of space, time becomes less significant.

Finally, globalization is more than internationalism, which is an older idea to describe the increasingly functionalized links between states and the emergence of 'world society'. The global age is widely held to be one in which states are no longer the sole actors, and in some formulations they have disappeared from a world of pure process and even of anarchy (Ohmae 1990, 1995; Horsman and Marshall 1994; Strange 1996). This position has led some to the conclusion that states have been usurped by markets, while others have drawn the conclusion that the end of the nation state has opened the door for cosmopolitan forms of governance (see Chapter 4). However, these arguments have been subject to a good deal of critical scrutiny (Dunn 1995; Berger and Dore 1996; Hirst and Thompson 1996; Holton 1998) and it might be concluded that the globalization thesis does not necessarily entail the end of the nation state and it is not a competitor to internationalism. It is clear that the internationalism of world society will continue to exist and that the crisis of sovereign state will increase. However, it is evident that we are still living in a world of states, but one of the growing importance of non-state actors, such as INGOs (Boli and Thomas 1999).

My contention is that globalization cannot be explained either by structure or agency. It is not a new structure or the work of a particular agent. Processes such as modernization, westernization and internationalism were all products of a world shaped by the nation state and the culture and institutions of modernity. Globalization must be seen as an expression of the interaction of different national centres and cultural systems, such as the interaction of modernity and postmodernity. This is not to deny the fact that westerniza-tion and, more recently, Americanization have been the dominant influences in global social change. As Arnason (1993) has argued, neither the concrete forms and consequences of Western hegemony, nor the limits to it, can be explained without taking into account the reactions and counter-projects on the civilizations on which it was imposed. The most fundamental aspects of Western modernity were co-determined by its interaction with the world beyond its original domain.

(Arnason 1993: 12)

Modernity as a global field has given rise to different versions of modernity, which means that westernization is only one particular form. A controversial version of this thesis is Huntington's (1993) well known essay on the civilizational conflict of the west and the Islamic-Confucian East which, in his terms, has replaced the older ideological conflict between capitalism and communism. A more differentiated version of this view is Barber's (1996) account of the conflict of 'Jihad vs. McWorld', the confrontation between the polarized scenarios of authoritarian communitarianism and individualististic consumerism. Globalization is best seen as a field of tensions in which cultures are more exposed to each other as a result of the diminishing limits of geography. The global age is simply an era of deterritorialized forms of communication. It is a field of interacting frameworks which are as likely to enhance the particular, the 'local', rather than the universal, the 'global'.

In sum, I see globalization as a meeting of cultures as a result of the diminishing importance of space. This can take the form of a violent conflict, the merging of cultures and the formation of a universal culture. Globalization simply facilities intercivilizational encounters.

The sociological analyses of globalization

The discussion in the preceding section raises a question that has confused many debates on globalization: does globalization lead to a global order, be it a global society or to a global culture? The literature on globalization tends to assume that globalization is more than a process or a dynamic but is also a condition – 'globality' – that has supplanted modernity, or even postmodernity. This is the view of Albrow (1997), for whom globalization is a particular condition which has succeeded modernity. Luhmann (1975, 1990) would also appear to hold such a position, as would Castells (1996). Agreeing with much of this, I prefer to theorize globalization simply as a dynamic that was intensified by modernity and postmodernity. I shall return to this in the following section on capitalism and democracy, which I shall be arguing are the two most important dynamics in globalization. The view that globalization is a successor age to the modern age makes the error of assuming that globalization is a condition, akin to the 'postmodern condition'. I believe that it is less a condition that can be attained than a process of accelerated social change arising out of the diminishing importance of space in defining cultural, political, social and economic ties. It is in this sense we can speak of a 'global age'.

Most theories of globalization fall into two groups, theories of political economic transformation and theories of socio-cultural transformation. I shall comment on each of these with respect to two points. First, I shall identify a strong and a weak argument in each position and second, the normative perspective on the positive or negative effects of globalization. The strong thesis is one that emphasizes globalization as leading to integration, homogeneity, standardization, or simply put, to a global order; the weak thesis is that globalization leads to fragmentation, plurality, even chaos.

In the first category, in many formulations, such as Guehenno (1995), Ohmae (1990, 1995) and Strange (1996), a picture is painted of global disorder, whereby, with the alleged decline of the nation state, a new global age will come into existence. Thus, in an extension of McLuhan's (1962) 'global village' thesis that the global age has abolished the village for a world society. The emphasis is on the economic undermining of the nation state. Many of these accounts exaggerate the dynamic of convergence, such as Fukuyama (1992), but others stress polarization and the growing chaos of the global order. Fukuyama's position could be seen as the strong thesis of globalization: the vision of the end of history in the universal victory of liberal democracy. The strong thesis asserts the integrative nature of globalization in the making of a homogeneous world society. Sassen (1992), in contrast, in her account of the rise of the 'global city', stresses the inherently fragmentary nature of the new capitalism, which tears the global city from its regional and national context. This might be said to be the weak thesis of globalization: globalization as chaos or a world in which states are 'losing control'. There are of course different normative appraisals of this. Marxist and critical theorists would see this as merely the expression of capitalism and westernization.

Susan Strange (1996) argued that one of the most fundamental changes is that today the state competes less over territory, which was the case in history, but for control over market shares in the world economy. Thus, rather than seeking military alliances, commercial ones are becoming more important. In this transformation the global order is about the competition for the favours of foreign firms. The 'new diplomacy' is triangular: while governments have to negotiate with other governments, they also have increasingly to negotiate with firms and adjust to the fact that firms negotiate between themselves (Strange 1996; see also Stoppard and Strange 1991; Dicken 1992). Bauman (1998) regards globalization as a destructive force in the world, producing new geopolitical patterns to inequality. Cosmopolitans, on the other hand, would like to see world society developing along the lines of a global civil society. Conservatives like Fukuyama (1992) see the global world as one of liberal democracy and free markets. Marxist-inspired accounts are more critical, but there are some that would see in the global economy new opportunities for the reinvention of trade unions and the recovery of the social project of labour (Munck and Watermann 1999).

Though not all theorists emphasize convergence or the interaction of international capital with counter-hegemonic projects, there is a pronounced tendency in the literature to see globalization as the expression of ever greater links in the world. Anthony Giddens (1990), for instance, sees globalization as the breaking down of the barriers of time and space which once separated peoples and whole societies from each other. In this sense, then, globalization entails a degree of universalization, though this does not necessarily lead to global convergences. For Giddens (1990) and Albrow (1997) the global age is not only a product of the modern age, but also its successor. This is in contrast to Robertson's (1992) view that globalization is prior to modernity, which is itself the expression of processes of globalization, for the dislocation of time and space are not specific to the contemporary period. In general, there is the assumption that globalization is both a process and a condition, or that a process leads to a particular condition. An assumption is made that globalization – the release of the economy from the geopolitical framework of the modern nation state – is leading to a global order. But the nature of this new condition remains unclear. Not too surprisingly, then, many theories have remained on a purely normative level of analysis on the possibility of a global civil society (I discussed these in Chapter 4).

To the second group of theorists belong those who emphasize the socio-cultural dynamics of globalization, for instance Featherstone (1990), Hannerz (1992b), Robertson (1992), Ritzer (1993), Friedman (1994), Lash and Urry (1994), Sousa Santos (1995, 1999), Appadurai (1996) and Jameson and Miyoshi (1998). I do not mean to suggest that these are two separate bodies of writing, but that there is, in general, a dominant tendency to see globalization as the worldwide expansion of capitalism and markets at the expense of the territorial nation state. Inspired by postmodernism and post-colonial studies, other theorists have written about cultural globalization as opposed to economic globalization. Here the normative emphasis is less on global civil society than on global culture, but there is also considerable ambivalence on whether this is some kind of universal condition, a 'secular ecumene' (Tenbruck 1990), or the latest version of cultural imperialism (Jameson and Miyoshi 1998). In these accounts, the strong thesis is that globalization brings about the progressive homogenization of all cultures and forms of communication. Inglehart (1977) has now generalized his older 'silent revolution' thesis to a global condition of a fundamental shift in values worldwide (Abramson and Inglehart 1995). However, the tendency, on the whole, seems to be increasingly towards a weaker thesis of the recalcitrance of the particular and the fragmentation of experience and meaning. Appadurai (1996) portrays globalization in terms of a chaotic flow of cultural 'scapes' – ethnoscapes, mediascapes, technoscapes, financescapes and ideoscapes – which provide particular cultural groups with models for their own organization and identity formation. His account of the global age is one that stresses the lack of order and direction. Robertson (1992) also writes of the relativization of societies and of national identities, on the one side and, on the other, the expansion of individual identities to the whole of humankind. He would appear to waver between the strong and the weak argument. The weak thesis of globalization sees it as leading as much to divergences as worldwide convergence around a single logic or driving force. Friedman (1994), too, sees globalization as a two-fold tendency 'towards a local encompassment of the global in cultural terms and at the same time an encompassment of the local by the global in material terms' (Friedman 1994: 12). Consequently, globalization is marked by a deep fragmentation of meaning and of cultural identity. This is also apparent in Robertson (1992), for whom one of the features of globalization is the particularism of the universal, such the local adaptation of universal ideas, as in creolization. Sousa Santos (1995: 262–96; 1999: 217–19) makes a distinction between 'globalized localism' (the globalization of a local phenomenon, such as the internationalization of English) and 'localized globalism' (the impact of global process on local practices, such as deforestation) as two forms of globalization emanating 'from above'. These can be contrasted to globalization 'from below', which he identifies with the counter-hegemonic discourses of cosmopolitanism (networks of INGOs and movements related to citizenship and democracy) on the one side and, on the other, 'the common heritage of humankind', which relates to the globe in its entirety. This distinction between hegemonic and counter-hegemomic forms of globalization is also made by Ulrich Beck, who associates new transnational actors operating beyond the system of parliamentary politics with the latter (Beck 1996: 16). These theorists, then, stress global convergence less than divergence and disjuncture within the global system, for globalization has more than one direction.

In contrast, the globalization theory of Lash and Urry (1994) puts the emphasis on the flow of economies and images and signs in a de-differentiated world in which the borders separating economy, politics and culture become diffuse. In their stronger version of the globalization argument, the distinctive feature of globalization is the rapid movement of information as a result of the 'disorganization' of capitalism, which is no longer able to constrain economy and culture within the national limits. Though they do not expressly claim that globalization leads to a global culture, this is clearly the implication of their analysis, a thesis that is also suggested by Ritzer's (1993) argument concerning McDonaldization as a global culture. Thus one of the main aspects of globalization is the formation of a transnational popular culture. O'Neill (1990) draws attention to AIDS as a feature of global culture. These developments raise major questions about what have been called cultural rights, or what Beck has termed 'global technological ethics' (Beck 1996: 22). The new global forms of communication and cultural transmission have raised fundamental questions that cannot be solved by the traditional forms of authority and which necessitate an entirely different kind of citizenship, for instance, the question of intellectual copyright, the censorship of the Internet and what in general might be called a socially responsible media (Lurry 1993; Pakulski 1997; Stevenson 1997; Trend 1997).

Other authors, such as Castells (1996) and Harvey (1989), take yet further the theme of globalization as the total separation of time from space in the making of a new global culture: time disappears into a timeless space. Thus, 'cybersociety' becomes the ultimate global society in which there is no distinction between time and space, for time has become compressed. While many accounts see globalization as leading to the unleashing of ethnic-nationalism, populist movements, religious fundamentalism, postmodernist-influenced theories, such as those of Harvey (1989), Lash and Urry (1994) and to an extent, too, Giddens (1990) and Castells (1996), see globalization as linked to the culture of reflexivity. In the new culture of flows, individuals and groups can create identities more easily. This does not lead to a homogeneous world but a world which is more or less positively appraised. Especially in Giddens's social theory, late modernity is seen as offering more possibilities for the construction of reflexive life projects and individuation.

The consensus in the very disparate sociological literature on globalization would suggest that a global age must be seen as one of diversity and fragmentation. In abolishing older systems of governance, a whole range of forces are released from the previously restraining forces of space. Globalization does not then lead to a global culture, still less to a global society. Though there are some empirical signs of a global culture, most theorists would see this in negative terms as the rule of the market. However, while recognizing this to varying degrees, many globalization theorists tend to emphasize too strongly the demise, or at least the massive restructuring, of the nation state, as a result of the transnationalization of capitalism. Castells is decidedly ambivalent on this, but his work has the merit of emphasizing the logic of fragmentation induced by globalization. In my view, his work makes the mistake of replacing capitalism with technology, and as a result his argument suffers from a technological determinism. But he has correctly recognized that the other side of the globalization is the recalcitrance of identity and the search for community. Rather than seeing this as reactive, it should be seen as embodying an immanent logic of development of its own. In any case, the extension of this communitarian identity has no direct connection to information technology. It is more helpful to see this as an expression of the spirit of democracy and the many different forms that it takes can be related to varieties of democracy.

Let us now consider two dynamics of globalization: capitalism and democracy.

Capitalism and democracy as global dynamics

My analysis emphasizes two dynamics to globalization: capitalism and democracy. That is, the dynamics of the worldwide extension of capitalism and, more generally, instrumental rationality, on the one side, and on the other, the equally worldwide extension of democratization, or what might be more broadly described as the rule of the self. These are the two most powerful forces in the world, which are also global. Before saying more on this I would like to reiterate a point made earlier, namely that underlying the logic of globalization are the logics of convergence and divergence. On the one side, globalization can be seen as a logic of convergence, the formation less of a world society than of homogeneous and interacting units and, on the other side, divergence, the fragmentation of common ties and the dislocation of life-worlds. Such logics have little to do with world society and can occur within nation states. Indeed, the very formation of the nation state was itself such a case of the confluence of logics of convergence and divergence, whereby a common unit emerged as a result of the divergence of its internal parts. I would also like to stress that globalization has the tendency to produce not just fragmentation but also polarization, the growing tension between geo-political units, such as those between north and south. Because globalization is an uneven process, the likelihood of fragmentation and polarization is very great. In what follows I shall illustrate this by reference to capitalism and democracy. My broader aim is to link the two paradigms in the sociology of globalization, the emphasis of capitalist restructuring and the socio-cultural emphasis on the counter-hegemonic currents of democratization.

Since the fall of communism and the liberation of many parts of the world from dictatorships, especially in Latin America, and the end of apartheid in South Africa, the spirit of democracy has penetrated everywhere. One might even go so far as to say that the spirit of democracy has penetrated even further than capitalism. It was democracy that had a greater impact on the communist system in the former USSR than capitalism, and in China since 1990, democracy has proved more troublesome than capitalism, to which the communist state has adjusted. Aside from the different impacts of demo-cracy and capitalism, it seems possible to describe these two forces as the most significant in the world today. It is also to be remarked that the penetration of capitalism and democracy cannot be explained by westernization or even by modernization.

The collapse of Soviet communism has been unsettling for the west, not least because both democracy and capitalism are deeply unstable forces. The global age, I would contend, is a post-colonial and post-totalitarian age, one which has been opened up to transformation by capitalism and democracy. It might also be termed it a 'posthegemonic' order (Keohane 1994). There is no doubt that capitalism is still a product of westernization, particularly in the developing world, though too much should not be made of this since many capitalist formations, for instance Japan, South East Asia, and the Chinese conversion to capitalism, as well as much of capitalist transition in the former Soviet bloc, cannot be attributed to western capitalism. Wallerstein's (1974, 1979) theory of the world-system is unable to explain the rise of a multiplicity of regional-systems, which are neither peripheries nor semi-peripheries of the west. The rise of the EU as a single trading bloc is also evidence within the west of more than one centre.

Capitalism did not alone transform the post-hegemonic world in the image of money and wealth accumulation. An equally and arguably more powerful force has been democracy, which is no longer just a political force but also a cultural movement. This is one of the main arguments of Alain Touraine (1997, 2000) and has also been argued by Manuel Castells (1997; see also Trend 1997). The worldwide penchant for democracy has rivalled capitalism in its ability to bring about social change. By democracy I do not simply mean liberal or parliamentary representative democracy, but the communitarian ideal of the rule of the people. In its pure form democracy is communitarian, even populist. Democracy is primarily an ideology of absolute equality and one which gives expression to the voice of the self. In the west, democracy has been contained within the political institutions of the state where it has been linked to the rule of law. Aside from various kinds of popular mobilization, democracy in the west has always been related to the institution of citizenship. Even in the radical democratic currents that transformed western politics since the late 1960s, the connection with citizenship was never entirely severed (see Chapter 3). In the global context it is a different story, for there democracy has not always been related to citizenship, which cannot exist without civil society, or the rule of law. But here, too, there are counterexamples. The students' revolt in Tiananmen Square was an example of a democratic movement connected with the pursuit of citizenship. But in much of the world, both in the west and beyond, the logic of democracy has been more allied to nationalism than to citizenship, and in many cases it is allied with religious fundamentalism.

Democracy gains its impetus from the idea of self-determination, and in its pure form it is the attempt to forge a perfect identity between self and other, the elimination of all differences in the pursuit of absolute equality. Smelser (1997) identifies one master impulse in the revolutions of the global age: 'the insistence on behalf of individual agency, free choice, and activism: the ennoblement of human affairs' (Smelser 1997: 81). The revolutions that he mentions as the most significant are the continuing revolution in economic growth, the continuing march of democracy, the revolution in solidarity and identity, and the environmental revolution. In this chapter I am principally concerned with the first, the worldwide extension of capitalism, and the middle two, democracy and identity, for democracy as used here refers to this wider impulse towards self-determination (Chapter 7 will discuss the implications of the environmental crisis). As argued in the introduction, it was inevitable that the quest for democracy as self-determination would be connected to a logic of violence, for the identity of the self had to sacrifice the autonomy of the other (de Vries and Weber 1997).

As a movement of the self, democracy and nationalism have not been too far apart. Nationalism stood for the assertion of the self in the name of the social bond; democracy stood for the assertion of the self in the name of the political bond. Together, the confluence of the national idea and the democratic ideal created the foundation for the modern configuration of geopolitical power. The essence of this was the coupling of nation and state. Democracy became absorbed into the state and thus lost its adversarial force; nationalism, too, was largely assimilated into the patriotism of what was to become a nation state. By means of the institution of citizenship, democracy and nationalism were domesticated. This has not always been the case, particularly where nationalism and democracy had different logics of development and where state formation was externally imposed. In the post-colonial world, national emancipation from imperialism and economic development led to different traditions in democracy. Nationalism was more important than democracy as a basis of legitimacy, and capitalism was less important than development. Where these projects failed, democracy and capitalism took over, and mostly have been less successful. In neo-imperialist forms of enforced dependency, capitalism has always been in the background but was rarely the basis of legitimacy. Given the relative weakness of post-colonial states, it was inevitable that popular democracy, on the one side, and, on the other, marketization would gain the upperhand. Throughout the period of decolonization in the aftermath of the Second World War, there were obvious limits to globalization: the cold war set limits to the diffusion of capitalism and democracy; despite the mass media, most communication systems were still national; economic development was largely controlled by national governments. The collapse of communism and the end of the cold war marked the beginning of the global era.

In the post-communist world, in contrast to the post-colonial world, the initial appeal for legitimacy was to both democracy and capitalism. Where the state was weak, or non-existent, and civil society destroyed by too rapid marketization, democracy quickly turned to nationalism. Democracy was a seedbed for nationalism, largely because democratization had to fit into a double transition: the transition to a market economy and a transition to a democratic state (Sakwa 1999). And, in many cases, there was the third transition, entailing geographical change in national borders (Offe 1997). Where democratization preceded marketization, the structures for a stable adjustment were often absent, particularly because of the incompletness of the transformation of the state. My point is that in much of the post-communist world, in particular in the more troubled parts, the failure of the state and civil society to harness the spirit of democracy and capitalism by the institution of citizenship had the effect of providing nationalism with a powerful impetus. Without a state rooted in citizenship and powerful enough to restrain capitalism, the dual forces of democracy and capitalism were responsible for shaping the direction of a good deal of social transformation.

Summary

I have argued that globalization is a movement of worldwide social transformation spearheaded by the dual forces of capitalism and democracy. Throughout the world in the 1990s the nation state has been weakened and, as a result, the forces it previously contained have been released to shape the world according to their own logic. I have identified capitalism and democracy. Others might stress technology, as has Castells (1996, 1997, 1998). However, I do not think that information-led technology alone has been the driving force in the world. In my view, far more powerful forces have been democracy and capitalism, power and wealth, which use the new information technology but are far from determined by it. Looking at globalization in terms of a conflict between these two forces has a number of advantages over approaches that reduce it to one central animus. I have tried to argue in this chapter that it has been the weakness of several theories of globalization that they reduce globalization to a logic of worldwide convergence while neglecting the other side of globalization, namely, the polarization of global units and their internal fragmentation.

In Chapter 7 I move on to a look at some of the consequences of globalization for cosmopolitan citizenship: nationalism, the city, multiculturalism and migration.

7

The transformation of the nation state: nationalism, the city, migration and multiculturalism

It has been a presupposition of cosmopolitan theories of citizenship that the nation state has been fundamentally transformed. The sociological analyses of globalization discussed in Chapter 6 share a common belief in the demise of the nation state. As I have argued, positions on this range from the extreme thesis of markets having supplanted states in the formation of a global capitalist world to a more moderate thesis of a loss of sovereignty in a world increasingly out of control. With respect to national culture, globalization theories range from the strong thesis of an emergent homogenizing global culture from 'above' to counter-cultural projects from 'below'. More generally, we can speak of a view of globalization ranging from global integration by technology to global fragmentation by capitalism or by democracy and its cultural currents, which include the new nationalism and populist mobilization. Whether by economic-led change or politico-cultural led change, globalization has been seen as having transformed the very possibility of society. Neither capitalism nor democracy are social in nature, for one is economic and the other is political and cultural. The social space of citizenship would appear to be eroded in these global transformations. Not surprisingly, cosmopolitan theorists have looked to the transnational level for a new citizenship capable of re-empowering civil society.

In this chapter I examine some aspects of global transformation with respect to the internal transformation of the nation state. My central concern is to explore the growing tension between nationality and citizenship within the nation state. In line with the argument in Chapter 6, I shall posit here that the principal change that is occurring today under the conditions of globalization is neither the end of the *nation* nor end of the *state* but the end of the *nation state*. Both the nation and the state are in strong positions – and may even be enhanced by globalization and its contradictory paths – but what is in fundamental crisis is the nation state, the fusion of nation and state in a single geopolitical entity. What in fact is occurring is the decoupling of nation and state. Once united in the unitary model of the nation state which served as a mechanism of social integration, the nation and state are drifting apart in an increasingly fragmented world. The world of the nation is being claimed by a resilient democracy, and the sphere of the state has been won over by capitalism unfettered by the geopolitical constraints. No longer exclusively confined to its role as provider, the state has found a new role as regulator. As a result, the position of citizenship is uncertain and in the context of increasing migration, citizenship is put even more on the defensive. No longer tied to nationality, citizenship has been alienated from the state. In new nationalist currents, the nation becomes tied to populist assertions of democracy, imposing further strains on citizenship.

What then is the fate of citizenship? With weakening national sovereignty, post-national citizenship is forced to align itself with transnational governance and with subnational governance. In this chapter I shall deal mostly with the latter. I have already suggested that the capacity for transnational or cosmopolitan governance is weak, a theme to which I shall return in Chapter 8. Too much of the debate on post-national citizenship has been focused on transnational governance to the neglect of other forms of post-nationalization. My thesis in this book is that cosmopolitan citizenship is meaningless unless it takes account of subnational forms of governance.

In the following analysis I first outline the nature of what is often taken to be the new nationalism, arguing that it can be seen as a corrupted form of democracy that has become divorced from citizenship. Second, I discuss other forms of subnational mobilization which are more closely related to citizenship, namely the resurgence of the city. Finally, I discuss the implications of immigration and multiculturalism for citizenship in an era of declining national sovereignty.

The new nationalism: from inclusion to exclusion

Today nationalism has become a major force in the world (Hobsbawm 1991, 1992; Kaldor 1993; Ignatieff 1994; Delanty 1999e; Kymlicka and Straehle 1999). As the nation state loses much of its previously unchallenged sovereignty, nationalism appears to be on the ascendancy. How are we to understand this apparent contradiction between rising nationalism and declining state sovereignty? I believe that this paradox can be explained by the weakening of state patriotism and the growing influence of a nationalism from 'below'. But this new nationalism from below is also related to post-national developments in general: the shifting of the nation code from the state to new reference points which allow for different kinds of identification. This, then, is the essence of the new nationalism: it is above all a nationalism of social discontent and not of state patriotism. What is at stake is less a question of ideology – comprehensive belief systems – than identity and social resources. It can take forms ranging from extreme racist xenophobia against immigrants to a renationalization of political discourse. Whatever form it takes, it cannot easily be harnessed for the purpose of the legitimation of state power. Throughout the world – from the United States to the Russian Federation – one of the main forms that nationalism is taking is opposition to the state. There are, of course, exceptions to this, such as Iraq, but in general nationalism has become a force not easily controlled by state authority and can undermine as much as enhance the state. Nationalism can thus be seen as a product of the internal crisis of the state in the age of globalization. But it is also a product of the postmodern search for community and identity. My thesis, then, is that nationalism is no longer contained within the categories of political community which equate a nation with a state, for the state has ceased to be the main embodiment of national community. What in fact is occurring is the release of the nation from the state. The nation code has become a free-floating signifier which can be used by many social actors: it is no longer contained by the state. It is this release of the nation code from the state that has multiplied the discourses of nationalism in recent years.

If the nation code is no longer contained by the state and has become a free-floating signifier in society, it will have lost its monopoly on collective identity. What this amounts to is post-nationalism: a national identity is only one particular form that collective identity takes. There are many collective identities, and national identity is only one such identity. In other words, nationalism today lives in a world of many identities. Thus, post-material environmental identities can be articulated alongside national and class identities. Let us try to specify more clearly what is new about nationalism today.

The main difference between the new and the old nationalism is that today nationalism has lost its connection with citizenship and has become a nationalism of exclusion. The old nationalism was based on an ideology of inclusion and was part of nation-state building (Bendix 1964). As Hobsbawm and other writers on nationalism have argued, nationalism prior to the early twentieth century was primarily a nationalism of state patriotism (Gellner 1983; Alter 1989; Hobsbawm 1990; Greenfeld 1992; Delanty 2000a). Even in the case of irredentist and secessionist nationalisms, there was always a strong connection with nation-state building (Hroch 1993). Nationalist ideology was mostly codified by political elites and intellectuals, having few roots in popular culture, and there are many who would argue that cultural nationalists invented popular genres, and even tradition itself, to give it a cultural basis that it might otherwise lack. In cases of national movements that successfully led to the creation of nation states, national identities were codified by new elites who merged cultural nationalism with the demand of the bureaucratic central state. The core components of the old nationalism were, variously, language, religion, territory and ethnicity. With the aid of national education systems, a monolinguistic culture, and social welfare programmes, the nation state consolidated around an internally homogenized population (E. Weber 1976). This was essentially a project that sought to transform rural communities into an urban industrial proletariat. Otherness, or cultural difference, was reduced by nationalizing programmes, which in fact exteriorized the 'other'. I will not comment further on the old nationalism other than to reiterate that it was part of a state-led project of nation state building in the context of societal modernization and was frequently part of 'social imperialism', the popular support for empire building, for the era of nation state building was also the age of empire. It was inevitable that the idea of the nation would come to reflect the central aim of modern citizenship, namely, social inclusion. No theory of nationalism can ignore the fact that in all its forms – whether secessionist nationalism or the state patriotism of the established states – it was connected to the formation of a national citizenry. The Enlightenment doctrine of self-determination combined with the international support for national self-determination, with the most influential calls being made by Woodrow Wilson and V.I. Lenin.

Nationalism in its most recent forms no longer tries to include by assimilation as much of the population as possible. The age of nation-state building is over, as are early nationalist projects to create culturally homogenous populations. Thus the 'other' in the discourses of the new nationalism is more likely to be immigrants than competing nation states. It is more a matter of xenophobia than of jingoism. Extreme nationalist movements in the developed world define national identity by reference to immigrants and not by reference to other western nationalities: the other is increasingly becoming the internal other. Nationalism today is more likely to be a product of the breakdown in social communication than a function of state building. The new nationalism is an expression of the crisis of the nation state as well as of the decomposition of industrial society and its system of social integration. As a totalizing ideology nationalism is certainly in crisis. This is perhaps one of the main differences between the old and the new nationalism. The universalistic ideology of national citizenship – embodied in the national idea of the United States, France's republican ideology, the old irredentist nationalism of Ireland and Italy, the state patriotism of Britishness and the ethnic nationalism of Germany and Russia – did involve an ideological dimension in the sense that the ideas of national identity were codified by elites into comprehensive and popular belief systems. What is in crisis today is this sense of ideology, as well as the connection with national identity and a shared political culture based on citizenship. This is not to say that exclusion played no role in the old nationalism. Clearly this was based on the ability to exclude by the legitimate monopoly over the means of violence, as well as in the articulation of nationalist ideology which clearly distinguished one national culture from another. However, this kind of exclusion was connected with internal state formation and the creation of modern citizenship.

Nationalism today no longer appeals to ideology but to identity and material interests. In the new nationalism ideology is refracted through the prism of identity and is mostly based on extra-legal powers. Thus, the predominant form that national identity takes in the Republic of Ireland is a neo-communitarian cultural nationalism and no longer the state seeking ideology of irredentism (Delanty 1997d; O'Mahony and Delanty 1998). This turn to culture can be described as a 'banal nationalism', as Billig (1995) terms it; it is a nationalism that pervades everyday discourse, frequently does not even understand itself as national, and may even see itself as post-national (Billig 1995). Material interests must not be excluded, for one of the main expressions of national identity is what Habermas (1991) has called welfare materialism. This is the nationalism of prosperity, namely that with diminishing material resources, such as welfare benefits, immigration controls must be strengthened.

Expressed in more general terms, we can say that there has been a decoupling of nation from state. With the gradual freeing of the state from some of its traditional functions, social identities, and in particular national culture, can reassert themselves in a variety of ways (Balibar 1991). The resurgence of nationalism can thus be seen in the context of the new processes of globalization, which have uprooted the state and set off a whole series of identity politics (Hedetoft 1995, 1999; Brubaker 1996; Calhoun 1997; Oommen 1997). The state is no longer dependent on a national culture and frequently it has rejected certain core elements of the national culture. Thus a major dimension to the new nationalism is its opposition to the state, an extreme example being the rise of the militias in the United States. Italy may also be cited as an example of how nationalism, as represented by the Northern League, can be divisive. For northern nationalists, the Italian state is corrupt and controlled by southern Italians. The new nationalism is more likely to derive from 'below', in contrast to the old nationalism, which was primarily a nationalism from 'above'. There are of course some exceptions, such as the ability of the Serbian state in 1999 to orchestrate nationalist mobilization. But in the majority of cases the new nationalism is expressed against marginal groups within the national territory. It is a discourse of exclusion. The increased incidence of civil wars as opposed to territorial wars between states is also part of this general tendency by which domestic conflicts replace international ones (Enzenberger 1994).

In the absence of a common enemy in the post-cold war era, and the more general decline in the ideological conflict between communism and the western democracies, the opportunities were ripe for cultural conflicts to emerge. The undermining of the state as a result of globalization, coupled with neoliberal attacks on the welfare state have provided further opportunities for nationalism to fill the void that has been opened up by the separation of the nation from state. According to this analysis, the state is far from being in demise. Although it has lost a considerable amount of its sovereignty to the new transnational processes, it has in many ways become strengthened as a result of globalization for it is no longer exclusively answerable to civil society. One of the main transformations of the state is the shift from a provisory to a regulatory role. There is a movement towards the emergence of regulatory states in much of the developed world (Majone 1996). The state is becoming increasingly the regulator of social interests than exclusively a provider, as was previously the case. Rather than seeing the retreat of the state and the end of big government, in fact we have seen more regulation in the growth of non-majoritarian forms of decision making. But this does not mean a return to the older social democracy of the post-war period. The new regime is a regulatory one, and as Majone (1996) argues, it leaves open the question of citizenship and democratic accountability. It is in this new regulatory kind of governance that nationalism, as a popular democracy, becomes a substitute for citizenship.

From this pessimistic scenario let us now look at an alternative expression of democracy, the city and the possibilities it offers for post-national citizenship in the context of subnational responses to globalization.

The city as the space of citizenship

In the most general sense, the crucial question of our time is the struggle between the forces of autonomy and fragmentation. This conflict has taken on a new dimension with the transformation of the world by globalization, which I have argued has led to the weakening of states by an internationalized capitalism. Nation states are suffering a decline in their sovereignty which is being transferred upwards to global institutions and downwards to the subnational. In the vacuum created by the erosion of the national level resurgent social forces, such as new nationalisms, regionalisms and various kinds of communal identities are being released which challenge the sovereignty of the state. In Chapter 4 I looked at the renaissance in discourses of human rights, which are increasingly overriding national citizenship in what is becoming a tendentially global order in which rights and identities are being recombined in new ways (Soysal 1994; Sousa Santos 1995; Jacobsen 1997). Regions, too, are beginning to surface as powerful new voices (Ohmae 1993; Sharpe 1993; P. Anderson 1994; Perulli 1998). Yet it is apparent, as I argued in Chapter 6, that globalization is not leading to a more homogeneous world. Indeed it would appear that the condition of late modernity is one of fragmentation. The most striking dimension to this is the collapse of 'the social'. We are witnessing the end of 'the social' in the sense of the decline of society as a meaningful concept (Touraine 2000). In its place are a variety of fragmentations, such as the atomized individual, the rule of the market, the victory of community over society and the invasion of the car.

These developments are particularly visible in the case of the city, whose form is fragmenting into increasingly separate spheres. In the transition from the city of modernity to the postmodern global city there is a fragmentation of the urban form. I am arguing that there is a separation of the cultural-aesthetic form of the city from the essentially urban form of life. The European city of modernity was constructed on the basis of a certain unity of aesthetic form, economic function and an integrated life-world (and as with the examples of the Hansa cities, the northern Italian cities of the Middle Ages and the cases of Bruges and Geneva, there was also a tradition of political sovereignty); or, the Greek belief in the possibility of a cosmopolis, the fusion of the human order of polis with the divine order of the cosmos. Today these domains have split apart and the hope of re-establishing a principle of unity is diminishing. Is there any chance of a new principle of unity emerging?

I do not think that the aesthetic form will achieve this, and the socially vulnerable life-world is unable to establish its autonomy over the systemic forces of economy and polity. Economic forces will not themselves bring about a principal unity. A more promising prospect, particularly as far as the European Union is concerned, is the possibility that the city in the post-national era will be able to assert its political voice against the state. However, it is unlikely that the political function of the city will succeed in re-establishing the autonomy of the city since politics in general has lost its ability to define sovereignty, which today, must be shared at many levels. The question of how the city can re-establish the unity of the urban form under the conditions of globalization is one of the central challenges for the recovery of citizenship (Eade 1996; Douglas and Friedmann 1998; Sandercock 1998; Holston 1999; Delanty 2000b; Isin 2000).

The fragmentation of the social in general, and urban life in particular, can be analysed in terms of the following four categories: accumulation, or material production (economic change); power, regulation and sovereignty (political change); meaning, identity and symbolic representation (cultural change); everyday life and social action (social change). I shall examine each of these in turn, relating them to the city as a possible space of citizenship.

Material production

The most striking development in economic production is the trend towards the spatial separation of production and consumption, the globalization of capital, and the increased importance of information technology. Economic production is becoming less controlled by national governments and many societies are experiencing de-industrialization. Those which are succeeding in adjusting to the conditions of information technology will be more versatile than those which have remained in the industrial mode of production (Castells 1994, 1996; Borgja and Castells 1997). We need not explore this any further here since these debates have been discussed in Chapter 6. My aim here is merely to point to the implications of changes in material production for cities. There is some evidence to suggest that cities are benefiting from global changes in the world's economy, with local initiatives becoming more and more important. With the loss of national governments' control over their economies, locally based economic policy is enjoying a new autonomy. Urban economic policy research stresses the role of local institutions in regenerating cities as economic units. Many cities have succeeded in greatly improving their economic performance independently of national governments, which can no longer guarantee the conditions of production. Formal and informal networks of cities are becoming more and more important as shaping factors in economic policy. Another crucial factor is the informational economy. The informational mode of production is of particular significance to cities allowing them to adapt to the conditions of de-industrialization (Castells 1989). The informational city can capture the ground from the centrifugal state since the (centreless) global economy is based less on expansive territories than on the interrelations of nodes.

Power, regulation and sovereignty

The erosion of national sovereignty has already been noted as a key dimension of the current situation. This does not imply that national governments will disappear but that they will have to share sovereignty with other levels, principally the transnational and the subnational. The struggle to control territory – which in former times was the goal of government – is being replaced by the drive to control a whole range of other forces, such as markets and international crime (Sassen 1996). In sum, we can declare the end of 'big government'. The chances for cities to assert their sovereignty will be dependent on two factors. First is, undoubtedly, their economic performance in defining locally or regionally based economic policy. The second is the ability of cities to form alliances with each other. The city in the global era will not be comparable to the state in high modernity; it can survive only by forging alliances with other cities. The role of local government is crucial in this since many problems can be solved only at the local and global levels. Cities will derive their strength from a world in which sovereignty is shared on many levels.

Meaning, identity and symbolic representation

Cultural transformation associated with globalization has been most pronounced in the 1990s. The cultural model of western societies is no longer shaped by nationally specific cultures. Moreover, the systems of meaning sustained by the cold war have collapsed, bringing about the release of a new politics of identity. We are living in a post-ideological age in the sense that ideology is no longer the defining feature of political culture (Delanty 1998c). However, this does not mean that ideology has come to an end but is being refracted through identity. Expressed in different terms we can say nation and state are being decoupled; the realm of symbolic representation and the political regulation of population are increasingly retreating into separated domains bringing about a major crisis in legitimacy. In the vacuum created by the collapse of ideology a new politics of identity has emerged, as is witnessed by the rise in a variety of new nationalisms. One of the central questions for the future of the city is whether it can capture this space in the articulation of a new political culture, and the recovery of a sense of civil society associated with the city. Today cities are fighting a battle over their symbolic representation. The dominant representations of the city are the motifs of helplessness, destruction, urban malaise, urban violence; in sum, fragmentation. But there is also a nascent discourse of the city as the site of autonomy, regeneration and of civil society.

Everyday life and social action

A central theme in recent social theory is the denial of the social. Communitarian and postmodern theories have undermined the coherence of society as a concept, replacing it with various conceptions of community. Communitarian thought, which has had its greatest impact in North America, stresses the exhaustion of society and the need for a retrieval of community (see Chapter 2). Postmodernism, too, has greatly contributed to the absorption of the social by the cultural. These movements of thought – while differing greatly – have given expression to a profound pessimism in the institutions of modernity. Perhaps it could be argued that the central question is the status of social space. Modernity entailed the separation of place from space; it brought about the creation of an abstract sense of space as an imagined domain. Today, in the postmodern and global era, space has been superseded by flows, the compression of time and space (Harvey 1989). The spatial categories of modernity, though not reducible to place, nevertheless preserved a relationship to place as a lived world, a life-world. The cities of modernity were both places and spaces, achieving a unity of form and function. In the space of flows which pervade the global city we are losing that crucial connection with place. Cities are becoming 'non-places', shaped by the flow of markets, capital and commodities. To recover a relationship between space and place is one of the main challenges facing the city today.

A new concept of space is needed to capture the space of the city under the conditions of globalization. I believe that it is possible to see cities in terms of 'discursive space'. The dominant conceptions of space stress either the visibility of space or representational space. Visible space is a static conception of the urban form and has been highly influential in the making of the city of high modernity. The more cognitive notion of representional space refers to cultural constructions of space and also entails an aesthetic orientation. The city of modernity in different ways gave expression to these two understandings of space, as is illustrated in the writings of Baudelaire, Joyce, Simmel and Benjamin, who all stressed the representational mode of space, while a more visible conception of space pervaded the designs of Le Corbusier or Baron Haussmann, for instance. In the search for a 'thirdspace', to use Edward Soja's (1996) term, we must go beyond these visions of space to embrace a sense of space more in tune with the current social realities, such as globalization, diversity, the postmodernization of culture and the informational society (Beall 1997). In my view, the notion of discursive space is more fruitful than the space of flows since it captures the connection between communication and action. Discursive space is the space of civic communication; it is the space of democracy and citizenship.

Immigrants and multiculturalism

In the period of nation-state building from the eighteenth century to the middle of the twentieth century, immigrants formed an integral part of the great national projects and their citizenship policies. Many countries, especially the United States, were formed out of the influx of huge numbers of immigrants. In several European countries migratory movements, within and across states, were common. Industralization and urbanization facilitated such movements, as did decolonization. In central and eastern Europe, the old territorial empires were based on the assimilation of a diverse population and migratory movements were commonplace. The USSR made ethnicity central to its citizenship policy. The period immediately after the Second World War saw the massive movements of people across Europe, with over 10 million ethnic Germans moving to West Germany from the Soviet occupied lands east of the Oder by the late 1940s. By the late 1950s nation state building projects were mostly completed and immigration policy determined the acquisition of citizenship. But migration continued, and many European countries imported immigrant labour from southern European countries. Though the incoming workers were not initially granted full citizenship, they acquired in time many rights and contributed to the formation of multiculturalism. Between the 1960s and 1980s many western countries became multicultural, largely as a result of immigration, due not only to decolonization and imported labour, but also to more open immigration policies.

Multiculturalism can be seen as an attempt to achieve a balance between inclusion and exclusion. In the mature nation state, as it consolidated in the period after the Second World War, citizenship became extended in different ways. Civic and political rights developed into social rights, as described by Marshall (1992), and immigrants, though denied political rights, were able to enjoy civic rights and, increasingly, social rights. But unlike the earlier period of nation state building, immigrants did not always enjoy the full benefits of citizenship and were frequently marginalized. In Germany in the 1960s immigrant workers were expected to return eventually to their home country, though, with the arrival of a second generation in the 1970s, this expectation diminished. Multiculturalism was the framework within which this was all possible. Immigrants were able to participate in both the national society as well as their own culture. Multiculturalism allowed a certain tolerance of difference and made possible a degree of equity. The fact that western multicultural societies had also created welfare states in this period, and were also enjoying relative economic prosperity in terms of economic growth, low unemployment, and general stability, greatly facilitated the fostering of multiculturalism. In this period a certain balance was achieved between the logic of inclusion (multiculturalism) and exclusion (citizenship) because the welfare state, as the 'social' face of national state, was able to reduce its exclusionary logic due to economic prosperity.

It is possible to identify three models of multiculturalism that existed in the developed world in this period: assimilation, pluralism and social integration. First, assimilation is the American model, which has also been called the 'melting pot' model. The basis of this is the view that all immigrants will become assimilated into the one society. This model in fact is not a model of multiculturalism since the aim is to have a common cultural identity. Second, marginalization: the paradigmatic model of this is the French republican policy of confining multiculturalism to the private sphere. In this model there can be no pubic recognition of cultural differences in the public domain of civil society, which is supposed to be a domain of equality. Third, pluralism: unlike the French model, pluralism, which is best represented by Canada, grants public recognition to different groups who are encouraged to retain their differences and will receive state support. Only a minimal commitment to the shared political culture of the public domain is required. Germany, which (unlike France) has not granted formal citizenship to its non-ethnic German immigrants, is officially committed to this kind of multiculturalism. While being very different, these models all reflect a common concern with striking a balance between inclusion and exclusion. To varying degrees this has been successful, though there is much to suggest that the first two models have been less successful than the third. However, in the present context what is important is the more general crisis of multiculturalism as a result of global-ization and the fragmentation of the nation state.

Several developments must be commented on. There is no doubt that the period of multiculturalism is coming to an end. The American model is now widely believed to be a failure, at least if we follow communitarian critiques (see Chapter 2). Assimilation has been possible only at the cost of gigantic ghettoization, and new forms of social exclusion have emerged (Wacquant 1993; Byrne 1999). This is not to deny the relative success of American multiculturalism, since there has been considerable assimilation (Patterson 1997; Smelser and Alexander 1999). What is apparent, however, is that this model may have reached its limits (Schleslinger 1992). A new multiculturalism has emerged as a result of the failure of assimilation, one that seeks to posit-ively empower groups through collective rights (Glazer 1997). The French republican model, which is also practised in Turkey where the state is offic-ally secular, is unable to stem the rising tide of religion and ethnic identity. This model presupposes widespread secularism. But one of the features of the current situation is the crisis of secularism (Juergensmeyer 1993). In China in 1999 the government was faced with the problem of the rise of the Falun Gong, a religious movement with over 100 million followers, just one of the many religious undercurrents challenging atheistic communism. Pluralist multiculturalism has been more successful. But as Soysal (1994) has argued, immigrants, at least within the countries of the European Union, have now extended their rights so far that they can challenge national governments by appealing directly to EU authorities (Soysal 1994; see also Cesarani and Fulbrook 1996). Moreover, ethnic groups are able to reaffirm their ethnic identities. With increasing rights, which no longer derive exclusively from the nation state but from human rights, identities can be reasserted. Soysal's (1994) thesis is that national citizenship is be-coming less important and national identities are articulated in new ways. In the context of my argument concerning citizenship and multiculturalism, what this means is that multiculturalism has ceased to be a container for immigrants.

As multiculturalism enters into a new phase, the modern institution of national citizenship is further undermined by the increasing restrictions that are imposed on the welfare state. The welfare state was the social basis of much of western multiculturalism, and the strong economies of the post-war period made possible widespread immigration. The new nationalism that I have discussed above must be seen as the product of the declining force of social citizenship: the logic of exclusion and inclusion no longer coincide. Extreme nationalist parties have gained huge support due less to the inherent belief in nationalism than to growing social discontent with the mainstream parties. This is evident in the tendency of nationalists, including extreme nationalists, to deny the racist component in their discourses. The issues, it is alleged, are merely about immigration, access to public goods and the restriction of citizenship to nationals. The new nationalism thus might be called a 'materialistic' nationalism as opposed to one that is explicitly cultural or political (Habermas 1991). Today the welfare state has reached its limits, and unemployment along with new kinds of poverty have challenged the older model of immigration. Nationalism has aroused hostility to immigrants who are seen as posing a risk to economic security. In many countries right-wing parties are more likely to succeed if they can link their xenophobia to material interests (Kitschelt 1995). It has been argued that right-wing voting can be explained less as an ideological phenomenon than as a reaction to economic insecurity. Economic crises combined with ideological predispositions channel support into the extreme right (Falter and Klein 1996). Thus the decline in support for the German extreme right in the 1994 and 1998 elections can be explained as a decline in political dissatisfaction rather than a decline in right-wing attitudes, the potential of which always exits. In other words, the real danger to democracy and multicultural citizenship is the erosion of the mainstream parties as they struggle to find a solution for unemployment. Nationalism and racism thrive when they can link themselves to the discourse of democracy and material interests. In a study of racism in Louisiana, Howell and Downing (1996) argue that David Duke (who ran for the governorship on an explicitly racist platform in 1991) is symptomatic of a new kind of symbolic racism which asserts that blacks are failing to live up to the work ethic and discipline. Duke combined this racist attitude with democratic populist hostility against the federal government which was, allegedly, elitist and too responsive to the demands of African Americans.

In sum, the presuppositions of multicultural citizenship no longer exist. Migration is increasing worldwide at a time when the developed world is becoming more concerned with exclusionary policies to restrict entry. With over 120 million immigrants worldwide and over 20 million refugees, the nation state is under pressure since the older model was not designed for such great numbers. As Sassen (1996) points out: 'Large-scale international migrations are highly conditioned and structured, embedded in complex economic, social, and ethnic networks. States may insist on treating immigration as the aggregate outcome of individual actions, but they cannot escape the consequences of those larger dynamics' (Sassen 1996: 75; see also Castells and Miller 1993; Sassen 1999). Western multiculturalism emerged on the basis of economic and social stability. Within the countries of the developed world multicultural citizenship has become unstable. Economic insecurity has risen, the welfare state is no longer able to absorb all kinds of social problems, and the cultural presuppositions of western multiculturalism have been undermined by rising nationalism and the emergence of second and third generation immigrants who no longer share the same commitments of the first generation and are becoming more integrated in the mainstream society.

Summary

We have now seen how the nation state is internally fragmenting under the pressure of globalization. I have looked at some dimensions of this with respect to the internal transformation of the nation state. Democracy is increasingly being claimed by populist movements such as nationalism as well as racist and neo-fascist movements. Multiculturalism is no longer the sole model for the containment of immigrants who are becoming more integrated into the mainstream society as a result of generational change and as a result of the acquisition of new rights and claims that can now be made beyond national governments. At the same time, citizenship is under strain by the weakening of the state in its new role as regulator rather than provider. There is one overall conclusion that can be drawn from this: citizenship is increasingly shifting from a right acquired at birth to a right acquired by virtue of residence. This situation has greatly changed the social situation of immigrants in particular. With the growing importance of residence as a criterion, nationality and citizenship are less strictly separated than they previously were.

In Chapter 8 we look at the impact of European integration on the decoupling of citizenship and nationality, for it is in the European Union that this tendency is most apparent having acquired a legal basis in post-national citizenship.

8

European integration and post-national citizenship: four kinds of post-nationalization

Towards the end of his classic work, *The Division of Labour in Society* (published in 1893), Emile Durkheim reflected on the possibility of a European society emerging out of the diversity of national societies. One of the conclusions of that work was:

> among European peoples there is a tendency to form, by spontaneous movement, a European society which has, at present, some idea of itself and the beginning of organization. If the formation of a single human society is forever impossible, a fact which has not been proven, at least the formation of continually larger societies brings us vaguely near the goal.
>
> (Durkheim 1960: 405–6)

Durkheim thought that the ever increasing division of labour was bringing into being a more differentiated and complex society, characterized by what he called 'organic solidarity' as opposed to the 'mechanical' forms of solidarity that had prevailed in earlier times. Illustrating the concept of organic solidarity with respect to Europe, he argued:

> today . . . the different nations of Europe are much less independent of one another, because, in certain respects, they are all part of the same society, still incoherent, it is true, but becoming more and more self-conscious. What we call the equilibrium of Europe is a beginning of the organization of this society.
>
> (Durkheim 1960: 121)

The fundamental question underlying Durkheim's work concerned the question of what holds a society together, or how is social integration possible? In his view, social integration in modern industrial society was leading towards the formation of a society which was, in its social and economic structures, characterized by differentiation, or the division of labour as he called it. Under such conditions, he believed, social integration required a particular kind of cultural cohesion that would be in harmony with social structures. The older forms of cultural cohesion were losing their hold because they were based on a too direct, or 'mechanical' as he called it, relationship between the individual and society. His question, then, related to the connection between social integration and cultural cohesion under the conditions of societal differentiation. More fundamentally, he wanted to know how was social order possible and what kind of cultural values made order reconcilable with the differentiated nature of social reality.

His answer was that a differentiated modern society requires generalized values and a form of solidarity based on cooperation between social groups, such as occupation and professional organizations and education. Such a generalized value system would not be based on the values of a particular social group but would be shared civic values. It is clear that Durkheim had in mind a republican conception of citizenship and believed the cohesion of a society rests on more than citizenship as a civic bond but also on identity. In his later work, *The Elementary Forms of the Religious Life*, Durkheim (1915) wrote about the formation of cultural representations which expressed the 'collective conscience'. These self-images were the objectified representations of society. In the present context, what is of great interest is whether Europe can articulate such a representation of itself: what is the collective conscience of European society? As early as *The Division of Labour in Society*, Durkheim has considered this question. What happens, he wondered, when two collective consciences confront each other? 'For one people to be penetrated by another,' he argued, 'it must cease to hold to an exclusive patriotism, and learn another which is more comprehensive'. Durkheim goes on to argue:

> this relation of facts can be directly observed in most striking fashion in the international division of labour history offers us. It can truly be said that it has never been produced except in Europe and in our time. But it was at the end of the eighteenth century and at the beginning of the nineteenth century that a common conscience of European societies began to be formed.
>
> (Durkheim 1960: 281)

But Durkheim was aware that Europe stood far from social integration and the cultivation of a European civic morality. It was no coincidence that he chose the theme of suicide for his great empirical treatise, *Suicide*, published in 1897 (Durkheim 1975). The phenomenon of suicide epitomized the anomie that Durkheim thought was creeping into European society in its transitional phase between traditional society and modern society. Anomie results when there is a breakdown in solidarity, when a discord emerges between culture and society, and as a result individuals no longer feel integrated into society. Suicide, in particular the phenomenon of 'anomic suicide', was symptomatic of the lack of coherence between cultural cohesion and social integration.

Durkheim was one of the first thinkers to reflect on the idea of a European society as an emergent reality. While many intellectuals from the Enlightenment onwards wrote about the possibility of a European federal polity and of European culture as a spiritual mission, he actually considered the question of the 'social' itself as a reality *sui generis*, to use Durkheim's own phrase. His central ideas remain of great importance today as European integration takes on a new momentum, in particular the idea of how a society represents itself and creates a cultural model which might be the 'meeting ground' between two collective consciences. One of his enduring themes concerned the relationship between the social and the cultural – the world of social institutions and cultural forms of identity and solidarity. A century later we have still not moved beyond Durkheim's fear that the degenerating forces of anomie are creeping into the vacuum created by the divergence of the social and the cultural. In this chapter I discuss European integration with a view to understanding the extent and significance of social transformation that it has brought about. I begin by outlining some of the background to European integration, with a brief account of the three main phases. Second, I look at the principal arguments against European post-nationalism. Third, I assess the extent to which we can say European integration is evolving in a post-national direction.

The three phases of European integration

The origins of European integration were in the circumstances surrounding the end of the Second World War: the need to solve the German problem, the desire to make lasting peace between France and Germany, and the need to contain the USSR. Inspired by the desire for peace and the cold war, the path to European integration was seen to lie in closer economic ties. As the memory of the war faded and as the structures of the cold war normalized, economic imperatives, fuelled by the post-war economic boom, increasingly came to the fore and, with the emergence of the European Economic Community (EEC), the political task of peacemaking finally receded. In general, the first phase was the project of rescuing the nation state, to use Milward's (1992) term. The key idea was reflected in the older realist philosophy of cooperation between sovereign and more or less autonomous states. According to this stance, only states are real and therefore supranational politics cannot be anything other than relations between states.

In the 1980s a second phase can be discerned. In this period the EEC became the European Community (EC), the adjective economic being dropped. In place of the exclusive priority of economic links and political cooperation, political steering now moved to centre stage. It was less a question of cooperation than of interdependence. In this period there was also enhanced legal and administration integration. This model has been reflected in neo-functional theories of European integration which stress the dimension of interdependence as opposed to mere cooperation. However, the emphasis was still on sovereign states (Milward *et al.* 1993). Despite the growing influence of federalist ideas, integration was rarely seen as leading towards unification. Growing interest in culture and questions of identity slowly emerged in the 1980s as a key dimension of European integration, and Jean Monnet is alleged to have stated that if he could start again he would start with culture (Wintle 1996).

By the early 1990s a third phase emerged and was marked by the name change to European Union (EU). The principal objective now became social integration, no longer purely economic or political cooperation. The older problem of peace has now been replaced by globalization as a justification of European integration (Rhodes *et al.* 1997). The emphasis on social integration is partly ironic in that the EC dropped the commitment to community in favour of the federalist notion of 'union' while advocating social integration as its overall aim. While the term is very obscure as far as EU policy is concerned, we can see a clear pattern of societal integration occurring in many policy areas. European integration is no longer a matter of economic and political steering but has penetrated into the social itself with a legal concept of European citizenship. As a result of the increased volume of EU law and regulatory policy, a real social impact is now evident. With full monetary union and market integration, the social integration of the EU countries will be even more pronounced. At the moment the EU is somewhere between regulatory policy making and social integration (Majone 1996).

With this brief sketch in mind we can address the question of the post-national transformation of European societies by European integration. Since the early 1990s the propect of a post-national European polity has been much discussed (Iivonen 1993; MacCormick 1993, 1996; Münch 1993; Touraine 1994; Delanty 1995a; Habermas 1998a). While views differed on the extent to which national sovereignty was being eroded and whether Europe was heading towards a more democratic 'Europe of Regions' or a post-sovereign federal state, there was widespread recognition of a major social transformation. The idea of a new role for citizenship emerged along with the declining significance of nationality, suggesting something like a post-national citizenship. It cannot be denied that a growing space has emerged on the European transnational level where an emergent civil society can be discerned. This is evident in the volume of lawmaking, lobbying activities, general public discourse and awarness of the limits of national politics. But the prospect of post-national citizenship also had its critics.

The argument against post-nationalism

Let us consider, in brief outline, the main objections to the post-national position. I shall mention four which are associated with liberalism, civil society, communitarianism and radical democracy.

The liberal critique

One of the most commonly heard objections is the view that supranational organizations, such as the European Union, will result in a loss of political sovereignty. This is essentially the liberal critique, which is based on the assumption that attempts to go beyond the constitutional state – that is, the institution of parliament – will result in a loss of democratic legitimation.

The civil society critique

An argument, associated with the civic republican position, is that the cosmopolitan dimension is devoid of a politics of participation. Citizenship entails a relationship to civil society and there is no civil society outside the parameters of national societies. No matter how hard we look, there is no transnational civil society. International society is not organized as a civic order.

The communitarian critique

An argument, associated with communitarianism but also to be heard from conservative 'Euro-sceptics', is that the cosmopolitan position neglects the question of identity and culture. A European polity would be devoid of collective identity. Without a substantive identity, there can be no political community.

The radical critiques

Those commited to radical democracy argue that the European polity will simply lead to the creation of new kinds of exclusion, in particular a 'Fortress Europe', and that there will consequently be a loss of solidarity. These perspectives tend to equate the regulatory policies of the Union with neo-liberalism. In this context, the absence of a European social order, for example a welfare state, is a major obstacle to integration (since this is also the social basis of western multiculturalism).

In sum, the most frequently heard critiques of European transnationalism is that any attempt to go beyond the sovereign nation states does not lead to: (1) a democratically based constitutional state rooted in the institution of parliament, (2) a civil society of participation, (3) a cultural identity and (4) a welfare state. These are all serious critiques of transnationalism and any defence of the possibilities for cosmopolitan citizenship must address them. In this chapter I shall demonstrate that something like a trade-off can be achieved between the respective loss of – to take the key terms in the critical positions – democratic legitimation, participation, identity and solidarity implied in these critiques.

Briefly stated, my argument is that cosmopolitan, or post-national citizenship, requires a specific kind of civic culture – a civic cosmopolitanism – of its own to provide it with a meaningful content (see Chapter 9). Rather than looking at national civic culture for a model, a civic cosmopolitanism is to be found in four 'post-national' kinds of governance, which I believe are demonstratively operative in European integration: (1) sustainability and regulatory policy making in the risk society, (2) new networks of communication,

(3) a citizenship of residence and (4) discourses of human rights. Thus, the loss of democratic legitimation conceived of in terms of parliamentary control can be compensated for with the institutionalization of a discourse on sustainability; the loss of active participation can be compensated by the creation of a transnational civil society based on flows of communication and 'voice'; the loss of cultural identity can be compensated by the creation of a legal identity based on a citizenship of residence; and the loss of solidarity can be compensated by a commitment to human rights.

European post-national society

To assess the extent of post-nationalization, it is useful to distinguish between four levels of community in order to discuss the different orders of governance that have implications for citizenship: political community, cultural community, civic community and cosmopolitan community. In each case I shall ask the question whether European transnationalism amounts to a substantial transformation of the nation state that has positive implications for cosmopolitan citizenship. The answer for all four will be a qualified affirmative. It will be demonstrated that so long as we look at European transnationalism merely as the reproduction of national models, then, the arguments given by the critics of post-nationalism have some force. But once we look for different criteria, then, we can indeed see something unique about the European integration process.

Political community

Political community is still almost entirely national. The Union has of course institutionalized a European citizenship, but this is derivative of national citizenship. While this is likely to increase in the future, the most striking feature of this kind of citizenship is that it is entirely codified in terms of highly formalistic rights. There is a notable absence of a participatory dimension in the current form of the European demos, which appears to have been based very much on the liberal-pluralist understanding of citizenship as rights. This is, of course, always the case with citizenship beyond the state: the more expansive citizenship becomes, the more formalized it is and the less substantive it can be.

As already noted, sovereignty is still largely in hands of the nation states who are the main actors in the international realm (Lepsius 1991). It may even be argued that the power of the state has been increased as a result of European integration rather than eroded, since the tendency does appear to be for the Union to take over from the state those functions which the state performs less well, for example regulation of financial markets and international trade. However, there is no disputing the tremendous transformation of sovereignty that has occurred and which points to the formation of a multi-levelled polity (Close 1995; Delanty 1997b). In this context the question of federalism is very important, but the chances of the Union to become a federation are hampered by the fact that many of the constituent units, that is the member states, are themselves internally federalized while others (for instance the UK and Ireland) are highly centralized, in particular the latter. The regions of the Union are more diverse than are states. The complex relations of sovereignty that this involves makes the idea of a unitary European demos an unlikely prospect. Since EU policies are implemented via the nation state, there will be limits to the erosion of national governance. However, the EU is forcing states to undergo internal change. States, which are not just passive, adjust to EU policy making simply because they benefit from it. Rather than seeing the end of the state we are in fact witnessing its redeployment.

Finally, as far as democracy is concerned there is the problem of legitimation. How is power legitimized in the Union? The kind of democracy institutionalized in the Union is more a kind of cartel democracy than one connected with citizenship. National governments are legitimized in the electoral system and are empowered to represent the electorate in the Union who do not exercise significant influence of a direct nature, and at the most is a kind of limited agenda setter (Tseblis 1994). The European Parliament, for instance, is not sovereign in the way that national parliaments are and the Council of Ministers have, relatively speaking, absolute power. The result is the much discussed democratic deficit.

We can say that the European demos is one that has achieved a low degree of citizenship participation, a high democratic deficit and has not solved the problem of sovereignty. Needless to say, this is not to suggest that the national governments score particularly high on these points. Is any kind of political community possible on the level of regulatory policy making? I would like to suggest that the notion of 'sustainable community' is one such model. The relative loss of national models of sovereignty that has occurred as a result of European integration can be viewed in positive terms if we see European integration as realizing a kind of politics that can no longer be conducted by national governance alone. It is in this context that the principle of subsidiarity is relevant: decision making proceeds from lower to higher levels only by functional necessity. A complex polity such as the EU, or indeed any nation state, cannot solve all problems at one level. Decision making must be conducted at different levels, depending on the nature of the problem.

In my estimation, the formation of a regulatory supra-state is an important development in the movement towards global governance. In particular, in the context of the problems of the 'risk society', the limits of national governance have been reached. With respect to European integration, an area of considerable progress has been in environmental regulation. The problem of regulating environmental destruction and creating an enviromentally sustainable economic development is one of the major challenges for the EU. The loss of legitimation that has come with the democratic deficit does not therefore force us to reject the possibility that a new kind of political community might be possible on the supranational level, provided that is linked to a transnational public sphere (the connection between transnational governance and the cosmopolitan public sphere will be discussed in Chapter 10). One might go so far as to suggest that traditional concepts of democratic governance – a political culture of electoral democracy and the direct accountability of politicians, via national parliaments, to electorates of individual citizens – is not the most effective way of solving many of the problems facing national governments. The institution of parliament, through the foundation of national politics, is a relatively ineffective means of exerting influence on the global level (Burns 1999). In conclusion, then, though European integration has greatly undermined the nation state and its model of sovereignty, which is based on the institution of parliament, the Union has led to the emergence of what Burns (1999) has aptly called 'meta-sovereignty', to describe the new kind of postnational governance.

European cultural community

It has long been recognized that European integration lacks a cultural dimension comparable to that of nation states (Garcia 1993; Schleslinger 1994; A. Smith 1995; Wintle 1996). Europe lacks the core components of national culture: language, a shared history, religion, an educational system and a press or media. Language is the main stumbling block. With some few exceptions, language has been the key dimension to the formation of national culture from the late nineteenth century onwards. Since the decline of Latin in the Middle Ages there is no common European language. The globalization of culture has, of course, led to the worldwide diffusion of the English language but it has also led to the relative strengthening, in Europe at least, of German and the decline of French. Even though the number of people in professions who speak more than one language is increasing, there will be no European language as such. An ethnos cannot be constructed on the basis of a polyglot elite. Religion is obviously not a criterion for a European identity, and there is no memory of a shared sense of history. To be sure, Christendom once served to unify the continent, but since the split between western Latin Christendom and eastern Orthodoxy in the early Middle Ages, and the subsequent split within western Christianity with the Reformation, religion has ceased to be coeval with European identity. European history has been the history of a great deal of division. Every attempt to unify the continent resulted in ever greater division (Fontana 1995; Delanty 1996a). As Therborn has argued, whatever resonances of Christianity remain are more likely to be exclusionary (Therborn 1995: 233–6).

The cultural integration of national societies was also very much dependent on national education programmes which provided a universal cultural reference framework. Europe does not have such a framework, apart from some programmes for cultural exchange (Wintle 1996). These programmes are based on the premise of temporary and subsidized mobility, which was not the case with nation state building in the past when mobility was often enforced and related to industrialization.

Attempts to create a European ethnos through a media policy are not particularly impressive when compared to the still mighty national press and media and American dominance of the global market in communications. Efforts made to articulate a sense of European identity by appeal to high culture or cultural heritage have been quite extensive, but these efforts have little resonance in the public. There is also a pronounced tendency to conflate a cultural idea with identities. At best, the European ethnos is emerging around highly mobile elites and consumers of cultural heritage. It is not possible to point to the existence of a European identity as a collective identity of European peoples (Cerutti 1992; Garcia 1993; Schleslinger 1994; Bodei 1995; Delanty 1995a; A. Smith 1995).

There is, of course, a sense of a European ethnos emerging around an identity based on exclusion. There is a growing sense of the need to express an identity of exclusion, a supranationality, when the reference point is the non-European. Uncertain of any internal commonalties and aware of the political vacuum in the institutions of the emerging polity, Europeans are inventing an ethnos of exclusion. In general, then, there is little to suggest that Europe is the basis of a substantive identity based on a sense of cultural community. However, one must also be mindful that all identities are based on some kind of exclusion, as the identity of the self can be defined only by reference to a non-self.

Despite attempts to construct an essentialistic kind of cultural identity, there are other possibilities. Identification can vary from positive to negative identification (Wendt 1994). A major question for Habermas (1998a, 1999a) is how are we to conceive of a European identity appropriate to the demands of a European polity in which national cultures and nation states will continue to exist, and where there is already a large immigrant population. I wish to suggest, following Habermas's arguments, that the only possible way we can conceive of a European identity as a specifically European identity is to define it by reference to what he has called a post-national identity or 'constitutional patriotism'. Constitutional patriotism, as the normative content of post-national identity, refers, then, to an identification with democratic or constitutional norms and not with the state, territory, nation or cultural traditions (see Chapter 3). It is essentially a legal identity, as opposed to a cultural identity. Since a modern society is characterized by both complexity and multiculturalism, there can be no simple form of consensus as a basis for integration. This must instead, therefore, be conceived in terms of the legal system's neutrality *vis-à-vis* cultural communities, while at the same time recognizing the diversity of the different forms of life: this is Habermas's central insight. One of its concrete implications is that post-national identity is compatible with multi-identities, since constitutional patriotism requires identification only with normative principles of argumentation. Habermas thus argues that Europe needs to create, what to an extent exists in Switzerland, a common political-cultural identity which would stand out against the cultural orientations of the different nationalities (Habermas 1996). But unlike Switzerland, this will involve creating a liberal immigration policy.

Habermas argues that a liberal immigration policy is an essential part of the task of defining the new Europe. Though Habermas does not explain the advantages of a liberal immigration policy, it could be mentioned in support of his position, as John Rex (1996) has argued, that immigrants do not come with non-negotiable identities, but have in fact complex relationships to both the country of origin and the home country. What is interesting in Habermas's reflection on the future of Europe is the implication that in fact immigration can challenge the cultural identity of Europe and open up the possibility of a post-national identity: in a multicultural Europe, all that needs to be expected of its citizens is a commitment to constitutional norms and not to cultural traditions. This implies, furthermore, a radical commitment to a discursive notion of democracy. While Habermas's formulation of this is somewhat abstract, it does suggest a political culture of openness and self-critical communities who recognize diversity as a positive feature of European societies.

Drawing on Habermas, my argument, then, is that European identity, conceived of as an identity in itself, is not a concrete identity rooted in cultural traditions but is focused on a commitment to discursively mediated principles and is an expression of multi-identification: one can simultaneously be a European and member of a community or nation. If we see things in this light, there is no serious trade-off between national and European citizenship. The latter is addressed to problems that cannot be solved on the national level. My contention is that European citizenship will become more and more important in cases of multi-belonging.

It is, furthermore, a mistake to assume that there is such a thing as a European essence or a European civic identity which must be protected from outside influences. European society is not homogeneous, neither at the level of the nation state nor at the wider European level. Variations are increasingly becoming apparent, not so such between nation states but in patterns of conflict between cores and peripheries. The idea of the social cohesion of European society and polity is also largely a myth: European integration is not leading to more cohesion but to increased opportunities for contentious action on the one side, and on the other to new forms of exclusion and polarization. In giving expression to new demands for rights, European citizenship could become the key to European integration, which is otherwise in danger of being defined in instrumentalist terms or by reference to essentialist constructs, such as cultural heritage, geography, history or language. Habermas (1998a) has put this succinctly:

> the initial impetus to integration in the direction of a postnational society is not provided by the substratum of a supposed 'European people' but by the communicative network of a European-wide political public sphere embedded in a shared political culture. The latter is founded on a civil society composed of interest groups, nongovernmental organizations, and citizen initiates and movements, and will be occupied by arenas in which the political parties can directly address the decisions of European

institutions and go beyond mere tactical alliance to form a European party system.

(Habermas 1998a: 153)

Civic community

Is there a European civil society (Perez-Diaz 1998)? What is the social in the project of social integration? This is a question of growing interest in social science (Münch 1993; Therborn 1997). Again, once we use conventional criteria borrowed from the nation state, we shall also come to a pessimistic conclusion. The specifically social dimension is almost entirely market driven, both in terms of commodities and labour. European integration has enhanced the flow of commodities and has made labour more flexible. But beyond the world of consumption and work there is little on the specifically European level to compare with national societies. Despite the intentions of the Treaty of Rome, the social areas of EU policy making – the Common Agricultural Policy, the Social Fund, labour market regulation – do not amount to a substantial kind of social citizenship.

What would be a principle of social integration? There is some evidence to suggest that the Union is creating a kind of consensus based on inclusion through work, in particular labour mobility. One of the principal expressions of consensus in the post-war period rested on the creation of welfare states. Yet nothing comparable exists on the European level. More important than the absence of a social citizenship on the European level is that at the national level the welfare state, while not being at an end, is experiencing severe restrictions, a development that is undoubtedly linked to the rise of nationalism in the member states. The welfare state was the basis of a certain consensus and provided social stability for the member states for much of the second half of the twentieth century. Since there is no European equivalent to this there can be no European society in the conventional sense of the term 'society' as a social domain.

I have argued that civic community has not been particularly manifest on the European level. There is no European civil society as such. However, I do think that there is a sense in which we can see a kind of civic community being realized on the transnational level. I would like to term this a 'civic communication community'. As a communication community, European integration is becoming a potentially important forum for what might broadly be termed, following Manuel Castells, the network society.

In the conclusion to the third volume of *The Information Age*, Castells (1998) applies the idea of the network society, originally outlined in the first volume to European integration (Castells 1996). A network society does not have a centre but nodes, which may be of different sizes and can be linked by asymmetrical relationships in the network. A network, then, is an open structure that expands in different directions. It is not a functionally integrated body with a central principle of organization essential to its survival. According to Castells, the distinctive feature of the network now emerging is that it is forming through the global diffusion of information: the network society is an informational society. Apart from this interesting suggestion, Castells does not develop further his notion of how European integration might be conceived of as a network society. He merely notes that the European polity is likely to be characterized by multi-levels of power. As a network state, authority will be shared along different points in the network. It is his overall thesis that the network is organized though flows of information. In my view, the emphasis on the diffusion of information is valuable but we will have to go beyond Castells's overstating of information. Undoubtedly the expansion in information technologies of communication has transformed economic relations and has opened up a whole new range of social and cultural possibilities, but I think there is more to the possibilities of communication than is indicated by the somewhat technocratic idea of information. I am suggesting that the notion of the 'knowledge society' might be a more appropriate model for the social dimension in European integration. The idea that we are living in a knowledge society has become a central tenet in recent sociology (Stehr 1992; Melucci 1996a; Bohme 1997; Delanty 1999a). In the sociology of Touraine (1977) we find one of the most elaborate attempts to theorize the confluence of knowledge, culture and production. The knowledge society is more than the information society, which is the application of knowledge in production. Knowledge pertains to the wider cognitive capacity of society to interpret itself and to imagine alternatives.

My analysis in this chapter has demonstrated the futility in transposing the conventional concepts of social integration borrowed from the nation state to the European level: Europe is neither a political nor a cultural community, and neither is it a society, in the conventional sense of the term, based on a principle of consensus. This leads to the conclusion that if Europe cannot be a 'real' community perhaps it can become a 'virtual' one. This virtual society is not one that is constituted as a system of values but as a discursive framework. Europe cannot become a democracy in the sense of being based on a citizenship of participation. Under the conditions of societal complexity, we can no longer take for granted a model of democratic participation on the supranational level. There is little point in holding on to a model that has already reached its historical limits on the national level and expecting that it will solve the democratic deficit on the European level. This also applies to the idea of cultural community: since under the conditions of multiculturalism and cultural diversity – which would be both impossible and undesirable to wish away, quite apart from being dangerous – Europe cannot be based on a cultural community. In my view, given the exhaustion of the demos and the ethnos on the European level, the challenge for further social transformation is to explore how the principle of discursivity can be given expression by European integration. In this context, a central question is that of the status and role of knowledge.

At the moment there is not much that is distinctive about the European project as a knowledge society in the making. In 1993 the European Commission published a White Paper on the information economy, and the Bangerman

Report of May 1994 focused on the broader idea of an information society and the need for a whole range of policies relating to economic, social, cultural and technical areas. Since then the Union has encouraged discussion on governance and citizenship in the 'virtual community' with projects for electronic communication between governments and citizens. However, these measures, which are still at the level of policy formation, are minimal and for the moment the Union is unlikely to compete with the US-dominated information society. Developments in the area of higher education, such as the Socrates programme of student and staff mobility, are perhaps more significant but do not amount to a knowledge society.

As I have argued, knowledge is wider than information and pertains to the very cultural self-understanding of a society. In what way can Europe become a knowledge society? Is it possible to create a civil society based on knowledge? Taking up Habermas's notion of communication as discursive, we can make the observation that knowledge today is increasingly taking the form of contested knowledge in such matters as group boundaries and in the fundamental codes of group membership, as well as in matters pertaining to scientific expertise. Thus, what is distinctive about current forms of collective identities is their ability to contest existing social frameworks and cultural codes. The culture of contestation in identity politics is rivalled only by that in knowledge production more generally. Both share the ability to exercise the power to define reality. In the risk society, knowledge is a matter of contestation and of the delegitimation of expertise. This can be seen in such instances as AIDS, BSE (bovine spongiform encephalopathy), radioactivity, biotechnological developments such as cloning, medical ethics, genetically modified foods and neurology, which have all opened scientific knowledge to public scrutiny bringing together discourses of nature, science, law and politics. These cases are also interesting in that the degree of contestation permeates to the cultural model of society itself and the discourses related to these issues are not dominated by any one particular social actor. The players are organized interests, professional bodies, experts, policy makers, regulatory agencies, media and social movements. In the absence of a key social actor, it is the public who is becoming more important as a social mediator in disputes which question the very foundations of a society's cognitive and cultural structures. Under these circumstances a model of consensus is being replaced by a model of dissensus and one in which the public is becoming increasingly vocal (Eder 1999). This all raises the role of what Karl-Dieter Opp (1996) calls 'voice' in European integration. Opp argues that while social movements may actually decrease in the EU, voice can continue to exert an influence on politics through citizen referenda. His thesis is that the claim that social movements can alleviate the democratic deficit of the EU is not tenable. The implications of his argument is that solutions of a different kind must be found. It is in this context that the role of discursive communication as described by Habermas may prove to be of crucial importance in linking European integration to a stronger kind of citizenship, that is the need for the 'legal institutionalization of citizens' communication' (Habermas 1998a: 161). At the moment there is not a European civil society as such, but there is a growing informal public sphere around European issues (Perez-Diaz 1998). Much of this takes the form of organized lobbying by a wide variety of interest organizations, INGOs and citizen movements. While it is far from having a legal basis, though many organizations have won the right to permanent consulation in particular areas, political communication that transcended the nation state is likely to continue to grow.

Cosmopolitan community

Finally, there is little to suggest that Europe is committed to world community in the sense of a cosmopolitan ethic of global citizenship. A strong emphasis on exclusion and the building of a 'fortress' mentality, it has frequently been noted, is central to its present project as well as a strong hostility to the former 'eastern' Europe. A security agenda and the tightening of border controls seem to be more central than a concern with human rights. However, this is an area where the Union has the potential to improve; it has transformed national citizenship, though this has on the whole remained on the margins, and has also made a contribution to a post-national citizenship for immigrants (Meehan 1993).

I have already commented on the institutionalization of a post-national citizenship on the European level. The main dimension to this is the codification of a supplementary citizenship based on residence, as opposed to one based on birth, albeit one that is still based on national citizenship. On the surface, it does not appear as though the EU is likely to extend the framework of European citizenship beyond this supplementary level. On the other hand, there are indications that something like a 'Fortress Europe' is emerging with the formation of a supranationality based on European citizenship, a European identity, and a security and immigration policy aimed at a high degree of internal cohesion. Thus, while the Union is not a replica of the nation state as such, it is seeking to give to citizenship an autonomous existence.

In sum, the case for a post-national European identity can be made in terms of trade-offs: the loss of legitimation, identity, participation and solidarity that has come with transnational governance can be viewed positively as a gain for new kinds of communities which can be realized to a better extent on the supranational level than on the national. However, these trade-offs make sense only if we see the European polity less as a zero-sum game than as multi-levels of governance.

Summary

I would like to conclude by addressing a crucial practical issue in definitions of European citizenship: the idea of citizenship based on residence rather than on birth. National models of citizenship, with some exceptions, are mostly based on birth (Brubaker 1989, 1992). Citizenship is thus equated with nationality.

In order to fully enfranchise immigrants from outside Europe, European citizenship would have to transcend national citizenship by defining citizenship in terms of residence. This would also enfranchise citizens of member states who do not live in their country of birth or nationality. At the moment citizens of member states not resident in their country of origin can vote only in local elections but not in national elections.

Though European citizenship is still highly limited in its function as a supplementary or third form of citizenship, complementing rather than undermining national citizenship, it can at the same time be seen as opening new institutional possibilities for democratic citizenship (da Burca, 1996; Preuss 1996; Lehning and Weale 1997). The most important challenges for citizenship are the double task of devolving national citizenship downwards to subnational units such as regions, cities and localities, on the one side, and on the other side transferring citizenship upwards to the European Union. The result would be a three-tier European polity, with power divided between national, subnational and supranational levels. European citizenship would be a formal kind of citizenship, not unlike the model of national citizenship, except that its normative reference point would be residence rather than birth. National citizenship would still remain, though in many cases it would have to adapt itself to European citizenship which would bring about increased convergence in national constitutions as far as formal citizenship is concerned. The substantive component of citizenship would be the empowering of regional and local authorities at the subnational level and increased involvement of social movements. My argument differs, then, from Euro-federal positions which stress the need for a transcendence of national citizenship by European supranational citizenship. As I have already argued, such citizenship is likely to be an even more formal citizenship than current national models.

The context, then, for discussing citizenship rights to residents of non-member states, as well as to potential immigrants, is the restructuring of citizenship: the splitting up of formal citizenship into national and European on the devolving of authority to subnational level. European citizenship would be a means of enfranchising immigrants while the growing autonomy of subnational regions would provide for more concrete means of inclusion. The question of a liberal immigration policy is a complex matter and cannot easily be solved. I wish merely to indicate that the issues it raises can be dealt with only through the establishment of a Euro-authority working in association with national and regional representatives as well as with social movements.

The multilayered model of citizenship that I am proposing is not at all divorced from the existing institutional structures of the European Union. The principle of subsidiarity for instance – that a larger unit assumes functions when smaller units are unable or less capable of fulfilling their role – can be applied to citizenship. The principle of subsidiarity still exists within the derivative model of European citizenship, but it is not inconceivable that it could be radicalized to include dimensions of citizenship excluded by the present model which privileges citizenship as nationality. According to Soysal

(1994), the idea of citizenship being formally determined by residence rather than birth or blood is no mere flight of the imagination, for it is already being partially realized in new conceptions of personhood on the European level (see also Baubock 1994; Jacobsen 1997). There are increasing forms of citizenship being shaped by global treaties. The European Union has itself partly institutionalized such forms of citizenship in recognizing immigrants as citizens, though they may not have access to national citizenship. The widening of the European Union to include over twenty potential members could force a new agenda. The European Union was established by large nation states who found in the principle of cooperation the paradoxical means of pursuing their individual interests. The question for the twenty-first century will be whether these nation states can be challenged by other social units and for purposes other than the maximization of economic goals?

PART THREE

Rethinking citizenship

9

The reconfiguration of citizenship: post-national governance in the multi-levelled polity

In Part two I presented some of the main challenges to the traditional liberal notion of citizenship as a set of rights. In Part one I outlined the older debates which revolved around the question of linking rights and duties to participation and identity, as in the communitarian critique. The most far-reaching critique of citizenship, in both its liberal and communitarian forms, was the radical democratic one, which seeks to link citizenship to democracy. However, as we have seen, the idea of democratic citizenship has itself been challenged by a relatively new conception of citizenship, cosmopolitan citizenship. I have attempted to demonstrate that this idea has acquired a new saliency as a result of globalization, which has led to the under-mining of the geopolitical and geocultural basis of citizenship in the territorial nation state. In Chapter 8 I argued that the European Union is the best example we have of a concrete kind of cosmopolitan public sphere. This is not to neglect one of the most pervasive challenges to national models of citizenship, the transformation in human rights, which no longer stand out-side the rights of citizenship, but cut across them. In general, we have much evidence of a legal cosmopolitanism and somewhat less evidence of a cosmo-politan political order.

In Chapter 10 I shall present a more complete analysis of the implications of the challenges emanating from globalization, with a view to assessing the relative strengths of cosmopolitanism on the level of the public sphere and on the level of civil society. In this chapter, my concern is to make sense of the arguments in the preceding chapters concerning the challenge of globalization for citizenship. I begin with an account of the fragmentation of citizenship and its reconfiguration in new kinds of group affiliations. Second, I discuss the crisis of citizenship in the context of the broader crisis of democracy of which it is a part. Finally, I look at the emerging structure of a post-national multi-levelled polity.

The fragmentation of citizenship?

Let us return to the definition of citizenship with which I began this book. Citizenship involves four components: rights, responsibilities, participation and identity. In the classic model of national citizenship these formed a unity of function. With the emphasis on rights, citizenship entailed a relationship between civil, political and social rights and duties, such as those of conscription, taxation and compulsory education, and the less legally obligatory ones such as the duty to vote. It was primarily a legal relationship between the individual and the state. However, citizenship also had an informal dimension as participation in the political community and was also linked to national identity. In the republican and communitarian tradition this informal dimension was stressed to a greater extent than in the liberal tradition. What has come about today, largely as a result of globalization, is the separation of these components from each other: they are no longer united by into a coherent national framework. Rights, responsibilities, participation and identity no longer constitute a unitary model of citizenship. For some this effectively means the end of citizenship (Soysal 1994; Touraine 2000). In contrast to this spectre of the total fragmentation of citizenship, I am stressing the reconfiguration of citizenship, for what is coming about is the constitution of entirely new discourses of citizenship. In short, it no longer makes sense to speak of citizenship as if it were just one single model. I shall illustrate this process of reconfiguration by reference to each of the four components of citizenship: rights, responsibilities, participation and identity.

Rights

The evolution of rights was related to the rise of the nation state and reflected the formal nature of modern law. Civil, political and social rights were formal entitlements granted by the state to its citizens. Today the politics of rights has taken rights discourse far from modern political culture. Beginning with the search for substantive citizenship in communitarian and in radical democratic discourses, citizenship has slowly moved away from a formal notion of rights. But the tie with nationality has only more recently been broken.

New conceptions of rights, such as collective rights, the rights of nature, and cultural rights have transformed the Marshallian evolutionary model. Social rights were conferred by the state upon individuals in order to dilute the inequalities of their class situation. The rise of cultural rights, for instance, cannot be located in the terms of this framework. In the past rights were won against the *ancien régime* in the name of a relatively intact and homogenous civil society. This was epitomized in the republican tradition, but is reflected in all modern demands for the extension of citizenship. What is different today is that the new kinds of rights, such as cultural rights and the collective rights of indigenous peoples, are aimed at other forces. Most states are no longer repressive in the way they once were. In the case of what I have been referring to as cultural rights, these principally derive from the dangers presented by technology, economy and the media. The early struggles assumed that economy, technology and the means of influence formed an integral part of civil society and were emancipatory, for in the early modern and Enlightenment movements the enemy of society was the state. Today that is no longer taken for granted, though state-supported forms of violence are still the most pervasive in the world. In a world transformed by globalization it is economic forces that present the greatest challenges to citizenship today. But economic transformation has now penetrated into the cultural sphere, a development recognized as Simmel and the Frankfurt School, and which has more recently been reiterated by postmodern critics (Jameson 1991). Civil society, Touraine (2000) therefore argues, is now defined in cultural terms, rather than in economic terms. As a result of the confluence of the economic and the cultural, citizenship is forced to become more cultural. One area of growing contestation concerns issues surrounding information, technology, environment and media (Dahlgren and Sparks 1991; Frankenfeld 1992; Lurry 1993; Dahlgren 1995; Irwin 1995; Selove 1995; Zimmerman 1995; Stevenson 1997; Isin and Wood 1999). With the globalization of cultural production, the autonomy of civil society is forced into conflicts over fundamental questions of cultural values. Citizenship has come to mean more than rights to access the public goods provided by the state but to a whole range of cultural resources. The older forms of citizenship took for granted that the citizen was a worker; whereas as the current reality is that the citizen is primarily a consumer.

The rise of cultural citizenship is visible in the new politics of human rights which have now come to mean not just belonging to an abstract humanity but rights to personal autonomy and individuation. In Chapter 5 I referred to the rise of an 'embodied self' in new conceptions of personhood, for instance the rights of children. With the growing interpenetration of national and international law, citizenship ceases to be synonymous with nationality. I have also argued that the discourse of the nation has become severed from the legitimation of the state. In the new nationalism, the nation code most often is asserted against the state.

Responsibilities

An area of considerable change concerns the rise of a new conception of responsibility. The classic model of citizenship often stressed the duties or responsibilities of citizens, that is the duty to be a good member of society. In return for rights, citizens had basic duties to perform, for the entitled citizen was also a dutiful citizen. This ranged from the conservative idea of obedience to authority to the communitarian sense of responsibility to the community and the civic republican emphasis on virtue. In general, responsibility was a neo-Tocquevillian notion of moral values and social obligations in the civic domain. The emphasis on personal responsibility had the effect of disburdening the state for responsibility for society. For instance, in Britain since the 1980s and 1990s a discourse of accountability has arisen, ostensibly in order to enhance transparency and a generally more responsible society. However, in reality, this has been tied to a right-wing ideology that seeks to disburden the state of responsibility and has the additional effect of leading to an explosion in social auditing (Mulgan 1994: Chapter 3; Power 1997). In the context of the risk society, a new idea of responsibility has arisen which bears very little resemblance with this older way of thinking.

Hans Jonas (1984) and Karl-Otto Apel (1987, 1988, 1990, 1996, 2000) introduced the need for a future-orientated planetary macro-ethics in modern thought. This marks a shift from individualistic notions of responsibility to collective or co-responsibility. As Strydom (1999a) has pointed out, Jonas and Apel, in effect, established a link between risk and responsibility, terms which play a key role in the societal semantics of our time. The idea of co-responsibility totally changes the entire discourse of responsibility. This has come with the recognition that individual responsibility is no longer able to find a solution to many problems facing society, in particular those emanating from technology. Habermas (1979) has alluded to the emergence of post-conventional individual morality and, in later works, has attached this to social movements, which are the carriers of societal responsibility in face of the massive retreat of the state for responsibility for society (Habermas 1987a). Today the perception of society in terms of risk, danger, safety and sustainability has grown enormously, a development that leads Strydom (1999a), following Beck (1992) and Luhmann (1989, 1995), to the conclusion that risk and responsibility have become the new master frame, even replacing the older emphasis on rights and justice. Beck (1992) takes this to the extreme in his view that the welfare state and class conflict have been replaced by the 'Safety State'. Even if one does not agree with the view that the ecological question concerning sustainability is supplanting the social question, there is much to suggest that the primary challenge for democratic citizenship is not merely justice, and some of the central assumptions of constitutional democracy may be at stake (Stein 1998). In any case, it is clear that the ecological question has caught the public imagination to the extent to which one can speak of co-responsibility as a new master frame. This concept, advanced in the work of Apel and Strydom, has the advantage in that it is able to reconcile the ideas of individual and collective responsibility. Co-responsibility does not preclude individual responsibility for some kind of collective responsibility but expresses the emergence of a moral consciousness that is beginning to have some effect on the cultural level of society.

Whether it is a question of responsibility for nature or for future generations, the emerging discourse has radicalized the older notion of individual responsibility either in the sense of the duties of citizenship or personal responsibility for moral decisions. For the critics of contemporary science and technology policies, the state is now the domain of 'organized irresponsibility', to use Beck's striking phrase, and consequently, responsibility has shifted to civil society.

Participation

One of the most discussed features of recent social change concerns the social transformation of space. The theme of space has become a key concern, uniting the disciplines of sociology, geography and international relations. Space is no longer dominated by the space of the state; other deterritorialized spaces have emerged along with the break-up of national society as the privileged codifier of social space. Modernity involved the dislocation of place and space. Postmodern conceptions of space suggest a recovery of place as a social space, but a space located in deterritorialized flows of communication (Castells 1996; Soja 1996; Thrift 1996). These spaces can offer more possibilities for participation as communicative interaction, in contrast with the passive model of the mass media in an earlier modernity. Contemporary societies are communication societies more than anything else (Delanty 1999a; Strydom 1999b). That is, communication has become more central to all spheres of life than ever before, from economy to technology and education. In the communication society, the public sphere occupies a more central role. It is not simply located in a particular space between state and private domain as in bourgeois society, but must be seen as a 'space of flows', as public communication. In Habermas's revised model, the public sphere 'represents a highly complex network that branches out into a multitude of overlapping international, national, regional, local, and subcultural arenas' (Habermas 1998a: 373). It is best viewed as a network of discursive spaces in society rather than occupying one particular location. But it is clear that this new public sphere, which differs from earlier ones in that it is tendentially more visual and rhetorical than discursive, can amount to the colonization of communication by consumption. Since most people are consumers more than they are producers, they are already participating in the communication society by virtue of the very logic of consumption. But there are other modes of social existence than consumption which, though all pervasive, are not monolithic and are part of what have become known as 'postmaterial values' (Abramson and Inglehart 1995). Late modern communication societies offer more and more possibilities for participation. This is because contemporary societies are characterized by an increasing number of actor locations and, consequently, social integration cannot be achieved by any one actor or dominant ideology.

In the present context what is of particular importance is the revival of civic participation as a politics of space. As a result of the erosion of national sovereignty by transnational processes associated with globalization, increased opportunities for subnational forms of governance have emerged. We are witnessing the revival of the role of regions, and cities are locuses of autonomy and political decision, according to Castells: 'The more national states fade in their role, the more cities emerge as a driving force in the making of a new European society' (Castells 1994: 23). In his view the strengthening of local governments is a precondition of the effective management of cities in a way conducive to maximizing citizen participation. But such a new citizenship of participation cannot succeed without engaging with transnational communication. As Castells argues, new information technologies make possible vital cooperation between local governments across national borders. Participation as a politics of citizenship can be viewed either in republican or radical democratic terms to be a matter of participation in the community or, as in radical democracy, in the making of a new society. Globalization has opened new opportunities for participatory politics. Linking local and regional forms of governance to global processes can strengthen subnational groups. While direct citizen participation is increasingly difficult at national and transnational levels, the emerging global civil society offers new opportunities for collective actors. In a society dominated by information, access to information and the ability to act upon it is one of the main dimensions to participation. There is no doubt that there has been a worldwide increase in contentious action, and therefore more demands for participation. Gamson (1992) finds that citizens develop ways of understanding public issues in ways that tend to support participatory forms of collective action, particularly in neighbourhood and community situations. He stresses the agency component of collective action as well as the identity component. The question of collective action does not preclude individualism, as Lichterman (1996) argues against a dominant tendency which sees personal fulfilment as detrimental to citizenship. In opposition to communitarian positions, he demonstrates that individualism can enhance common goals and active participation in society.

There is no doubt that there has been an increase in participatory politics in the past few decades. But participation has been rendered diffuse by social change and takes many different forms, ranging from new age alternative movements to nationalism to environmentalism and a whole range of NGOs, operating nationally and internationally. For present purposes we simply need to stress the opening up of local and regional forms of governance to a more participatory kind of citizenship. For instance, within the European Union a striking development is the increasing importance of residence as a criterion for citizenship. Though the dominant model of national citizenship still remains the underlying criterion, there is increasing recognition that residence entails a right to citizenship and to participation in civic community. Along with dual citizenship, this points to a growing fluidity in the relationship between citizenship and nationality.

In sum, I am arguing that current developments, arising partly out of radical democracy and processes related to globalization, facilitate forms of citizen participation irreducible to nationality. Today's citizens can participate in world society and in their local life-world as much as in the social framework of the nation state.

Identity

In many respects identity has replaced ideology as the codification of political communication. Ideology has not of course disappeared but it has certainly become refracted through the prism of identity. The older ideologies of modernity – capitalist liberal democracy and state socialism – and their geo-political foundations in east versus west appear to have dissolved into new kinds of binary opposites, such as those of *self* and *other*. New images of otherness confront us daily, be it those of suffering, the socially excluded or marginalized, political extremists, or multiculturalism. What has changed may indeed be something in the nature of reality – the collapse of the cold war consensus which sustained the older political culture – but it might quite well be a result of a shift in cultural-cognitive structures, for today we have more means at our disposal to image and witness otherness. This is not unconnected with the fact that we are living in a globalized culture of voyeurism. The encounter with the other is more likely to be a highly mediated one. This is true, too, of the discovery of the self, which, if we follow a range of theorists (Giddens 1991; Maffesoli 1996; Melucci 1996a), is constructed by various kinds of cultural practices, such as therapy, the culture of experience, the aestheticization of everyday life, all of which allow the self to be objectified.

The decoupling of citizenship and nationality is strikingly evident in the question of identity. Rights and identity are entering more into tension with each other (Soysal 1994). With identity increasingly becoming the basis of participatory politics, rights discourse is under attack. I have drawn attention to the challenge of collective rights as a new development arising largely out of a third generation of human rights. With the shift from civic and political human rights to social and developmental rights, the increasing prevalence of collective and cultural rights has greatly undermined national citizenship. This can be partly explained in terms of the power of identity. But the politics of identity is more than just the assertion of identity; it is also an expression of the culture of personhood. What is different about the search for identity today is the dimension of reflexivity: identity is very much about itself. For instance, it is frequently to be heard from groups and individuals struggling to assert their identity that identity is not an inherent personality of cultural condition but something that can be freely chosen and is not exclusive. This emphasis on multiple identities is one of the main changes in identity formation today.

Identity must be seen as essentially contested and above all multilayered. With respect to issues relating to citizenship, this is particularly important in the context of immigrants and the growing pluralization of cultural groups. One of the great challenges facing democratic citizenship is to accommodate diversity (Tully 1995; Touraine 1998, 2000; Calhoun 1999). To be equal and yet different defines the challenge of cultural citizenship today, argues Touraine. Citizenship is no longer exclusively about the pursuit of equality; it is also about finding ways to preserve difference.

There are differences between personal and collective identity. An integrated personal identity may provide the individual with the means of survival and coping with choice. However, a strong collective identity can present problems in accommodating diversity. In such cases, there is likely to be the danger that the collective identity will become too focused on hostility, that the self can be affirmed only by the denial of otherness. There is no evidence to indicate that societies, or large groups, actually require strong collective identities, and it might be suggested that such identities are often closely connected with xenophobia, or hatred of the other. As has been frequently noted, identities, are highly contested, overlapping and negotiable (Melucci 1996a; Calhoun 1999). Polyethnicity and multilingualism have been the norm in world history, according to William McNeill (1986). In situations where personal identities are weak and collective identities strong, there is likely to be a very real danger of major cultural pathologies emerging. This would appear to be one of the central theses of the famous study led by Theodor Adorno (1959), *The Authoritarian Personality*. The social psychology of the Freudian-influenced Frankfurt School believed that with the weakening of the bourgeois ego under the conditions of mass society, there was a weakening of authority, which was displaced onto the political level where authoritarian forms of political leadership were able to find an outlet. Though much of this kind of social Freudianism has been discredited, the fundamental question of the relation between the personal and the collective remains a pressing problem. It will suffice to reiterate here that with the dissolution of integrated national cultures with their unitary models of identity, developments in contemporary society suggest that there is an opening up of discursive spaces in which groups and individuals engage with otherness.

In conclusion, taking the components of rights, responsibilities, participation and identity, we can see how the discourse of citizenship has become fragmented. Citizenship has ceased to be a unitary framework reflecting the geopolitics and geoculture of the nation state; its components have become separated from each other having become taken up in other discourses. Rights have become embodied in discourses that extend far beyond the legal reach of the nation state; responsibility has shifted from a discourse of personal obligation focused on the state to a discourse of co-responsibility for nature and for future generations; participation is less focused on the national community than on others' spaces, which have been opened up as a result of subnational mobilization linked to globalization; and identity has become pluralized to the extent that citizenship must now contend with reconciling the pursuit of equality with the recognition of difference.

Citizenship and the crisis of democracy

The scenario I have sketched in the previous section might have led some to the conclusion that citizenship is now at an end. The limits of citizenship have been reached with the deterritorialization of rights and the release of identity politics (Soysal 1994). Citizenship presupposed a principle of unity, that political society could impose unity on society. Touraine (2000) has argued that this is no longer a realistic aspiration. Effectively declaring the end of citizenship, he has argued for an entirely different principle of unity focused on the recovery of the 'subject' (Touraine 2000). Citizenship was once connected with social integration and was integral to democracy. But what is democracy? Democracy is both a political and legal project. Its most basic idea is self-determination, but democracy cannot be reduced to the 'rule of the people' for it is also associated with the legal order of a state and is also related to civil society. Democracy can be said to consist of self-determination, the rule of law, and civil society.

According to Touraine (1997: 26–8), who offers a more specific definition of the institutional nature of democracy as a political, legal and civic order, democracy consists of three principles: the limitation of state power (constitutionalism), the representation of conflicting interests (pluralism) and the political participation of citizens in the political community (citizenship). Democracy must be a combination of all of these principles; it must be liberal and constitutionalist, pluralist and participatory. The first two are predominantly procedural while the latter connects democracy to civil society. They are all central to democracy as an institutional system, though different traditions will give more prominence to one principle over the other. In this book I have been mainly concerned with the relationship of the democratic idea with citizenship and argued that once democracy is severed from citizenship there is the danger that nationalism will fill the void.

Following Touraine, I am arguing that there is no natural trend towards democracy today because these principles are not developing alongside each other. They have become fragmented. First, with the rise of new kinds of technological and economic power, the idea of constitutional democracy is increasingly helpless. The original idea of constitutional democracy was to limit the power of the state in order to provide civil society with an autonomous space. In the early theories of liberal government in England, and later in American constitutional democracy, the idea of a restricted government was based on natural rights and gave expression to what has become known as 'negative liberty' (Berlin 1969). With the rise of notions of citizenship based on social justice and the need for economic intervention, the state was required to take a more affirmative role in society. But the basic idea of constitutional democracy has remained as a relationship between state and society, a relationship which the early theories called a social contract and was designed for the purpose of preserving basic individual liberties. As we have seen in earlier chapters, one of the main developments today is that the primary struggle is no longer between state and society, but to use Habermas's term, a struggle between life-world and system, or as Touraine would put it, between the culture and economy – the symbolic and instrumental worlds. In order to accommodate these challenges, an entirely different kind of social contract is required. John O'Neill (1994) thus speaks of the civic recovery of the nation as entailling a social contract between state, community, economy and household.

Second, there is also a profound crisis in political representation. Democracy in the twentieth century was principally concerned with the representation of competing interests by means of the principle of majority rule within the electoral system. Largely in the form of party politics within the structures of representative government, democracy was the means by which a multiplicity of interests was resolved. Though democratic theories differ greatly on this question of pluralism, there is general agreement that the basic idea of democracy as self-determination must be modified by the reality of competing interests. Without pluralism there can be no democracy. One of the main problems today concerns the emergence of a deeper and more cultural form of pluralization. Critics of pluralism have often pointed out the problems of pluralist democracy and the limits of the institutionalized channels of parliament for the social representativity of all social interests. But with the rise of the new social movements, a whole range of other problems have become manifest. Though many of these movements are now less opposed to democratic pluralism than in the previous decades, there is still a major tension between the politics of everyday life, which the new social movements highlight, and the institutionalized politics of government. This ongoing crisis is directly related to the crisis in citizenship.

Third, as a result of the decoupling of citizenship and nationality, the relationship between citizenship and democracy is no longer straightforward. Citizenship, as I have argued, has ceased to be defined by the unitary framework of the state: rights, duties, identity and participation have become disjointed. The idea of citizenship as participation in the political community was central to democracy, which was never entirely procedural but always had a relationship to civil society. With the growing alienation of much of the institutional system of democracy in the crisis of pluralism and the apparent irrelevance of constitutionalism, citizenship loses its primary legitimation. In the absence of a democratic political system, citizenship is meaningless. Citizenship is not merely membership of society but of civil society, that is a civic order that mediates between society and state. When this link is broken, citizenship retreats into privatism. Without its roots in citizenship, on the other side, democracy withdraws more and more into a communitarian assertion of identity and community.

Citizenship in the multi-levelled polity

It may be felt that I have stressed too strongly the fragmentation of citizenship. There is another way of looking at this, which is to see this fragmentation as a process of reconfiguration. The components of citizenship are becoming part of a complex reconfiguration of the democratic field. The state no longer dominates the discourses and politics of citizenship, whose components are being taken up by a broad spectrum of social actors. The democratic order is itself being reconfigured as a multi-levelled polity, for it is no longer possible to see governance in terms of one level. National governance exists alongside two other levels, subnational and transnational. This development is most apparent in the EU, where transnational governance is embodied in a formal institutional structure, but tendencies towards post-national governance are more broadly evident in the growing salience of international law. The EU is unique in being both a political and a legal order of governance.

With the emergence of three levels of governance – subnational, national and transnational – democratic citizenship is likewise decentred. Rather than speaking of the end of citizenship, it makes more sense to look at its restructuring on these levels of governance. This approach will have the advantage of being able to reconcile the various components of citizenship and the different dimensions of democracy with the emergent reality of the multi-levelled polity. In the EU the principle of subsidiarity, though used to legitimize the relationship between the national and transnational, offers a political metaphor to describe links between democratic citizenship and levels of governance. The following is a model of these links.

A decentred, multi-level citizenship is one that does not seek to concentrate all components of citizenship at one level. In a societally complex world, functional differentiation also applies to citizenship and democracy. Thus we can begin to see how participatory forms of democracy are best suited to subnational forms of governance. Direct citizenship participation is more suitable to local and regional democracy than to national and transnational levels of governance. There is some truth to the criticism that complexity and participation are incompatible. While some have taken this to the extreme in rejecting all forms of citizenship participation, a more plausible position might be to relate participatory democracy to the subnational.

National governance is still one of the most important levels of governance. For instance, with respect to social rights there is no equivalent model on either the subnational nor transnational. The welfare state remains an important dimension of social citizenship. Radical critics of the national state neglect this and appeal too easily to a politics beyond the state. Decentralization is conducive to democratic citizenship only if the state continues to be responsible for society. The state is not only a welfare state but also a constitutional state. It is still the most important institution within society and in the international order for the protection of rights, be they civil, political, social or cultural rights.

Transnational governance, as we have seen, is an area of growing importance. This can take either a political or a legal form. At the moment transnational governance is based mainly on a legal order. Exceptions to this are the UN and the EU. The former is a weaker example of political governance while the EU is the only tangible example we have of a transnational political order, albeit it one that that is very reluctant to extend its geographical limits. This is perhaps the nature of transnational political governance: it must be self-limiting. However, in general, transnational governance predominantly takes the form of legal cosmopolitanism. Transnational political governance, that is cosmopolitan democracy, mediates between, on the one side, legal cosmopolitanism and, on the other, national and subnational governance. It is becoming an important domain for social movement actors. I would like to suggest that the appropriate kind of democratic citizenship for the transnational level of governance is collective or group citizenship. Social actors are operative on all levels of governance, in particular on the national level where they are particularly effective (Tarrow 1995). But with respect to some of the key challenges to democratic citizenship, such as the question of an economically sustainable society, the global regulation of justice, migration, human rights and security, it is only on the transnational level that such problems can be solved. It is evident that transnational governance is moving in the direction of regulatory governance. This is particularly so with respect to the European Union, as I argued in Chapter 8, and since this is the best example we have of a cosmopolitan political order, it is reasonable to suppose that other transnational processes will also be of a regulatory nature. Regulatory orders are not incompatible with democracy, though it is the nature of regulatory regimes to sidestep much of the democratic process. However, there is no reason why regulatory and democratic politics cannot be linked. A crucial factor in this is civil society and the culture of citizenship. With respect to transnational forms of regulation, there is much to suggest that international governmental organizations, along with states, are playing a leading role in shaping transnational governance in areas ranging from human rights to security to environment (Shaw 1994b). At the moment it must be left an open issue as to whether their role will increase in the future or whether the transnational level will continue to be dominated by organized interests and states. In the present context, what needs to be stressed is that the transnational level is less important for a citizenship as individual participation than of collective participation. It is also at this level that some of the responsibilities of citizenship reach their highest level of expression in the articulation of an ethic of global responsibility. Thus, responsibility is not confined to the national level or the level of local communities but has a wider global significance.

Summary

The main conclusion to be drawn from this analysis is that the debate on citizenship must address the wider transformation of democracy. The challenge for citizenship is not merely linking citizenship to democracy, as radical democrats argue. In Chapter 3 I outlined some of these positions which argue for the need for not just more participation and the recognition of identity but for the linking of these to democracy. Unless citizenship is linked to democracy, citizenship will be reduced to being a pre-political privatism and, on the other side, democracy will be separated from civil society. However, there is an additional challenge today. This is the challenge to respond to the internal fragmentation of citizenship and to the emergence of a multi-levelled polity in which democracy operates at different levels and according to different models. Rather than locating democratic citizenship at one level, it must be seen as operating on the subnational, national and transnational levels. The implication of this is that there are different levels of inclusion and that the model of inclusion on the transnational level, for instance that of the European Union, is more likely to be one closer to the liberal model than the republican or radical democratic models of participation.

Conclusion: the idea of civic cosmopolitanism

Having discussed the growing discord between citizenship and nationality as a result of globalization, we now need to consider some of the implications of this for cosmopolitanism. Is a cosmopolitan citizenship possible, and if so, is it desirable?

In my estimation cosmopolitan citizenship can succeed only if it re-establishes a relationship to community. We must rethink the relationship between community and cosmopolitanism. At the moment nationalism is able to claim the idea of community for itself. Very much a feature of the current situation is the spectre of a new nationalism, ranging from violent separatist movements, religious nationalism to neo-fascism and the more subtle cultural nationalisms which have become an integral part of late political culture. Faced with this scenario we can ask the questions how is a post-nationalism possible and of what does it consist. Is it possible to have nations without nationalism, as Kristeva (1993) suggests? Is it possible to separate cosmopolitanism from globalization? In my view, the answer to these two questions is related: cosmopolitanism must be rooted in a civic concept of the nation.

It is indeed paradoxical that modernity was both the age of the national idea and also the age of cosmopolitanism, for the transcendence of the national idea in cosmopolitanism was made possible precisely by nation states which were relatively culturally homogeneous and founded on a constitutionally based legal order. To be cosmopolitan was to participate in a wider order beyond the national culture – one which could also be appealed to as the universalistic foundation of all national cultures, be it universal humanity, Europe, or western civilization (Meinecke 1970; Schlereth 1977; Delanty 1995a). Thus, a certain universalism went with modernity, which cultivated a cosmopolitanism ostensibly capable of transcending self, other and world – the basic components of human community. Today, in an increasingly global world and a postmodernized culture, the nation is being awakened in many guises and in forms that are apparently antithetical to the universalistic cultural aspirations of modernity. Instead of being integrative, elite orchestrated and ideologically coherent, nationalism is becoming more divisive, recalcitrant and anti-statist. With the declining differences between nation states, the focus of hostility is shifting onto immigrants. Exactly what it means to be a post-national cosmopolitan is far from clear, particularly given the diffuse nature that nationalism is taking and the fact that the new media of communication and consumption have made everybody cosmopolitan. My argument is that unless cosmopolitanism can articulate a notion of community, it will be unable to challenge nationalism which is increasingly profiting from the neo-liberal order that has destroyed solidarity, commitment and community.

One of the most important representatives of the post-national position is Habermas (1984), whose notion of a 'constitutional patriotism' offers a conception of a kind of national identity which is confined to an identification with the principles of the constitution as opposed to territory, history or the state. In this way a minimal kind of nationalism is possible, but at the price of severing any connection with self, other and world, which are the basic ingredients of community. In my view, Habermas's idea of constitutional patriotism is an immensely important idea but it has its weaknesses. For instance, a constitutional patriotism is ultimately possible in the context of the constitutional state. Habermas's model was originally proposed in the context of debates on national identity in West German political culture in the 1980s. It will be recalled from Chapter 3 that it was Habermas's argument that the only defensible form of German nationalism after the Holocaust was a patriotism of the constitution. In short, it was a nationalism that could show its face only at the cost of self-denial. In the wider context of a world over which the constitutional state has less and less jurisdiction, it is not apparent how a constitutional patriotism might work. Moreover, the cosmopolitan point of view ultimately rests on the call to abandon identity and community. In the context of (West) Germany this may have made sense; given the relative homogeneity and stability of its social, economic and political structures, a certain degree of cultural scaling down could be possible. But the hopelessly fragmented global world is a different scenario. Habermas's conception of the post-national is a negation of nationalism and in a world in which nationalism has become a real force, it can be only an ineffective residue of Enlightenment cosmopolitanism seeking to hold on to the last strands of universalism. In this final chapter I want to reflect on how cosmopolitan post-nationalism and nationalism can be seen, not as antithetical discourses fundamentally opposed to each other, but as expressions of the same discourses, and that something like nations without nationalism might be possible and serve as a foundation for a civic cosmopolitanism.

To put this in slightly different terms, we need to rethink the relationship between the cosmos and the polis. If nationalism is the expression of the human order of the polis and post-nationalism the expression of the higher order of the cosmos, how are we to find a point of mediation? Either we retreat to the communitarian world of the polis or take flight to the intellectualized spheres of the cosmos. Stephen Toulmin (1990) writes of the modern world since the Enlightenment as the imposition of a universalizing and depersonalized pursuit of 'cosmopolis', to which he contrasts the humanizing worldview of an earlier modernity. Against Toulmin's idealization of Renaissance humanism, I believe that a self-limiting kind of cosmopolitanism is possible, one that can reconcile polis with cosmos. This seems to me to be the only rejoinder to the critics of cosmopolitanism, such as Zolo (1997) and Toulmin (1990). Zolo dismisses cosmopolitan arguments, seeing cosmopolitanism as no different from globalization:

> What western cosmopolitans call 'global civil society' in fact goes no further than a network of connections and functional interdependencies which has developed within certain important sectors of the 'global market', above all finance, technology, automation, manufacturing industry and the service sector. Nor, moreover, does it go much beyond the optimistic expectation of affluent westerners to be able to feel and be universally recognised as citizens of the world – citizens of a welcoming, peaceful, ordered and democratic 'global village' – without for a moment or in any way ceasing to be 'themselves', i.e. western citizens. The rhetoric of civil globalization and of a rising 'cosmopolitan citizenship' underestimates one of the most characteristic and most serious consequences of the way in which westernization is cultural homogenization without integration: namely the antagonism between the esteemed citizenships of the West and the countless masses belonging to regional and subcontinental areas without development and with a high rate of democratic growth.
>
> (Zolo 1997: 137)

For Zolo, so long as a billion individuals worldwide live below a minimum level of literacy there can be no global civil society. Such a entity would produce only further fragmentation. There is much that is true in this and the argument presented in this book has been mindful of such issues. However, I believe that it is possible both normatively and empirically to distinguish between cosmopolitanism and globalization. I have also drawn a distinction between legal cosmopolitanism and political (or democratic) cosmopolitanism. There is much to suggest that there is a sufficient amount of transnational developments to warrant the designation of one of these terms, for instance the growing discourses of human rights, ecological politics, security, crime and humanitarian aid. To an extent international law now has a genuinely cosmopolitan role in the world today, but it is in the dimension of governance, democratic politics, that the real impetus towards cosmopolitan civil society can be found.

From a different perspective, there is the more conservative communitarian critique which calls for the priority of the human order of the polis over the cosmos, the defence of community against univeralisms and cosmopolitanism (Walzer 1987; Smith 1995). My argument is one that recognizes the communitarian critique of the post-national, as well as the post-national critique of the communitarian (Bellamy and Castiglione 1998; Thompson 1998). Both positions, therefore, are invalid in so far as they are alternatives. We need both the polis and the cosmos in order to protect us from the excesses of both. I am calling this position 'civic cosmopolitanism', for what it entails is a recognition that unless it expresses substantive content, the cosmopolitan position is ineffective. The success of nationalism is due less to the popularity and force of its ideology than to the absence of an equally compelling counter-ideology from the left and, in particular, from post-national cosmopolitan currents in contemporary society. Nationalism has been able to monopolize the pathos of solidarity, commitment and community because these have found no expression in other discourses. As Touraine (1997: 129) argues, the real danger is that a globalized world market might become divorced from communities. 'Democracy', he argues, 'is now more uncertain because globalization is crushing cultural diversity and personal experiences and because the citizen is being transformed into a consumer' (see also Touraine 1997: 68). In my view, to reconcile community and globalization is the task of cosmopolitanism.

Cosmopolitans would urge us to abandon the distinction between friend and foe, inclusion and exclusion, for a discourse which transcends culture and the life-world. The problem with world community or universal humanity is that it ignores the plurality of communities and presupposes moral and cultural detachment. A minimal cosmopolitanism can find a certain expression in human rights, which are abstract and for the most part are not the basis of concrete identities. At the most they are resources for identities. The postnational cosmopolitan is somebody who is sufficiently uncommitted to be able to be detached and is generally taken to be the intellectual. In this conventional understanding of the term the cosmopolitan – as opposed to the immigrant – is a universal citizen, mobile, autonomous and choosing to be transnational. Cosmopolitans have no sense of self and therefore no notion of an other since these have been rendered transparent – and have no feeling for a world which they have voluntarily abandoned. However, there is another way of looking at the problem and it is to see the idea of the nation – as opposed to nationalism – and cosmopolitanism as mutually reinforcing. Only in this way can we bridge the futile divorce of polis and cosmos, community and world, ethnicity and universalism.

One way of approaching this is to see cosmopolitanism as a real force in the world, manifest in the multiple alliances and identities that people have. In particular, diasporas, immigrants and transnational communities of all descriptions embody a cosmopolitanism that cannot be compared with the Enlightenment notion of cosmopolitanism or that of bourgeois detachment. This sense of the term may be called 'cultural cosmopolitanism' and is represented in the work of Charles Taylor and in post-colonial writings (see Chapter 4). It is of course evident that this kind of cosmopolitanism is compatible with ethno-nationalism. An emphasis on multiculturalism will not provide us with a viable means of rethinking cosmopolitanism so long as multiculturalism does not entail a commitment to a shared political culture. The tendency everywhere is that there are limits to the shared political culture of the public domain. Tolerance has become indifference and indifference has become cynicism (Hollinger 1995). Multiculturalism has become an expression of the failure of late modern societies to achieve social integration by means of a common moral and public culture. A strict Habermasian or a left liberal – such as Rawls – would argue that there is still enough ground to make cosmopolitanism viable, though this is likely to be a minimal meeting point, as is suggested by Habermas's 'patriotism of the constitution' or Rawls's 'overlapping consensus'. The existence of such a common ground is one of the main arguments of Smelser and Alexander (1999) in a recent volume on the viability of multiculturalism. The problem still remains how this meeting ground can be made more central to the constitution of society. Cautious of equating cosmopolitanism with transnational communities, I believe that this is the best concrete example we have of post-national consciousness, even if what is affirmed is a multiplicity of nationalisms.

An alternative model is suggested by what Held (1995) calls 'cosmopolitan democracy', an essentially political conception of cosmopolitanism, and whose origins, it is sometimes held, lie in Kant (though Kant was more concerned with the relationship between states). Held's model is based on a reformed General Assembly of the United Nations where IGOs, INGOs, citizens' groups and social movements could be represented and where international problems would be debated (Held 1995: 274). The premise underlying this is that democratic law can be effective only if it becomes international law. While the state is far from being in decline as a result of globalization, and in many senses its power has increased, it is evident that the state is no longer the sole site of democratic politics. The crisis of national models of sovereignty creates new opportunities for radical democracy. Like Habermas, Held seems to assume that radical democracy must extend beyond the nation state, but unlike Habermas his notion of cosmopolitan democracy challenges the model of the constitutional state tendentially presupposed by Habermas. Though Held does not use the idea of collective citizens, the concept is central to his insistence that a cosmopolitan democratic order would grant a central place not merely to states but to other collectivities such as INGOs, citizens' groups and social movements. Given the multi-levelled nature of transnational democracy – which involves complex relations between regions, national governments and the transnational agencies – it may become the case that collective actors will be more operative on the transnational level.

The normative idea underlying Held's cosmopolitan democracy is the principle of autonomy, a notion which seems to owe much to Habermas: it 'connotes the capacity of human beings to reason self-consciously, to be reflective and to be self-determining' (Held 1995: 146). Radical democracy not only must be cosmopolitan, but must also be freed from cultural tradition: democracy does not presuppose agreement on diverse values. Rather, it suggests a way of relating values to each other and of leaving the resolution of value conflicts open to participants in a public process, subject only to certain provisions protecting the shape and the form of the process itself (Held 1995: 298). Like Habermas, Held recognizes the limits of the older radical conceptions of democracy, such as those associated with Rousseau and the Marxist tradition, for these do not have the principle of autonomy at the heart of their projects, appealing instead to essentialistic notions of the 'general will'. Held defends the principle of autonomy as a project preoccupied with the capability of persons to determine and justify their own actions, and if necessary to delimit democracy. In this respect, like Habermas, his notion of democracy is one that recognizes the achievements of modern liberal democracy.

Held's notion of cosmopolitan democracy, which is focused on creating new political institutions within the legal framework of international law, offers an important perspective for the institutionalization of discursive democracy in the global context, but it is an exclusively normative model and is based on the unrealistic assumption of the reform of the UN. However, to speak of institutionalization at this level is premature since we are living in a period in which the nation state is still one of the main actors in the global context, even if its power has been considerably eroded in some areas of its jurisdiction. A more important issue may indeed be the creation of a global 'constitution' which does not presuppose national sovereignty (Habermas 1999b). A global constitution cannot be just about rights but must be a discursive framework to create a social order. We can already see some indications of the growing importance of discursivity in global order. Applying Habermas's theory to the global order, it may be suggested that the emergence of global discourses of law and regulation provide radical democracy with an institutional space in which to bring about increased democratization by granting a central place to new definitions of citizenship. Essential to this is a notion of collective actors. Habermas takes the individual as his starting point, as is suggested by dialogue as the model for communicative action. In the global context of post-national democracy, we need to go beyond this dialogic model of communicative action if we are to address the complex nature of social change today.

In sum, this approach to the question of what might be the basis of cosmopolitanism has much going for it. Cosmopolitanism is tied less to transnational communities and therefore the tie with nationalism is weakened. Conceiving of cosmopolitanism in terms of democracy has the merit that it allows us to envisage post-national forms of citizenship.

While I am not rejecting the three positions – Habermas's constitutional patriotism, cultural cosmopolitanism and a cosmopolitan of democracy and law – I wish to add one crucial dimension to our conceptions of cosmo-politanism. I have argued that both the position of constitutional patriotism and cosmopolitan democracy ignore the cultural foundations of cosmopolitanism and that, on the other side, the argument for transnational cosmopolitanism makes too many concessions to culture for any of these to be adequate. The position I am arguing for may be termed civic cosmopolitanism to signify the fact that it is a cosmopolitanism rooted in civic communities, communities which are also discursively constituted. I do not think equating the cosmo-politan moment with the transnational is an adequate alternative to the pure Habermasian universalism of the constitution. Missing from both is the loca-tion of cosmopolitanism in real lived communities. In short, cosmopolitanism ends with the transnational (as in Kant or in Held's version of the Kantian argument) but has its roots in civic communities. These communities may be those of transnational communities but the essence of community is not mobility but communication.

One of the most important challenges today is to articulate a form of community that is capable of capturing the ground from nationalism. Unless the left can give expression to the discourses of self, other and world, nationalism will continue to thrive. Civic cosmopolitanism is necessary in order to combat ethnonationalism and state nationalism, to mention the two most common forms that nationalism takes. The problem with many varieties of cosmopolitanism is that they are conceived as discourses that transcend the nation and are therefore impotent in the face of nationalism. There is much truth in Rorty's (1998) critique of the (American) academic left which has become devoid of a political project because it has rejected the belief in the nation:

> In America, at the end of the twentieth century, few inspiring images and stories are being proffered. The only version of national pride encouraged by American popular culture is a simple minded chauvinism. But such chauvinism is overshadowed by a widespread sense that national pride is no longer appropriate. In both popular and elite culture, most descriptions of what America will be like in the twenty-first century are written in tones either of self-mockery or self-disgust.
>
> (Rorty 1998: 4)

Rorty's aim is to redirect the left away from the culture battles to embrace a commitment to social goals, and to do this he believes that a sense of national pride, commitment and national hope are essential to that task. In other words, unless left-wing progressive politics can capture the discourse of the nation, it is unlikely to be able to resist either neo-liberalism or nationalism. This is a position which I would endorse, for there is much to suggest that there is a relationship between the new nationalism and social discontent. As I argued in Chapter 7, the logic of exclusion (nationalism, the market) is no longer compensated by the logic of inclusion (citizenship and multiculturalism).

Another factor is undoubtedly the reaction to the global context. In Europe the momentum towards European integration (which is a dynamic of inclusion) occurred at a time when welfare states were under attack from neo-liberal influenced strategies of exclusion. Combined with the spectre of large-scale immigration following the collapse of communism, the secure foundations of western societies suddenly became questioned. Transnational processes, such as European integration, appeared to undermine the cultural models of national societies which were also reaching the limits of their capacity to provide an enduring form of social citizenship. The motivational forces of nationalism are fear, resentment and disappointment. Nationalism provides an ethos of security in a world which is fraught with anxiety, risk and insecurity. In the former communist countries the loss of economic security that communism provided and exposure to neo-liberal economics and a culture of consumption led to a major feeling of economic and cultural insecurity.

If my analysis is correct, the chances for a genuine post-national cosmopolitanism are good simply because the new nationalism is standing on thin ground, albeit one that is bolstered by global capitalism. My proposal is for a strengthening of the civic dimensions of citizenship in order to combat nationalism, which cannot command support solely on the basis of either a cultural politics of ethnicity or a politics of state patriotism. Following Habermas, I would argue that there is no culture which is not able to withstand critique and self-confrontation. Unlike in the past when nationalism had few adversaries – its main competitor being class – today it is forced to live in a world in which many identities exist. According to Habermas (1984), modernity contains a self-reflective component that cannot simply be avoided: the critique of cultural traditions and reflexivity of ideology is built into the modern understanding of the world. The post-national perspective would argue that no cultural tradition is able to withstand self-examination, for the critical power of self-scrutiny and self-confrontation are not extraneous to all modern value systems but are built into them. Even though there is much empirical evidence to the contrary – for modernity has also witnessed the rise of fundamentalism – it could be argued in defence of this position that every cultural tradition – in particular nationalism – can be seen both in terms of constructivism and essentialism, a reflected mode of thinking and a taken-for-granted mode. The culture of tradition and the culture of reflection are not exclusive but interwoven.

It is one of the conclusions of recent work in nationalism that essentialism and constructivism can be theorized as two perspectives, the former being that of the participant or social actor and the latter that of the theorist (Benhabib 1998; Delanty 2000a). Thus the question is not whether there are two kinds of nationalism – constructivist or essentialist – but whether the essentialist mode can be rendered reflective in a consciousness of the inventiveness of all identity. In other words: can a reflective consciousness be available to social actors? Or if we prefer: can the theoretical aspect be open to social actors? My contention is that post-national cosmopolitanism entails not cultural negation or moral indifference but the ability to render cultural traditions transparent. To put it in different terms, since Benedict Anderson (1983) the imaginary component of national identity is something that is now taken for granted in theories of nationalism, though views certainly do differ on whether this is to be seen as a fabrication (Gellner 1983; Hobsbawm and Ranger 1983) or an integral and authentic expression of collective identity (Smith 1995). It is one of the great lessons of modern social and political thought – as is illustrated in the work of Adorno, Derrida, Gadamer, Habermas and Taylor – that critical reflective and transformative dialogue is built into the very self-understanding of the modernity. I do not think that there is a particular cultural tradition that can withstand the power of critique and self-renewal. If we accept the relevance of the concept of the imaginary – if not the affirmative conception of Anderson (1983) but the radical imaginary of Castoriadis (1987) – then we can say that national identity contains a self-transcending dimension. To give expression to the discursive space within the national imaginary is one of the tasks of civic cosmopolitanism.

The main difference between my conception of cosmopolitanism and others is that I believe a cosmopolitan civil society is meaningless in the absence of a cosmopolitan public sphere. Many of the existing conceptions of cosmopolitanism conflate civil society with the public sphere. While I am of the view that a cosmopolitan legal order is preferable to a cosmopolitan political order, a far more important question concerns the prior existence of a cosmopolitan public sphere, as the civic space of public communication. Civil society, on the other hand, comes into existence only when a public sphere has already been created, for civil society cuts across the domain of the state and the civic realm of the public sphere. Without a cosmopolitan public sphere, legal and political forms of global civil society will not be rooted in the civic dimension of community that is necessary in order to resist homogeneizing forms of globalization. The public sphere is a more basic form of community than the political and the legal domains of civil society. The public sphere is a domain of communication and cultural contestation. A cosmopolitan public sphere is not necessarily a global public sphere as such, though this can be one dimension to it, but is located in national and subnational public spheres which have been transformed by interaction with each other. In short, we need to distinguish between subnational, national and transnational public spheres with respect to the degree of cosmopolitanism that they exhibit. Once these civic cosmopolitan public spheres become evident, the distinct question of the legal and political forms of a cosmopolitan civil society can be addressed.

The idea of civic cosmopolitanism I am arguing for can be understood as a self-limiting kind of cosmopolitanism. It is a 'thin' cosmopolitanism and can be contrasted to the 'thick' cosmopolitanism of global civil society. This civic conception of cosmopolitanism ties in with the communitarian critique of universalism, as well as the radical democratic critique of communitarism (Connolly 1991, 1995; Habermas 1998a; Linklater 1998; Isin and Wood 1999). As Linklater argues, cosmoplitanism seeks to extend the ethical horizons of political community until a point is reached at which no group is excluded (Linklater 1998: 57). This modest kind of cosmopolitanism does not seek the transcendence of political community in an international organization of states but a pluralist world of political communities. The cosmopolitan moment occurs when context-bound cultures encounter each other and undergo transformation as a result. Only in this way can the twin pitfalls of the false universalism of liberalism's universalistic morality and the communitarian retreat into the particular be avoided. This differentiated particularism requires a cosmopolitan critique of globalization in so far as the latter is a discourse that succumbs to the false universalism of an empty world culture or the romanticism of the particular.

Bibliography

Abramson, P. and Inglehart, R. (1995) *Value Change in Global Perspective*. Ann Arbor, MI: University of Michigan Press.

Adorno, T., Frenkel-Brunswik, E., Levinson, D.J. and Nevitt-Stanford, R. (1959) *The Authoritarian Personality*. New York: Norton.

Albrow, M. (1997) *The Global Age*. Cambridge: Polity.

Alejandro, R. (1993) *Hermeneutics, Citizenship and the Public Sphere*. New York: State University of New York Press.

Alter, P. (1989) *Nationalism*. London: Arnold.

Anderson, B. (1983) *Imagined Communities*. London: Verso.

Anderson, P. (1994) *The Invention of the Region, 1945–1990*, EUI working paper no. 94/2. Florence: European University Institute.

Apel, K.-O. (1978) The conflicts of our time and the problem of political ethics, in F. Dallymar (ed.) *From Contract to Community: Political Theory at the Cross Roads*. New York: Dekkar.

Apel, K.-O. (1987) The problem of a macroethic of responsibility to the future in the crisis of technological civilization, *Man and World*, 20: 3–40.

Apel, K.-O. (1988) *Diskurs und Verantwortung: Das Problem des Übergangs zur postkonventionellen Moral*. Frankfurt: Suhrkamp.

Apel, K.-O. (1990) The problem of a universalistic macroethics of co-responsibility, in S. Griffioen (ed.) *What Right Does Ethics Have?* Amsterdam: VU University Press.

Apel, K.-O. (1992) The ecological crisis as a problem for discourse ethics, in A. Ofsti (ed.) *Ecology and Ethics*. Trondheim: Nordland Akademi for Kunst og Vitenskap.

Apel, K.-O. (1993) How to ground a universalistic ethics of co-responsibility for the effects of collective actions and activities, *Philosophica*, 52(2): 9–29.

Apel, K.-O. (1996) A planetary macroethics for humankind: the need, the apparent difficulty and the eventual possibility, in *Karl-Otto Apel: Selected Essays*, vol. 2. Atlantic Highlands, NJ: Humanities Press.

Apel, K.-O. (2000) Globalization and the need for universal ethics: the problem in light of discourse ethics, *European Journal of Social Theory*, 3(2).

Appadurai, A. (1996) *Modernity at Large: Cultural Dimensions of Globalization*. Minneapolis, MN: University of Minnesota Press.

Appiah, K.A. (1998) Cosmopolitan patriots, in P. Cheah and B. Robbins (eds) *Cosmopolitics: Thinking and Feeling Beyond the Nation*. Minneapolis, MN: University of Minnesota Press.

Arendt, H. (1958) *The Human Condition*. Chicago: University of Chicago Press.

Aristotle (1962) *The Politics*. Harmondsworth: Penguin.

Arnason, J. (1990) Nationalism, globalization and modernity, *Theory, Culture and Society*, 7: 207–36.

Arnason, J. (1993) *The Future that Failed: Origins and Destinies of the Soviet Model*. London: Routledge.

Avineri, S. and De-Shalit, A. (eds) (1992) *Communitarianism and Individualism*. Oxford: Oxford University Press.

Axford, B. (1995) *The Global System: Economics, Politics and Culture*. Cambridge: Polity.

Balibar, E. (1991) Es Gibt keinen Staat in Europa: racism and politics in Europe today, *New Left Review*, 186: 5–19.

Barbalet, J. (1988) *Citizenship*. Milton Keynes: Open University Press.

Barber, B. (1984) *Strong Democracy: Participatory Politics for a New Age*. Berkeley, CA: University of California Press.

Barber, B. (1996) *Jihad vs. McWorld*. New York: Ballantine Press.

Barbieri, W. (1998) *Ethics of Citizenship: Immigration and Group Rights in Germany*. Durham, NC: Duke University Press.

Baubock, R. (1994) *Transnational Citizenship: Membership and Rights in International Migration*. Aldershot: Edgar Elgar.

Bauman, Z. (1993) *Postmodern Ethics*. Oxford: Blackwell.

Bauman, Z. (1997) *Postmodernity and its Discontents*. Cambridge: Polity.

Bauman, Z. (1998) *Globalization*. Cambridge: Polity.

Beall, J. (ed.) (1997) *A City for All: Valuing Difference and Working with Diversity*. London: Zed Books.

Beck, U. (1992) *The Risk Society*. London: Sage.

Beck, U. (1996) World risk society as cosmopolitan society?, *Theory, Culture and Society*, 13(4): 1–32.

Beck, U. (2000) *What is Globalization?* Cambridge: Polity.

Beetham, D. (1998) Human rights and cosmopolitan democracy, in D. Archibugi, D. Held and M. Köhler (eds) *Re-Imagining Political Community: Studies in Cosmopolitan Democracy*. Cambridge: Polity.

Bellamy, R. and Castiglione, D. (1998) Between cosmopolis and community: three models of rights and democracy within the European Union, in D. Archibugi, D. Held and M. Köhler (eds) *Re-Imagining Political Community: Studies in Cosmopolitan Democracy*. Cambridge: Polity.

Bellamy, C. and Taylor, J. (eds) (1998) *Governing in the Information Age*. Buckingham: Open University Press.

Bendix, R. (1964) *Nation-Building and Citizenship*. New York: John Wiley.

Benhabib, S. (1992) *Situating the Self*. Cambridge: Polity.

Benhabib, S. (ed.) (1996) *Democracy and Difference: Contesting the Boundaries of the Political*. Princeton, NJ: Princeton University Press.

Benhabib, S. (1998) Democracy and identity: in search of civic polity, *Philosophy and Social Criticism*, 24(2/3): 85–100.

Berger, S. and Dore, R. (eds) (1996) *National Diversity and Global Capitalism*. Ithaca, NY: Cornell University Press.

Berlin, I. (1969) Two concepts of liberty, in Berlin, *Four Essays on Liberty*. Oxford: Oxford University Press.

Beyer, P. (1994) *Religion and Globalization*. London: Sage.

Bhabha, H. (1990) *Nation and Narration*. London: Routledge.

Billig, M. (1994) *Banal Nationalism*. London: Sage.

Bobbi, N. (1995) *The Age of Rights*. Cambridge: Polity.

Bodei, R. (1995) Historical memory and European identity, *Philosophy and Social Criticism*, 21(4): 1–13.

Bohman, J. (1996) *Public Deliberation: Pluralism, Complexity and Democracy*. Cambridge, MA: Harvard University Press.

Bohman, J. (1997) The public spheres of the world citizen, in J. Bohman and W. Rehg (eds) *Deliberative Democracy: Essays on Reason and Politics*. Cambridge, MA: MIT Press.

Bohman, J. (1998) The globalization of the public sphere, *Philosophy and Social Criticism*, 24(2/3): 199–216.

Bohman, J. and Lutz-Bachmann, M. (eds) (1997) *Perpetual Peace: Essays on Kant's Cosmopolitan Ideal*. Cambridge, MA: MIT Press.

Bohman, J. and Rehg, W. (eds) (1997) *Deliberative Democracy: Essays on Reason and Politics*. Cambridge, MA: MIT Press.

Bohme, G. (1997) The structure and prospects of the knowledge society, *Social Science Information*, 36(3): 447–68.

Boli, J. and Thomas, G. (1997) World culture in the world polity: a century of international non-governmental organization, *American Sociological Review*, 62(April): 171–90.

Boli, J. and Thomas, G. (eds) (1999) *Constructing World Culture: International Non-Governmental Organizations since 1875*. Stanford, CA: Stanford University Press.

Borgja, J. and Castells, M. (1997) *Local and Global: Management of Cities in the Information Age*. London: Earthscan.

Boulding, E. (1990) *Building a Global Civic Culture: Education for an Independent World*. Syracuse, NY: Syracuse University Press.

Brubaker, R. (ed.) (1989) *Immigration and the Politics of Citizenship in Europe and North America*. Lanham, MD: University Press of America.

Brubaker, R. (1990) Immigration, citizenship, and the nation-state in France and Germany, *International Sociology*, 5(4): 379–407.

Brubaker, R. (1992) *Citizenship and Nationhood in France and Germany*. Cambridge, MA: Harvard University Press.

Brubaker, R. (1996) *Nationalism Reframed: Nationhood and the National Question in the New Europe*. Cambridge: Cambridge University Press.

Buchstein, H. and Dean, J. (eds) (1997) Special issue: democratizing technology/technologizing democracy, *Constellations*, 4(2).

Bull, H. (1977) *The Anarchical Society*. London: Macmillan.

Burca, G. da (1996) The question of legitimacy in the European Union, *Modern Law Review*, 59(3): 349–76. .

Burns, T. (1999) The evolution of parliaments and societies in Europe: challenges and prospects, *European Journal of Social Theory*, 2(2): 167–94.

Burton, J. (1972) *World Society*. Cambridge: Cambridge University Press.

Byrne, D. (1999) *Social Exclusion*. Buckingham: Open University Press.

Calhoun, C. (ed.) (1993) *Habermas and the Public Sphere*. Cambridge, MA: MIT Press.

Calhoun, C. (1997) *Nationalism*. Buckingham: Open University Press.

Calhoun, C. (1999) Nationalism, political community and the representation of society, *European Journal of Social Theory*, 2(2): 217–31.

Canovan, M. (1999) Trust the people! Populism and the two faces of democracy, *Political Studies*, 47: 2–16.

Castells, M. (1983) *The City and the Grassroots*. Berkeley, CA: University of California Press.

Castells, M. (1989) *The Informational City*. Oxford: Blackwell.

Castells, M. (1994) European cities, the informational society, and the global economy, *New Left Review*, 204: 18–12.

Castells, M. (1996) *The Information Age: Vol. 1, The Rise of the Network Society*. Oxford: Blackwell.

Castells, M. (1997) *The Information Age: Vol. 2, The Power of Identity*. Oxford: Blackwell.

Castells, M. (1998) *The Information Age: Vol. 3, End of Millennium*. Oxford: Blackwell.

Castells, S. and Miller, M. (1993) *The Age of Migration: International Population Movements in the Modern World*. London: Macmillan.

Castoriadis, C. (1987) *The Imaginary Institution of Society*. Cambridge: Polity.

Cerutti, F. (1992) Can there be a supranational identity?, *Philosophy and Social Criticism*, 18(2): 147–62.

Cesarani, D. and Fulbrook, M. (eds) (1996) *Citizenship, Nationality and Migration in Europe*. London: Routledge.

Cheah, P. and Robbins, B. (eds) (1998) *Cosmopolitics: Thinking and Feeling Beyond the Nation*. Minneapolis, MN: University of Minnesota Press.

Chen, X. (1995) *Occidentalism: A Theory of Counter-Discourse in Post-Mao China*. Oxford: Oxford University Press.

Clarke, P. (1996) *Deep Citizenship*. London: Pluto.

Close, P. (1995) *Citizenship, Europe and Change*. London: Macmillan.

Cohen, J. (1999) Does voluntary association make democracy work?, in N. Smelser and N. Alexander (eds) *Diversity and Its Discontents: Cultural Conflict and Common Ground in Contemporary American Society*. Princeton, NJ: Princeton University Press.

Cohen, J. and Arato, A. (1992) *Civil Society and Political Theory*. Cambridge, MA: MIT Press.

Collins, R. (1997) *The Sociology of Philosophies: A Global Theory of Intellectual Change*. Cambridge, MA: Harvard University Press.

Connolly, W.E. (1991) *Identity/Difference: Democratic Negotiations of Political Parodox*. Ithaca, NY: Cornell University Press.

Connolly, W.E. (1995) *The Ethos of Pluralization*. Minneapolis, MN: University of Minnesota Press.

Dahl, G. (1999) *Radical Conservatism and the Future of Democracy*. London: Sage.

Dahlgren, P. (1995) *Television and the Public Sphere: Citizenship, Democracy and the Media*. London: Sage.

Dahlgren, P. and Sparks, C. (eds) (1991) *Communication and Citizenship: Journalism and the Public Sphere*. London: Routledge.

Dallymayr, F. (ed.) (1978) *From Contract to Community: Political Theory at the Crosswords*. New York: Marcel Dekker.

de Tocqueville, A. (1969) *Democracy in America*. New York: Doubleday.

de Vries, H. and Weber, S. (eds) (1997) *Violence, Identity, and Self-Determination*. Stanford, CA: Stanford University Press.

Delanty, G. (1995a) *Inventing Europe: Idea, Identity, Reality*. London: Macmillan.

Delanty, G. (1995b) The limits and possibility of a European identity: a critique of cultural essentialism, *Philosophy and Social Criticism*, 21(4): 15–36.

Delanty, G. (1996a) The frontier and identities of exclusion in European history, *History of European Ideas*, 22(2): 93–103.

Delanty, G. (1996b) The resonance of Mitteleuropa: a Habsburg myth or anti-politics?, *Theory, Culture and Society*, 14(4): 93–108.

Delanty, G. (1997a) Habermas and Occidental rationalism: the politics of identity, social learning and the cultural limits of moral universalism, *Sociological Theory*, 15(3): 30–59.

Delanty, G. (1997b) Models of citizenship: defining European identity and citizenship, *Citizenship Studies*, 1(3): 285–303.

Delanty, G. (1997c) *Social Science: Beyond Realism and Constructivism*. Buckingham: Open University Press.

Delanty, G. (1997d) Social exclusion and the new nationalism: European trends and their implications for Ireland, *Innovation: The European Journal of Social Sciences*, 10(2): 127–43.

Delanty, G. (1998a) The idea of the university in the global era: from knowledge as an end to the end of knowledge?, *Social Epistemology*, 2(1): 3–25.

Delanty, G. (1998b) Rethinking the university: the autonomy, reflexivity and contestation of knowledge, *Social Epistemology*, 12(1): 103–13.

Delanty, G. (1998c) Redefining political culture in Europe today: from ideology to the politics of identity, in U. Hedetof (ed.) *Political Symbols, Symbolic Politics: Europe between Unity and Fragmentation*. Aldershot: Ashgate.

Delanty, G. (1999a) *Social Theory in a Changing World*. Cambridge: Polity.

Delanty, G. (1999b) Self, other and world: discourses of nationalism and cosmopolitanism, *Cultural Values*, 3(3): 365–75.

Delanty, G. (1999c) Biotechnology in the risk society: the possibility of a global ethic of societal responsibility, in P. O'Mahony (ed.) *Nature, Risk and Responsibility: Discourses of Biotechnology*. London: Macmillan.

Delanty, G. (1999d) The foundations of social theory: origins and trajectories, in B.S. Turner (ed.) *The Blackwell Companion to Social Theory*, 2nd edn. Oxford: Blackwell.

Delanty, G. (1999e) Die Transformation nationaler Identitaet und die kulturelle Ambivalenz europaeischer Identitaet, in R. Viehoff and R. Seger (eds) *Kultur, Identitä, Europa*. Frankfurt: Suhrkamp.

Delanty, G. (2000a) Nationalism, in G. Ritzer and B. Smart (eds) *Handbook of Social Theory*. London: Sage.

Delanty, G. (2000b) The resurgence of the city: the spaces of European integration, in E. Isin (ed.) *Politics and the City*. London: Routledge.

Delanty, G. (2000c) *Modernity and Postmodernity: Knowledge, Power, and the Self*. London: Sage.

Deleuze, G. and Guattari, F. (1983) *Anti-Oedipus*. Minneapolis, MN: University of Minnesota Press.

Derrida, J. (1977) *Of Grammatology*. Baltimore, MD: Johns Hopkins University Press.

Derrida, J. (1978) *Writing and Difference*. London: Routledge and Kegan Paul.

Dicken, P. (1992) *Global Shift: The Internationalization of Economic Activity*. London: Chapman.

Donnelly, J. (1989) *Universal Human Rights in Theory and Practice*. Ithaca, NY: Cornell University Press.

Douglas, M. and Friedmann, J. (eds) (1998) *Cities for Citizens: Planning and the Rise of Civil Society in a Global Age*. New York: Wiley.

Drucker, P. (1994) *Postcapitalist Society*. New York: HarperCollins.

Dryzek, J. (1990) *Discursive Democracy: Politics, Policy and Political Science*. Cambridge: Cambridge University Press.

Dryzek, J. (1999) Transnational democracy, *Journal of Political Philosophy*, 7(1): 30–51.

Dunn, J. (ed.) (1995) *Contemporary Crisis of the Nation State?* Oxford: Blackwell.

Durkheim, E. (1915) *The Elementary Forms of the Religious Life*. London: Allen & Unwin.

Durkheim, E. (1957) *Professional Ethics and Civic Morals*. London: Routledge and Kegan Paul.

Durkheim, E. (1960) *The Division of Labour in Society*. Glencoe, IL: Free Press.

Durkheim, E. (1975) *Suicide: A Study in Sociology*. London: Routledge and Kegan Paul.

Eade, J. (ed.) (1996) *Living the Global City: Globalization as Local Process*. London: Routledge.

Eder, K. (1993) *The New Politics of Class*. London: Sage.

Eder, K. (1996) The institutionalisation of environmentalism: ecological discourse and the second transformation of the public sphere, in S. Lash, B. Szerszynski and B. Wynne (eds) *Risk, Environment and Modernity*. London: Sage.

Eder, K. (1999) Integration durch Kultur? Das Paradox der Suche nach einer europaeischen Identitaet, in R. Viehoff and R. Seger (eds) *Kultur, Identitä, Europa*. Frankfurt: Suhrkamp.

Enzenberger, H.M. (1994) *Civil War*. London: Granta.

Etzioni, A. (1995) *The Spirit of Community*. London: Fontana.

Falk, R. (1987) *The Promise of World Order: Essays in Normative International Relations*. Philadephia, PA: University of Pennsylvania Press.

Falk, R. (ed.) (1993) *The Constitutional Foundations of World Peace*. New York: State University of New York Press.

Falk, R. (1994) The making of global citizenship, in B. Steenbergen (ed.) *The Condition of Citizenship*. London: Sage.

Falk, R. (1995a) The world order between inter-state law and the law of humanity: the role of civil society institutions, in D. Archibugi and D. Held (eds) *Cosmopolitan Democracy*. Cambridge: Polity.

Falk, R. (1995b) *On Humane Governance: Toward a New Global Politics*. Cambridge: Polity.

Falter, J. and Klein, M. (1996) The mass basis of the extreme right in contemporary Europe in a comparative perspective, in F. Weil (ed.) *Extremism, Protest, Social Movements and Democracy*. Greenwich, CT: JAI Press.

Featherstone, M. (ed.) (1990) *Global Culture: Nationalism, Globalization and Modernity*. London: Sage.

Fisher, R. and Kling, J. (eds) (1993) *Mobilizing the Community: Local Politics in the Era of the Global City*. London: Sage.

Fiskin, J. (1991) *Democracy and Deliberation*. New Haven, CT: Yale University Press.

Fontana, J. (1995) *The Distorted Past: A Reinterpretation of European History*. Oxford: Blackwell.

Foucault, M. (1986) Of other spaces, *Diacritics*, 16(1): 22–7.

Frankenfeld, P. (1992) Technological citizenship: a normative framework for risk studies, *Science and Technology and Human Values*, 17(4).

Fraser, N. (1989) *Unruly Practices*. Cambridge: Polity.

Fraser, N. (1992) Rethinking the public sphere: a contribution to the critique of actually existing democracy, in C. Calhoun (ed.) *Habermas and the Public Sphere*. Cambridge, MA: MIT Press.

Fraser, N. and Gordon, L. (1994) Civil citizenship against social citizenship?, in B. van Steenbergen (ed.) *The Condition of Citizenship*. London: Sage.

Frazer, E. and Lacey, N. (1993) *The Politics of Community*. Hemel Hempstead: Harvester Wheatsheaf.

Freeman, M. (1995) Are there collective rights?, *Political Studies*, 43: 25–40.

Friedman, J. (1990) Being in the world: globalization and localization, in M. Featherstone (ed.) *Global Culture: Nationalism, Globalization and Modernity*. London: Sage.

Friedman, J. (1994) *Cultural Identity and Global Process*. London: Sage.

Friedman, J. (1995) Global system, globalization and the parameters of modernity, in M. Featherstone, S. Lash and R. Robertson (eds) *Global Modernities*. London: Sage.

Fukuyama, F. (1992) *The End of History and the Last Man*. Harmondsworth: Penguin.

Galbraith, J.K. (1992) *The Culture of Contentment*. Boston, MA: Houghton Mifflin.

Gamson, W. (1992) *Talking Politics*. Cambridge: Cambridge University Press.

Garcia, S. (ed.) (1993) *Europe and the Search for Identity*. London: Pinter.

Garcia Canelini, N. (1995) *Hybrid Cultures: Strategies for Entering and Leaving Modernity*. Minneapolis, MN: University of Minnesota Press.

Garnham, N. (1990) *Capitalism and Communication: Global Culture and the Economics of Information*. London: Sage.

Gellner, E. (1983) *Nations and Nationalism*. Oxford: Blackwell.

Gessner, V. and Schade, A. (1990) Conflicts of culture in cross-border legal relations, *Theory, Culture and Society*, 7: 253–77.

Giddens, A. (1981) *A Contemporary Critique of Historical Materialism*. London: Macmillan.

Giddens, A. (1982) Class division, class conflict and citizenship rights, in Giddens, *Profiles and Critiques in Social Theory*. London: Macmillan.

Giddens, A. (1985) *The Nation State and Violence*. London: Macmillan.

Giddens, A. (1990) *The Consequences of Modernity*. Cambridge: Polity.

Giddens, A. (1991) *Modernity and Self-Identity*. Cambridge: Polity.

Giddens, A. (1998) *The Third Way: The Renewal of Social Democracy*. Cambridge: Polity.

Glazer, N. (1997) *We Are All Multiculturalists Now*. Cambridge, MA: Harvard University Press.

Goldblatt, D. (1996) *Social Theory and the Environment*. Cambridge: Polity.

Goldman, M. (ed.) (1998) *Privatizing Nature: Political Struggles for the Global Commons*. London: Pluto.

Greenfeld, L. (1992) *Nationalism: Five Roads to Modernity*. Cambridge, MA: Harvard University Press.

Grusky, D. and Sorensen, J. (1998) Can class analysis be salvaged?, *American Journal of Sociology*, 103: 1187–234.

Guehenno, J. (1995) *The End of the Nation State*. Minneapolis, MN: University of Minnesota Press.

Gutmann, A. (1993) The challenge of multiculturalism in political ethics, *Philosophy and Public Affairs*, 22(3): 171–206.

Haas, E. (1964) *Beyond the Nation-State: Functionalism and International Organization*. Stanford, CA: Stanford University Press.

Habermas, J. (1976) *Legitimation Crisis*. London: Heinemann.

Habermas, J. (1979) *Communication and the Evolution of Society*. London: Heinemann.

Habermas, J. (1984) *The Theory of Communicative Action, Vol. 1, Reason and the Rationalization of Society*. London: Heinemann.

Habermas, J. (1987a) *The Theory of Communicative Action, Vol. 2, Lifeworld and System: A Critique of Functionalist Reason*. Cambridge: Polity.

Habermas, J. (1987b) *The Philosophical Discourse of Modernity*. Cambridge, MA: MIT Press.

Habermas, J. (1989a) *The Structural Transformation of the Public Sphere*. Cambridge: Polity.

Habermas, J. (1989b) *The New Conservatism: Cultural Criticism and the Historians' Debate*. Cambridge, MA: MIT Press.

Habermas, J. (1989c) The new obscurity, in Habermas, *The New Conservatism: Cultural Criticism and the Historians' Debate*. Cambridge, MA: MIT Press.

Habermas, J. (1991) Yet again, German identity – a unified nation of angry DM-burghers, *New German Critique*, 12: 1–19.

Habermas, J. (1996) *Between Facts and Norms: Contributions to a Discourse Theory of Law and Democracy*. Cambridge: Polity.

Habermas, J. (1998a) *The Inclusion of the Other: Studies in Political Theory*. Cambridge, MA: MIT Press.

Habermas, J. (1998b) Remarks on legitimation through human rights, *Philosophy and Social Criticism*, 24(2/3): 157–71.

Habermas, J. (1998c) *Die postnationale Konstellation*. Frankfurt: Suhrkamp.

Habermas, J. (1999a) The European nation-state and the pressures of globalization, *New Left Review*, 235: 46–59.

Habermas, J. (1999b) The war in Kosovo: bestiality and humanity: a war on border between legality and morality, *Constellations*, 6(3): 263–72.

Hannerz, U. (1990) Cosmopolitans and locals in world culture, *Theory, Culture and Society*, 7: 237–51.

Hannerz, U. (1992a) The global Eecume as a network of networks, in A. Kuper (ed.) *Conceptualizing Society*. London: Routledge.

Hannerz, U. (1992b) *Cultural Complexity: Studies in the Social Organization of Meaning*. New York: Columbia University Press.

Hannerz, U. (1996) *Transnational Connections: Culture, People, Places*. London: Routledge.

Harvey, D. (1989) *The Condition of Postmodernity*. Oxford: Blackwell.

Hayek, F.A. (1973–9) *Law, Legislation and Liberty*, 3 vols. London: Routledge and Kegan Paul.

Hedetoft, U. (1995) *Signs of Nation: Studies in the Political Semiotics of Self and Other*. Aldershot: Dartmouth.

Hedetoft, U. (1999) The nation-state meets the world: national identities in the context of transnationality and cultural globalization, *European Journal of Social Theory*, 2(1): 71–94.

Held, D. (1989) Citizenship and autonomy, in D. Held (ed.) *Political Theory and the Modern State*. Stanford, CA: Stanford University Press.

Held, D. (1995) *Democracy and the Global Order: From the Modern State to Cosmopolitan Governance*. Cambridge: Polity.

Held, D. (1996) *Models of Democracy*, 2nd edn. Cambridge: Polity.

Held, D., McGrew, A., Goldblatt, D. and Perraton, J. (1999) *Global Transformations: Politics, Economic and Culture*. Cambridge: Polity.

Heller, A. and Feher, F. (1988) Citizen ethics and civic virtues, in Heller and Feher, *The Postmodern Political Condition*. Cambridge: Polity.

Henkin, L. (1990) *The Age of Rights*. New York: Columbia University Press.

Hindess, B. (1987) *Freedom, Equality and the Market*. London: Tavistock.

Hindess, B. (1993) Citizenship in the modern West, in B.S. Turner (ed.) *Citizenship and Modern Social Theory*. London: Sage.

Hindess, B. (1998) Divide and rule: the international character of modern citizenship, *European Journal of Social Theory*, 1(1): 57–70.

Hirst, P. (1994) *Associative Democracy: New Forms of Economic and Social Governance*. Cambridge: Polity.

Hirst, P. and Thompson, G. (eds) (1996) *Globalization in Question*. Cambridge: Polity.

Hobsbawm, E. (1990) *Nations and Nationalism Since 1870*. Cambridge: Cambridge University Press.

Hobsbawm, E. (1991) The perils of the new nationalism, *The Nation*, 4 November: 555–6.

Hobsbawm, E. (1992) Ethnicity and nationalism in Europe today, *Anthropology Today*, 8: 3–8.

Hobsbawm, E. and Ranger, T. (eds) (1983) *The Invention of Tradition*. Cambridge: Cambridge University Press.

Hoffman, M. (1995) *Beyond the State*. Cambridge: Polity.

Hollinger, D. (1995) *Postethnic America: Beyond Multiculturalism*. New York: Basic Books.

Holmwood, J. (2000) Three pillars of welfare state theory: T.H. Marshall, Karl Polanyi and Ava Myrdal in defence of the national state, *European Journal of Social Theory*, 3(1): 23–50.

Holston, J. (ed.) (1999) *Cities and Citzenship*. Durham, NC: Duke University Press.

Holton, R. (1998) *Globalization and the Nation-State*. London: Macmillan.

Honneth, A. (1995) *The Struggle for Recognition: The Moral Grammar of Social Conflicts*. Cambridge: Polity.

Horsman, M. and Marshall, A. (eds) (1994) *After the Nation-State*. London: HarperCollins.

Howell, S. and Downing, L. (1996) David Duke: democracy under stress in Louisiana, in F. Weil (ed.) *Extremism, Protest, Social Movements and Democracy*. Greenwich, CT: JAI Press.

Hroch, M. (1993) From national movement to fully-formed nation, *New Left Review*, 198: 1–20.

Huntington, S. (1993) The clash of civilizations, *Foreign Affairs*, 72(3): 22–50.

Ignatieff, M. (1994) *Blood and Belonging: Journeys into the New Nationalism*. London: Chatto and Windus.

Iivonen, J. (ed.) (1993) *The Future of the Nation State in Europe*. London: Edward Elgar.

Inglehart, R. (1977) *The Silent Revolution: Changing Values and Political Styles among Western Publics*. Princeton, NJ: Princeton University Press.

Irwin, A. (1995) *Citizen Science: A Study of People, Experience and Sustainable Development*. London: Routledge.

Isin, E. (ed.) (2000) *Politics in the Global City*. London: Routledge.

Isin, E. and Wood, P. (1999) *Citizenship and Identity*. London: Sage.

Jackson, J. (1998) *National Minorities and the European Nation-States*. Oxford: Oxford University Press.

Jacobsen, D. (1997) *Rights Across Borders: Immigration and the Decline of Citizenship*. Baltimore, MD: Johns Hopkins University Press.

Jameson, F. (1991) *Postmodernism, or, the Cultural Logic of Late Capitalism*. Durham, NC: Duke University Press.

Jameson, F. (1998) Globalization as philosophical issue, in F. Jameson and M. Miyoshi (eds) *The Cultures of Globalization*. Durham, NC: Duke University Press.

Jameson, F. and Miyoshi, M. (eds) (1998) *The Cultures of Globalization*. Durham, NC: Duke University Press.

Janoski, T. (1998) *Citizenship and Civil Society: A Framework of Rights and Obligations in Liberal, Traditional, and Social Democratic Regimes*. Cambridge: Cambridge University Press.

Jonas, H. (1984) *The Imperative of Responsibility: In Search of an Ethics for the Technological Age*. Chicago: University of Chicago Press.

Jones, C. (1999) *Global Justice Defending Cosmopolitanism*. Oxford: Oxford University Press.

Joseph, M. (1999) *Nomadic Identities: The Performance of Citizenship*. Minneapolis, MN: University of Minnesota Press.

Juergensmeyer, M. (1993) *New Cold War? Religious Nationalism Confronts the Secular State*. Berkeley, CA: University of California Press.

Kaldor, M. (1993) Yugoslavia and the new nationalism, *New Left Review*, 197: 44–51.

Kant, I. (1970) Perpetual peace, in H. Reiss (ed.) *Kant: Political Writings*. Cambridge: Cambridge University Press.

Keane, J. (1984) *Public Life and Late Capitalism*. Cambridge: Cambridge University Press.

Keane, J. (1988a) *Democracy and Civil Society*. London: Verso.

Keane, J. (ed.) (1988b) *Civil Society and the State*. London: Verso.

Keohane, R. (1994) *After Hegemony: Cooperation and Discord in the World Political Economy*. Princeton, NJ: Princeton University Press.

Keohane, R. and Nye, J. (eds) (1973) *Transnational Relations and World Politics*. Cambridge, MA: Harvard University Press.

King, A.D. (ed.) (1991) *Culture, Globalization and the World-System*. London: Macmillan.

King, D. (1987) *The New Right: Politics, Markets and Citizenship*. London: Macmillan.

Kingdom, E. (1991) *What's Wrong with Rights? Problems for Feminist Politics of Law*. Edinburgh: Edinburgh University Press.

Kitschelt, H. (1995) *The Radical Right in Western Europe*. Ann Arbor, MI: University of Michigan Press.

Klausen, J. and Tilly, L. (eds) (1997) *European Integration in Social and Historical Perspective*. London: Rowman and Littlefield.

Köhler, M. (1998) From national to the cosmopolitan public sphere, in D. Archibugi, D. Held and M. Köhler (eds) *Re-Imagining Political Community: Studies in Cosmopolitan Democracy*. Cambridge: Polity.

Konrad, G. (1984) *Antipolitics*. New York: Harcourt Brace Jovanovich.

Kooiman, J. (ed.) (1993) *Modern Governance: New Government–Society Interactions*. London: Sage.

Kriesi, H., Porta, D. and Rucht, D. (eds) (1998) *Social Movements in a Globalizing World*. London: Macmillan.

Kristeva, J. (1993) *Nations without Nationalism*. New York: Columbia University Press.

Kukathas, C. (1992) Are there any cultural rights?, *Political Studies*, 20(1): 105–39.

Kymlicka, W. (1989) *Liberalism, Community and Culture*. Oxford: Clarendon Press.

Kymlicka, W. (1995) *Multicultural Citizenship: A Liberal Theory of Minority Rights*. Oxford: Clarendon Press.

Kymlicka, W. and Straehle, C. (1999) Cosmopolitanism, nation-states, and minority nationalism: a critical review of recent literature, *European Journal of Philosophy*, 7(1): 65–88.

Laclau, E. and Mouffe, C. (1985) *Hegemony and Socialist Strategy: Toward a Radical Democracy*. London: Verso.

Lasch, C. (1995) *The Revolt of the Elites and the Betrayal of Democracy*. New York: Norton.

Lash, S. and Urry, J. (1994) *Economies of Signs and Space*. London: Routledge.

Lehning, P. and Weale, A. (eds) (1997) *Citizenship, Democracy and Justice in the New Europe*. London: Routledge.

Lepsius, R. (1991) Beyond the nation-state: the multinational state as model for the European Community, *Telos*, 91: 57–76.

Lichterman, P. (1996) *The Search for Political Community: American Activists Reinventing Commitment*. Cambridge: Cambridge University Press.

Linklater, A. (1998) *The Transformation of Political Community*. Cambridge: Polity.

Lipschutz, R. (1992) Reconstructing world politics: the emergence of global civil society, *Millennium*, 21(3): 389–420.

Lipschutz, R. (1995) *Global Civil Society and Global Environmental Governance*. New York: State University of New York Press.

Lister, R. (1995) Dilemmas in engendering citizenship, *Economy and Society*, 24(1): 1–40.

Lister, R. (1997) *Citizenship: Feminist Perspectives*. London: Macmillan.

Lister, R. (1998) Citizenship and difference: towards a differentiated universalism, *European Journal of Social Theory*, 1(1): 71–90.

Lowe, S. (1986) *Urban Social Movements: The City After Castells*. London: Macmillan.

Luard, E. (1990) *International Society*. London: Macmillan.

Luhmann, N. (1975) Die Weltgesellschaft, in Luhmann, *Soziologische Aufklaerung*, vol. 2. Frankfurt: Suhrkamp.

Luhmann, N. (1989) *Ecological Communication*. Chicago: University of Chicago Press.

Luhmann, N. (1990) The world society as a social system, in Luhmann, *Essays in Self-Reference*. New York: Columbia University Press.

Luhmann, N. (1995) *Risk: A Sociological Theory*. Berlin: de Gruyter.

Lurry, C. (1993) *Cultural Rights*. London: Routledge.

Lyons, F.S.L. (1963) *Internationalism in Europe, 1815–1914*. Leyden: Sythoff.

Lyotard, J.-F. (1984) *The Postmodern Condition*. Manchester: Manchester University Press.

MacCormick, N. (1993) Beyond the sovereign state, *Modern Law Review*, 56(1): 1–18.

MacCormick, N. (1996) Liberalism, nationalism and the postsovereign state, *Political Studies*, 44(3): 553–67.

McGrew, A. and Lewis, P. (eds) (1992) *Global Politics*. Cambridge: Polity.

MacIntyre, A. (1981) *After Virtue*. London: Duckworth.

McLuhan, M. (1962) *The Gutenberg Galaxy*. Toronto: University of Toronto Press.

McNeill, W. (1986) *Polyethnicity and National Unity in World History*. Toronto: University of Toronto Press.

MacPherson, C.P. (1962) *The Political Theory of Possessive Individualism*. Oxford: Clarendon Press.

Maffesoli, S. (1996) *Time of the Tribes*. London: Sage.

Majone, G. (1996) *Regulating Europe*. London: Routledge.

Mann, M. (1987) Ruling class strategies and citizenship, *Sociology*, 21(3): 339–54.

Mann, M. (1999) The dark side of democracy: the modern tradition of ethnic and political cleansing, *New Left Review*, 235: 18–45.

Marshall, T.H. (1965) *Social Policy*. London: Hutchinson.

Marshall, T.H. (1992) *Citizenship and Social Class*. London: Pluto.

Marx, K. (1977) On the Jewish question, in D. McLellan (ed.) *Karl Marx: Selected Writings*. Oxford: Oxford University Press.

Marx, K. and Engels, F. (1967) *The Communist Manifesto*. Harmondsworth: Penguin.

Matustik, M. (1993) *Postnational Identity*. London: Gulford.

Mayall, J. (1990) *Nationalism and International Society*. Cambridge: Cambridge University Press.

Mazlish, B. and Buultjens, R. (eds) (1993) *Conceptualizing Global History*. Boulder, CO: Westview Press.

Meehan, E. (1993) *Citizenship and European Community*. London: Sage.

Meinecke, F. (1970) *Cosmopolitanism and the Nation State*. Princeton, NJ: Princeton University Press.

Melucci, A. (1989) *Nomads of the Present: Social Movements and Individual Needs in Contemporary Society*. Philadelphia, PA: Temple University Press.

Melucci, A. (1996a) *Challenging Codes: Collective Action in the Information Age*. Cambridge: Cambridge University Press.

Melucci, A. (1996b) *The Playing Self: Person and Meaning in the Planetary Age*. Cambridge: Cambridge University Press.

Menand, L. (1993) Human rights as global imperative, in B. Mazlish and R. Buultjens (eds) *Conceptualizing Global History*. Boulder, CO: Westview Press.

Mestrovic, S. (1994) *The Balkanization of the West: The Confluence of Postmodernism and Postcommunism*. London: Routledge.

Meyer, J. (1987) The world polity and the authority of the nation-state, in G. Thomas, J. Meyer, F. Ramirez and J. Boli (eds) *Institutional Structure: Constituting State, Society and the Individual*. London: Sage.

Miller, D. (1992) Community and citizenship, in S. Avineri and A. de–Shalit (eds) *Communitarianism and Individualism*. Oxford: Oxford University Press.

Miller, D. (1995) *On Nationality*. Oxford: Oxford University Press.

Miller, D. and Walzer, M. (eds) (1995) *Pluralism, Justice, and Equality*. Oxford: Oxford University Press.

Milward, A. (1992) *The European Rescue of the Nation State*. London: Routledge.

Milward, A., Sorensen, V. and Ranieri, R. (1993) *The Frontier of National Sovereignty*. London: Routledge.

Moore, B. (1972) *Reflections on the Cause of Human Misery and on Certain Proposals to Eliminate Them*. London: Allen Lane.

Moore, W.E. (1966) Global sociology: the world as a singular system, *American Journal of Sociology*, 71: 475–82.

Mouffe, C. (1992) Feminism, citizenship and radical democratic politics, in J. Butler and J.W. Scott (eds) *Feminists Theorize the Political*. London: Routledge.

Mulgan, G. (1994) *Politics in an Antipolitical Age*. Cambrige: Polity.

Mulhall, S. and Swift, A. (1996) *Liberalism and Communitarianism*, 2nd edn. Oxford: Blackwell.

Münch, R. (1993) *Das Projekt Europa*. Frankfurt: Suhrkamp.

Münch, R. (1996) Between nation-state, regionalism and world society: the European integration process, *Journal of Common Market Studies*, 34(3): 379–401.

Munck, R. and Waterman, P. (eds) (1999) *Labour Worldwide in the Era of Globalization*. London: Macmillan.

Nederveen Pieterse, J. (1995) Globalization as hybridization, in M. Featherstone, S. Lash and R. Robertson (eds) *Global Modernities*. London: Sage.

Nisbet, R. (1974) Citizenship: two traditions, *Social Research*, 41: 612–37.

Nozick, R. (1974) *Anarchy, State, and Utopia*. Oxford: Blackwell.

Nussbaum, M. (ed.) (1996) *For Love of Country: Debating the Limits of Patriotism*. Boston, MA: Beacon.

Nussbaum, M. (1997) Kant and cosmopolitanism, in J. Bohman and M. Lutz-Bachmann (eds) *Perpetual Peace: Essays on Kant's Cosmpolitan Ideal*. Cambridge, MA: MIT Press.

Oakeshott, M. (1975) *On Human Conduct*. Oxford: Clarendon Press.

Oakeshott, M. (1996) *The Politics of Faith and the Politics of Scepticism*. New Haven, CT: Yale University Press.

Offe, C. (1984) *Contradictions of the Welfare State*. London: Hutchinson.

Offe, C. (1997) *Varieties of Transition: The East European and East German Experience*. Cambridge: Polity.

Ohmae, K. (1990) *The Borderless World*. London: Collins.

Ohmae, K. (1993) The rise of the region, *Foreign Affairs*, 71(2): 78–87.

Ohmae, K. (1995) *The End of the Nation State*. New York: Free Press.

Oldfield, M. (1990) *Citizenship and Community: Civic Republicanism and the Modern World*. London: Routledge.

O'Mahony, P. and Delanty, G. (1998) *Rethinking Irish History: Nationalism, Identity, Ideology*. London: Macmillan.

O'Neill, J. (1990) AIDS as a globalizing panic, in M. Featherstone (ed.) *Global Culture*. London: Sage.

O'Neill, J. (1994) *The Missing Child of Liberal Theory: Towards a Covenant Theory of Family, Community, Welfare and the Civic State*. Toronto: University of Toronto Press.

O'Neill, J. (ed.) (1996) *Hegel's Dialectic of Desire and Recognition: Texts and Commentary*. Cambridge: Cambridge University Press.

O'Neill, J. (1997) The civic recovery of citizenship, *Citizenship Studies*, 1(1): 19–32.

Ong, A. (1998) Flexible citizenship among Chinese cosmopolitans, in P. Cheah and B. Robbins (eds) *Cosmopolitics: Thinking and Feeling Beyond the Nation*. Minneapolis, MN: University of Minnesota Press.

Oommen, T. (1997) *Citizenship, Nationality and Ethnicity*. Oxford: Blackwell.

Opp, K.-D. (1996) The role of voice in a future Europe, in F. Weil (ed.) *Extremism, Protest, Social Movements and Democracy*. Greenwich, CT: JAI Press.

Pakkuski, J. (1997) Cultural citizenship, *Citizenship Studies*, 1(1): 73–86.

Parekh, B. (1994) Discourses on national identity, *Political Studies*, 42(3): 492–504.

Parekh, B. (1995) Cultural pluralism and the limits of diversity, *Alternatives*, 20: 431–57.

Parekh, B. (1997) Dilemmas of a multicultural theory of citizenship, *Constellations*, 4(1): 54–62.

Patterson, O. (1997) *The Ideal of Integration: Progress and Resentment in America's 'Racial' Crisis*. Washington, DC: Counterpoint.

Pegg, C. (1983) *Evolution of the European Idea, 1914–1945*. Chapel Hill, NC: University of North Carolina.

Perez-Diaz, V. (1998) The public sphere and a European civil society, in J. Alexander (ed.) *Real Civil Societies*. London: Sage.

Perulli, P. (ed.) (1998) *Neo-Regionalismo*. Turin: Bollati Borghieri.

Peterson, M. (1992) Transnational activity, international society and world politics, *Millennium: Journal of International Studies*, 21(3): 371–88.

Phillips, A. (1993) *Democracy and Difference*. Cambridge: Polity.

Pocock, J.G.A. (1975) *The Machiavellian Moment: Florentine Political Thought and the Atlantic Republican Tradition*. Princeton, NJ: Princeton University Press.

Pocock, J.G.A. (1995) The ideal of citizenship since modern times, in R. Beiner (ed.) *Theorizing Citizenship*. New York: State University of New York Press.

Pogge, T. (1992) Cosmopolitanism and sovereignty, *Ethics*, 103: 48–75.

Pogge, T. (1997) How to create supra-national institutions democratically: some reflections on the European Union's democratic deficit, *Journal of Political Philosophy*, 5: 163–82.

Power, M. (1997) *Audit Society*. Cambridge: Cambridge University Press.

Preuss, U. (1996) Two challenges to European citizenship, *Political Studies*, 44(3): 534–52.

Preuss, U. (1998) Migration – a challenge to modern citizenship, *Constellations*, 4(3): 307–19.

Putnam, R. (1993) *Making Democracy Work: Civic Traditions in Modern Italy*. Princeton, NJ: Princeton University Press.

Rawls, J. (1971) *A Theory of Justice*. Cambridge, MA: Harvard University Press.

Rawls, J. (1987) The idea of an overlapping consensus, *Oxford Journal of Legal Studies*, 7: 1–25.

Rawls, J. (1993) *Political Liberalism*. New York: Columbia University Press.

Rawls, J. (1999) *The Law of Peoples*. Cambridge, MA: Harvard University Press.

Regan, T. (1983) *The Case for Animal Rights*. Berkeley, CA: University of California Press.

Rehg, W. (1994) *Insight and Solidarity: A Study in the Discourse Ethics of Jürgen Habermas*. Berkeley, CA: University of California Press.

Rengger, N. (ed.) (1999) Special issue on global justice, *International Affairs*, 75(3).

Renteln, A. (1990) *International Human Rights: Universalism versus Relativism*. London: Sage.

Rex, J. (1996) National identity in the democratic multicultural state, *Sociological Research Online*, 1(2) http://www.socresonline.org.uk/socresonline1/2/1.html

Rhodes, M., Heywood, P. and Wright, V. (eds) (1997) *Developments in West European Politics*. London: Macmillan.

Rimmerman, C. (1997) *The New Citizenship: Unconventional Politics, Activism and Service*. Boulder, CO: Westview.

Ritzer, G. (1993) *The McDonaldization of Society*. London: Sage.

Robbins, B. (ed.) (1993) *The Phantom Public Sphere*. Minneapolis, MN: University of Minnesota Press.

Roberston, R. (1992) *Globalization: Social Theory and Global Culture*. London: Sage.

Roche, M. (1992) *Rethinking Citizenship: Welfare, Ideology and Change in Modern Society*. Cambridge: Polity.

Roche, M. (1995) Rethinking citizenship and social movements: themes in contemporary sociology and neo-conservative ideology, in L. Maheu (ed.) *Social Movements and Social Classes*. London: Sage.

Rorty, R. (1993) Human rights, rationality and sentimentality, in S. Shute and S. Hurley (eds) *On Human Rights*. New York: Basic Books.

Rorty, R. (1998) *Achieving our Country: Leftist Thought in Twentieth-Century America*. Cambridge, MA: Harvard University Press.

Rose, N. (1989) *Governing the Soul: The Shaping of the Private Self*. London: Routledge.

Rosenau, J. (1990) *Turbulence in World Politics*. Brighton: Harvester.

Rosenau, J. and Czempiel, E. (eds) (1992) *Governance without Government: Order and Change in World Politics*. Cambridge: Cambridge University Press.

Rousseau, J.-J. (1968) *The Social Contract*. Harmondsworth: Penguin.

Ruggie, J. (1983) Human rights and the entire international community, *Daedalus*, 112(4).

Ruggie, J. (1993) Territoriality and beyond: problematizing modernity in international relations, *International Organization*, 47(1): 139–74.

Sakwa, R. (1999) *Postcommunism*. Buckingham: Open University Press.

Sandel, M. (1982) *Liberalism and the Limits of Justice*. Cambridge: Cambridge University Press.

Sandercock, L. (1998) *Towards Cosmopolis: Planning for the Multicultural Cities*. New York: John Wiley.

Sassen, S. (1992) *The Global City: New York, London, Tokyo*. Princeton, NJ: Princeton University Press.

Sassen, S. (1996) *Losing Control: Sovereignty in an Age of Globalization*. New York: Columbia University Press.

Sassen, S. (1999) *Guests and Aliens*. New York: New Press.

Schlereth, T. (1977) *The Cosmopolitan Ideal in Enlightenment Thought: Its Form and Function in the Ideas of Franklin, Hume, and Voltaire, 1694–1790*. Notre Dame, IN: University of Notre Dame Press.

Schleslinger, A. (1992) *The Disuniting of America*. New York: Norton.

Schleslinger, P. (1994) Europe a new battlefield?, in J. Hutchinson and A. Smith (eds) *Nationalism*. Oxford: Oxford University Press.

Selove, R. (1995) *Democracy and Technology*. New York: Guilford Press.

Selznick, P. (1992) *The Moral Commonwealth: Social Theory and the Promise of Community*. Berkeley, CA: University of California Press.

Shapiro, I. and Kymlicka, W. (eds) (1997) *Ethnicity and Group Rights*. New York: New York University Press.

Sharpe, L. (ed.) (1993) *The Rise of MesoGovernment in Europe*. London: Sage.

Shaw, M. (1994a) *Global Society and International Relations*. Cambridge: Polity.

Shaw, M. (1994b) Civil society and global politics: beyond a social movements Approach, *Millennium: Journal of International Studies*, 21(3): 647–67.

Skinner, Q. (1978) *The Foundation of Modern Political Thought*, 2 vols. Cambridge: Cambridge University Press.

Skinner, Q. (1992) The Italian republics, in J. Dunn (ed.) *Democracy: The Unfinished Journey, 508BC to AD 1993*. Oxford: Oxford University Press.

Sklair, L. (1991) *Sociology of the Global System*. London: Harvester Wheatsheaf.

Smelser, N. (1997) Global sociology, in N. Smelser *Problematics of Sociology: The Georg Simmel Lectures, 1995*. Berkeley, CA: University of California Press.

Smelser, N. and Alexander, N. (eds) (1999) *Diversity and Its Discontents: Cultural Conflict and Common Ground in Contemporary American Society*. Princeton, NJ: Princeton University Press.

Smith, A. (1995) *Nations and Nationalism in a Global Era*. Cambridge: Polity.

Smith, B.J. (1985) *Politics and Remembrance: Republican Themes in Machiavelli, Burke and Tocqueville*. Princeton, NJ: Princeton University Press.

Smith, J. (1998) Global civil society? Transnational social movement organizations and social capital, *American Behavioral Scientist*, 42(1): 93–107.

Smith, J., Chatfield, C. and Pagnucco, R. (eds) (1997a) *Transnational Social Movements and Global Politics: Solidarity Beyond the State*. Syracuse, NY: Syracuse University Press.

Smith, J., Pagnucco, R. and Lopez, G. (1997b) Globalizing human rights: the work of transnational human rights NGOs in the 1990s, *Human Rights Quarterly*, 20: 379–412.

Soja, E. (1996) *Thirdspace: Journeys to Los Angeles and Other Real and Imagined Places.* Oxford: Blackwell.

Somers, M. (1995) Narrating and naturalizing civil society and citizenship theory: the place of political culture and the public sphere, *Sociological Theory*, 13(3): 229–74.

Sousa Santos, B. de (1995) *Toward a New Common Sense: Law, Science and Politics in the Paradigmatic Transition.* London: Routledge.

Sousa Santos, B. de (1999) A multicultural conception of human rights, in M. Featherstone and S. Lash (eds) *Spaces of Culture.* London: Sage.

Soysal, Y.N. (1994) *Limits of Citizenship: Migrants and Postnational Membership in Europe.* Chicago: University of Chicago Press.

Springborg, P. (1992) *Western Republicanism and the Oriental Prince.* Cambridge: Polity.

Steenbergen, B. (1994) Towards a global citizenship, in B. Steenbergen (ed.) *The Condition of Citizenship.* London: Sage.

Stehr, N. (1992) *Knowledge Societies.* London: Sage.

Stein, T. (1998) Does the constitutional and democratic system work? The ecological crisis as a challenge to the political order of constitutional democracy, *Constellations*, 4(3): 420–49.

Stevenson, N. (1997) Global media and technological change: social justice, recognition and the meaningfulness of everyday life, *Citizenship Studies*, 1(3): 365–88.

Stewart, A. (1995) Two conceptions of citizenship, *British Journal of Sociology*, 46(1): 63–78.

Stoppard, J. and Strange, S. (1991) *Rival States, Rival Firms: Competition for World Markets.* Cambridge: Cambridge University Press.

Strange, S. (1996) *The Retreat of the State: The Diffusion of Power in the World Economy.* Cambridge: Cambridge University Press.

Strydom, P. (1999a) The challenge of collective responsibility for sociology, *Current Sociology*, 47(3): 65–82.

Strydom, P. (1999b) Triple contingency – the theoretical problem of the public in communication societies, *Philosophy and Social Criticism*, 25(2): 1–25.

Strydom, P. (2000) *Discourse and Knowledge: The Making of Enlightenment Sociology.* Liverpool: Liverpool University Press.

Taguieff, P.-A. (1995) Political science confronts populism, *Telos*, 103(spring): 9–43.

Tarrow, S. (1994) *Power in Movement: Social Movements, Collective Action and Politics.* Cambridge: Cambridge University Press.

Tarrow, S. (1995) The Europeanization of conflict: reflections from a social movement perspective, *West European Politics*, 18(2): 223–51.

Taylor, C. (1989) Cross-purposes: the liberal–communitarian debate, in N. Rosenblum (ed.) *Liberalism and the Moral Life.* Cambridge, MA: Harvard University Press.

Taylor, C. (1990) *Sources of the Self.* Cambridge, MA: Harvard University Press.

Taylor, C. (1994) *Multiculturalism: Examining the Politics of Recognition.* Princeton, NJ: Princeton University Press.

Tenbruck, F. (1990) The dream of a secular ecume: the meaning and limits of development, *Theory, Culture and Society*, 7: 193–206.

Tester, K. (1991) *Animal Rights.* London: Routledge.

Therborn, G. (1977) The rule of capital and the rise of democracy, *New Left Review*, 103.

Therborn, G. (1995) *Beyond European Modernity: The Trajectory of European Societies, 1945–2000.* London: Sage.

Therborn, G. (1997) Europe in the twenty-first century: the world's Scandinavia, in P. Gowan and P. Anderson (eds) *The Question of Europe.* London: Verso.

Thompson, J. (1998) Community identity and world citizenship, in D. Archibugi, D. Held and M. Köhler (eds) *Re-Imagining Political Community: Studies in Cosmopolitan Democracy.* Cambridge: Polity.

Thrift, N. (1996) *Spatial Formations*. London: Sage.

Tiryakian, E. (ed.) (1984) *The Global Crisis: Sociological Analyses and Responses*. Leiden: Brill.

Tönnies, F. (1957) *Community and Society*. East Lansing, MI: Michigan State University Press.

Torpey, J. (2000) *The Invention of the Passport: Surveillance, Citizenship and the State*. Cambridge: Cambridge University Press.

Toulmin, S. (1990) *Cosmopolis: The Hidden Agenda of Modernity*. Chicago: University of Chicago Press.

Touraine, A. (1977) *The Self-Production of Society*. Chicago: University of Chicago Press.

Touraine, A. (1994) European countries in a post-national era, in C. Rootes and H. Davies (eds) *A New Europe: Social Change and Political Transformation*. London: UCL Press.

Touraine, A. (1995) *Critique of Modernity*. Oxford: Blackwell.

Touraine, A. (1997) *What is Democracy?* Oxford: Westview.

Touraine, A. (1998) Can we live together, equal and different?, *European Journal of Social Theory*, 1(2): 165–78.

Touraine, A. (2000) *Can We Live Together? Equal and Different*. Cambridge: Polity.

Trend, D. (1997) *Cultural Democracy: Politics, Media, New Technology*. New York: State University of New York Press.

Tseblis, G. (1994) The power of the European Parliament as a conditional agenda setter, *American Political Science Review*, 88: 128–42.

Tully, J. (1995) *Strange Multiplicity: Constitutionalism in an Age of Diversity*. Cambridge: Cambridge University Press.

Turner, B.S. (1986a) *Citizenship and Capitalism: The Debate over Reformism*. London: Allen & Unwin.

Turner, B.S. (1986b) Personhood and citizenship, *Theory, Culture and Society*, 3(1): 1–16.

Turner, B.S. (1990) Outline of a theory of citizenship, *Sociology*, 24(2): 189–217.

Turner, B.S. (1993a) Contemporary problems in the theory of citizenship, in Turner (ed.) *Citizenship and Social Theory*. London: Sage.

Turner, B.S. (1993b) Outline of a theory of human rights, in Turner (ed.) *Citizenship and Social Theory*. London: Sage.

Turner, B.S. (1994) Postmodern culture/modern citizens, in B. van Steenbergen (ed.) *The Condition of Citizenship*. London: Sage.

Turner, B.S. (2000) Globalization, religion and cosmopolitan virtue, *European Journal of Social Theory*, 3(2).

Twine, F. (1994) *Citizenship and Social Rights*. London: Sage.

Urry, J. (2000) *Sociology Beyond Societies: Mobilities for the Twenty-first Century*. London: Routledge.

Vajda, M. (1988) East-Central European perspectives, in J. Keane (ed.) *Civil Society and the State*. London: Verso.

Vincent, R.J. (1992) Modernity and global rights, in A. McGrew and P. Lewis (eds) *Global Politics*. Cambridge: Polity.

Vincent, R.J. (1986) *Human Rights and International Relations*. Cambridge: Cambridge University Press.

Voet, R. (1998) *Feminism and Citizenship*. London: Sage.

Wacquant, L. (1993) Urban outcasts: stigma and division in the black American ghetto and French urban periphery, *International Journal of Urban and Regional Research*, 17(3): 336–83.

Walby, S. (1990) *Theorizing Patriarchy*. Oxford: Blackwell.

Walker, R.B.J. (1991) On the spatiotemporal conditions of democratic practice, *Alternatives*, 16: 243–62.

Walker, R.B.J. (1994) Social movements/world politics, *Millennium: Journal of International Studies*, 23(3): 669–700.

Wallerstein, I. (1974) *The Modern World System*. New York: Academic.

Wallerstein, I. (1979) *The Modern World System II*. New York: Academic.

Wallerstein, I. (1992) *Geopolitics and Geoculture*. Cambridge: Cambridge University Press.

Walzer, M. (1983) *Spheres of Justice*. New York: Basic Books.

Walzer, M. (1987) *Interpretation and Social Criticism*. Cambridge, MA: Harvard University Press.

Walzer, M. (1994) *Thick and Thin: Moral Argument at Home and Abroad*. Notre Dame, IN: University of Notre Dame Press.

Walzer, M. (ed.) (1995) *Toward a Global Civil Society*. Oxford: Berghahn.

Wapner, P. (1996) *Environmental Activism and World Civic Politics*. New York: State University of New York Press.

Waters, M. (1995) *Globalization*. Cambridge: Polity.

Watson, A. (1992) *The Evolution of International Society: A Comparative Historical Analysis*. London: Routledge.

Weber, E. (1976) *Peasants into Frenchmen: The Modernization of Rural France, 1877–1914*. Stanford, CA: Stanford University Press.

Weber, M. (1958) *The City*. New York: Free Press.

Wendt, C. (1994) Collective identity formation and the international state, *American Political Science Review*, 88(2): 384–96.

Wexler, P. (1990) 'Citizenship in the semiotic society, in B. Turner (ed.) *Theories of Modernity and Postmodernity*. London: Sage.

Whittington, K. (1998) Revisiting Tocqueville's America: society, politics, and association in the nineteenth century, *American Behavioral Scientist*, 42(1): 21–32.

Wilson, R. (ed.) (1997) *Human Rights, Culture and Context: Anthropological Perspectives*. London: Pluto.

Wilson, R. and Dissanayake, W. (eds) (1996) *Global/Local: Cultural Production and the Transnational Imaginary*. Durham, NC: Duke University Press.

Wintle, M. (ed.) (1996) *Culture and Identity in Europe*. Aldershot: Avebury.

Yearley, S. (1996) *Sociology, Environmentalism, Globalization*. London: Sage.

Yeatman, A. (1993) Voice and representation in the politics of difference, in S. Gunew and A. Yeatman (eds) *Feminism and the Politics of Difference*. London: Allen & Unwin.

Young, I.M. (1989) Polity and group difference: a critique of the ideal of universal citizenship, *Ethics*, 99: 250–74.

Young, I.M. (1990) *Justice and the Politics of Difference*. Princeton, NJ: Princeton University Press.

Young, O. (1994) *International Governance: Protecting the Environment in a Stateless Society*. Ithaca, NY: Cornell University Press.

Zimmerman, A. (1995) Toward a more democratic ethics of technological governance, *Science, Technology and Human Values*, 20(1).

Zolo, D. (1992) *Democracy and Complexity*. Cambridge: Polity.

Zolo, D. (1993) Citizenship in a postcommunist era, in D. Held (ed.) *Prospects for Democracy*. Cambridge: Polity.

Zolo, D. (1997) *Cosmopolis: Prospects for World Government*. Cambridge: Polity.

Index

WORK, CONSUMERISM AND THE NEW POOR

Zygmunt Bauman

- Can poverty be fought and conquered by orthodox means?
- Should we seek new solutions like 'decoupling' the right to livelihood from the selling of labour and extending the socially recognized concept of work?
- How urgent is it to confront these social questions and find practical answers?

It is one thing to be poor in a society of producers and universal employment; it is quite a different thing to be poor in a society of consumers, in which life projects are built around consumer choice rather than work, professional skills or jobs. If 'being poor' once derived its meaning from the condition of being unemployed, today it draws its meaning primarily from the plight of a flawed consumer. This is one difference which truly makes a difference – in the way living in poverty is experienced and in the chances and prospects to redeem its misery.

This absorbing book attempts to trace this change, which has been taking place over the duration of modern history, and to make an inventory of its social consequences. On the way, it tries also to consider to what extent the well remembered and tested means of fighting back advancing poverty and mitigating its hardships are fit (or unfit) to grasp and tackle the problems of poverty in its present form. Students of sociology, politics and social policy will find this to be an invaluable text on the changing significance and implications of an enduring social problem.

Contents

Introduction – Part one – The meaning of work: producing the work ethic – From the work ethic to the aesthetic of consumption – Part two – The rise and fall – The work ethic and the new poor – Part three – Prospects for the new poor – Notes – Index.

128pp   0 335 20155 5 (Paperback)   0 335 20156 3 (Hardback)

SOCIAL EXCLUSION

David Byrne

- What does the term 'social exclusion' mean and who are the 'socially excluded'?
- Why has there been such a significant increase in 'social exclusion'?
- How can we attempt to tackle this and the problems associated with it?

'Social exclusion' is the buzz phrase for the complex range of social problems which derive from the substantial increase in social inequality in Western societies. This timely and engaging volume examines these problems in societies where manufacturing industry is no longer the main basis for employment and the universal welfare states established after the Second World War are under attack. It reviews theories of social exclusion, including the Christian democratic and social democratic assertions of solidarity with which the term originated, Marxist accounts of the recreation of the reserve army of labour, and neo-liberal assertions of the sovereignty of the market in which the blame for exclusion is assigned to the excluded themselves.

Drawing on a wide variety of empirical evidence, the author concludes that the origins of social exclusion lie with the creation of a new post-industrial order founded on the exploitation of low paid workers within western capitalism, and that social policies have actually helped to create an unequal social order as opposed to simply reacting to economic forces. This controversial but accessible text will be essential reading for undergraduate courses on social exclusion within sociology, politics, economics, geography and social policy, as well as students on professional courses and practitioners in social work, community work, urban planning and management, health and housing.

Contents

Introduction – Part one – The possessive individualists: blaming the poor – Order and solidarity: collectivist approaches – Exploitation matters: Marxist approaches to exclusion – Part two – Dynamic society – dynamic lives – The dynamic of income inequality – Divided spaces: social divisions in the post-industrial city – Conclusion: what is and what is to be done about it – Notes – Bibliography – Index.

176pp   0 335 19974 7 (Paperback)   0 335 19975 5 (Hardback)

THE GOVERNANCE OF SCIENCE

Steve Fuller

- What does social and political theory have to say about the role of science in society?
- Do scientists and other professional enquirers have an unlimited 'right to be wrong'?
- What are the implications of capitalism and multiculturalism for the future of the university?

This ground-breaking text offers a fresh perspective on the governance of science from the standpoint of social and political theory. Science has often been seen as the only institution that embodies the elusive democratic ideal of the 'open society'. Yet, science remains an elite activity that commands much more public trust than understanding, even though science has become increasingly entangled with larger political and economic issues. Fuller proceeds by rejecting liberal and communitarian ideologies of science, in favour of a 'republican' approach centred on 'the right to be wrong'. He shows how the recent scaling up of scientific activity has undermined the republican ideal.

The centrepiece of the book, a social history of the struggle to render the university a 'republic of science', focuses on the potential challenges posed by multiculturalism and capitalism. Finally, drawing on the science policy of the US New Deal, Fuller proposes nothing short of a new social contract for 'secularizing' science.

Contents

192pp   0 335 20234 9 (Paperback)   0 335 20235 7 (Hardback)